The Story of Jesus

The Story of Jesus

A Mosaic

ROY A. HARRISVILLE

foreword by Mark Mattes

RESOURCE *Publications* • Eugene, Oregon

THE STORY OF JESUS
A Mosaic

Copyright © 2021 Roy A. Harrisville. All rights reserved. Except for brief quotations in critical publications or reviews, no part of this book may be reproduced in any manner without prior written permission from the publisher. Write: Permissions, Wipf and Stock Publishers, 199 W. 8th Ave., Suite 3, Eugene, OR 97401.

Resource Publications
An Imprint of Wipf and Stock Publishers
199 W. 8th Ave., Suite 3
Eugene, OR 97401

www.wipfandstock.com

PAPERBACK ISBN: 978-1-7252-8103-5
HARDCOVER ISBN: 978-1-7252-8102-8
EBOOK ISBN: 978-1-7252-8104-2

01/05/21

The text of this volume is dedicated to the memory of my wife, Norma, and to my grandchildren.

Contents

Foreword by Mark Mattes	ix
Preface	xiii
Acknowledgments	xv
Introduction	xvii

Part One: Beginnings

The Conception and Birth of Jesus	3
The Prologue in John	7
The Boyhood of Jesus	9
The Forerunner	11
The Baptism of Jesus	14

Part Two: The Begininings of Jesus' Ministry

Jesus' Appearing and Preaching	19
Calling of the Disciples	28
The Exorcisms	31
Miracles of Healing	35
The Nature Miracles	45
The Parables	53
The Hard Sayings	74

Part Three: Schooling the Disciples

The Sermon on the Mount	113
The Call to Discipleship.	117
The Marks of Discipleship	120
The Conditions of Discipleship	122

The Specifics of Disciplesip	128
The Last Things	140
The Inner Life of Jesus	143

Part Four: The Passion

The Passover	151
Gethsemane	154
Jesus before the High Priest	160
Peter's Denial	161
Jesus before the Council	162
Jesus before Pilate and Judas' Death	164
Jesus or Barbabas	166
Jesus Flogged	169
The Soldiers Mock	170
The Crucifixion of Jesus	171
Jesus between Two Thieves	173
The Death of Jesus	174
The Burial of Jesus	177
The Resurrection	179

Part Five: Summary

Summary	193
A Final Reflection on the Resurrection of Jesus	200

Appendix

Glossary	207
Questions for Reflection	211
Bibliography	215
Index	219

Foreword

Of the many questions that can be posed, asking who Jesus Christ is may be the most important. Even among the increasing number of "nones," those who identify with no specific faith tradition, including atheists, agnostics, and a good many who are "spiritual but not religious," Jesus as a teacher, ethical model, and martyr is held in high esteem. It is easy to give lip service to the importance of Jesus, but unless we investigate who he was, how will we know if our appreciation for him is justified?

Roy Harrisville, professor emeritus of New Testament at Luther Seminary and the author, editor, and translator of numerous books and articles, is one of America's foremost scholars of the New Testament. For over eight decades he has reflected on the import of Jesus both for those who confess Jesus as Savior and those who do not.

This book succinctly and energetically gives us the results of Harrisville's extensive lifetime of research. Harrisville meticulously and fearlessly walks us through what the four gospels tell us about Jesus, all so that we can come to an awareness of who Jesus is and what claim he may have on us. For many Christians, the Bible is taken as an authoritative source which provides proof texts of pure doctrine, its miracles are accepted at face value, and its stories are regarded as a stimulus for the practice of genuine piety. Harrisville is certainly aware of this stance, since he was raised in it. But he is just as much aware of the rise of "historical consciousness," that is, the tendency among scholars to situate the Bible within history, with no privileged status, as one religious text among many. Such an historical consciousness, for instance, does not accept the miracles recorded in the Bible at face value, since they do not comport with the uniformity of experience that the natural sciences assume about the world. This approach to the Bible is far less apt to assume that the gospels are in harmony, instead highlights the differences between each.

Harrisville does not dismiss these concerns. In our current secular context, it would be intellectually dishonest to do so. Instead, he feels their full force, faces them fearlessly, brings them to the fore, and allows us to feel their weight. That said, he recognizes that the naturalistic assumptions embedded within this historicizing are not without bias. If the gospels are to be heard on their own terms, we find ourselves and our scientific bent challenged, particularly to the degree that we hold such a naturalistic bias against miracles and supernatural interventions. Harrisville provokes us to be "open to transcendence," and unless we are, we will fail to understand Jesus on his own terms.

Harrisville describes his project as a wager. If Jesus proves not to be the Savior of the world, we will only be mistaken about history. But if Jesus in fact is the Savior, and we wager against that, then we lose out on his redemption. How we should wager can only be determined by our combing through the scope of Jesus' life, teachings, ministry, and opposition to the political and religious leaders of his time. Indeed, the gospels are written from the standpoint of faith. But that does not disqualify them as historically accurate documents, because the early church was less inventive, and more receptive, of Jesus' stories and sayings handed on by his earliest followers. We need not cede preference to skepticism about the overall portrayal of Jesus by the gospel authors. Such skepticism is mere bias against the proposal that God exists and that God intervenes in worldly affairs. If Jesus is the redeemer, such naturalistic bias is unjustified.

As he portrays Jesus' life, teachings, death, and resurrection, what Harrisville shows us is that C.S. Lewis was quite accurate to describe Jesus' life as a "true myth," that is, that the events to which the gospels witness, scripted as they are within a narrative of redemption for the world, actually happened. Specifying this redemption, Harrisville does not understand Jesus apart from his willingness to die, not just as a martyr for the truth, but as a sacrifice, an act of love to expiate human sin. Such self-sacrifice on the part of Jesus effectuates nothing other than a "rupture" within God himself as Jesus takes on human trespasses. Thereby, Jesus' own righteousness, not human sin, defines those who belong to Christ. As risen, Christ continuously and constantly grants such grace to sinners. In a word, God seeks to "win back" the world he has made.

In Harrisville's work, Jesus is no unknown figure lost to us because we simply project our own ideals onto him, as Albert Schweitzer critiqued the attempt to describe Jesus' life by scholars in his era. Instead, through carefully sifting through the gospels, examining divergencies in their portraiture of Jesus, and weighing their information in light of ancient Judaism and the various religious traditions of the ancient Roman empire, Jesus comes to light. As Jesus called people to discipleship so he still bids them follow him today. In Harrisville's work we sense that Jesus calls you as well. We do well to heed his call!

MARK MATTES
Grand View University
Des Moines, Iowa

Preface

This book is intended for the college or seminary age reader. The pieces and fragments of the "mosaic" are gathered from more than thirty years of teaching the New Testament. The reader will soon discover that the book reflects a point of view. Honesty in scholarship requires it. But so also does the New Testament itself. From its reader it intends a response that cannot help but affect its interpretation. The interpretation may be flawed, but the requirement stands. The message of the New Testament intends the assent of its reader if it is not to be truncated. Whether or not there is agreement with the point of view reflected here is quite another matter, but that there is a point of view answers to the requirement of the New Testament. My hope is that my answer is faithful, and that the reader will allow it!

ROY A. HARRISVILLE

Acknowledgments

The English translation used in this volume is the New Revised Standard Version (NRSV). The Greek text is that of Nestle-Aland, 27th edition, Deutsche Bibelgesellschaft, 1993.

For repair and editorial work, I am greatly indebted to my daughter, Dr. Randi Lundell.

Introduction

Thousands of books have been written about Jesus, so one might ask, "Why another? Why add to the clutter?" My answer, in part, is that the same could be said of books about Abraham Lincoln or Napoleon Buonaparte. Writers, essayists, historians, psychologists never tire of writing about them, to the point where our libraries are groaning under the weight of their stories. I hear no one calling to end the spate of biographies of Lincoln or Napoleon, for the simple fact that they were, not merely arguably, but indisputably, world-changing figures. Among those in the farthest reaches of the world there has been fascination with the figure of Abraham Lincoln, and, states and countries south of our borders have been led by revolutionaries, such as, for example, Simon Bolivar, whose dreams of a united South America had Napoleon for their father. As for Jesus of Nazareth, fascination with him has never flagged, to say nothing of allegiances to him over the centuries that have resulted in the forming of communities world-wide. Whether in blessing or cursing, in invoking or blaspheming, his name is on the lips of millions. This fact alone is surely an argument for telling about him again.

My answer to the question "why another book about Jesus?" is, also in part, that despite the decline, and in some instances, collapse of mainline Christian denominations, the fascination with Jesus of Nazareth is still existent, particularly among the youth. Disinterested in institutional churches with their traditional dogmas and liturgies, many still spending millions to heap up brick and mortar for columns and apses and flying buttresses, the youth still nurse interest in the one in whose name all this consumption of time, energy, and money occurs.

In addition, my answer to the question is that due to the influx of people from the Middle East and Asia, who hold religious affiliations once thought alien, debate has arisen as to what place Jesus of Nazareth deserves or does not deserve to occupy among those varied persuasions. It is clear, for example, that in Islam, Jesus ranks as a forerunner of Mohammed, that in Hinduism he enjoys merely one niche alongside its innumerable deities, or that in Buddhism he is commended principally for his ethical teaching. How, for example, does Jesus "add up" over against the Qur'an, the Bhagavad-Gita, the Zend-Avesta, or the Sutras, to say nothing of the analogies between his life and career and those of the redeemers of ancient Greece or Rome? In the fourth volume of his *A Study of History*, in which he listed the various saviors throughout human history, the British historian and philosopher Arnold Toynbee wrote: "As we stand and gaze with our eyes fixed on the farther shore of history, a simple figure arises from the flood and straightway fills the whole horizon. There is the Savior." But is that "single figure" that "Savior" an idea, of which Jesus is merely the illustration?

No doubt, large portions of this story will not meet with agreement from that aggregate we call the scholarly world. The "quest for the historical Jesus" has undergone more phases than time could tell, has earned many an academic a chair, though precious few have revealed the presuppositions leading them to undertake the study and arrive at the conclusions they have drawn. I admit to being a disciple of Jesus of Nazareth, have been drawn to him since my earliest years, and have lodged in him all the trust and confidence I am able to give. This cannot help affect my judgment respecting the historical genuineness of the events I describe, but I believe the affirmation of their verity at the least deserves a status equal to their denial, since neither I nor all those on the other side of this argument are eye-witnesses. As an old friend and noted scholar once put it, skepticism need not assume pride of place in our methodology. To nuance Pascal's wager: if what I describe belongs, for the most part, to the world of myth and legend, I have suffered only finite loss (my historical reflections), whereas if what I describe, for the most part, belongs to what actually happened, I have received infinite gain (factuality of the life and career of my Redeemer), and avoided infinite loss (absence from the disciples of the crucified).

This story depends exclusively on the witness to Jesus in the New Testament as contained in the four Gospels. In the last century radical skepticism was raised against the credibility of that witness. It was assumed that prior to the writing of the Gospels the oral tradition that underlay them had gone through such revision and emendation by the Christian community that the possibility of constructing a coherent and cohesive "Life" of Jesus was simply out of the question. In recent years, that earlier suspicion has been challenged. For example, parallels have been drawn between the oral and written transmission of the Jesus tradition in early Christianity and the transmission of the oral Torah in Pharisaic Judaism. In the period prior to the composition of the Gospels, so the argument goes, the disciples of Jesus came from this Jewish tradition, known for its extreme care in the handling of the oral Torah. The conclusion drawn is that since the transmission of the Jesus-tradition reflected such a conservative pedagogic, there can have been little scope for alteration. Add to this the fact that the Church which nursed this tradition believed the one whose sayings and doings it was transmitting was the Messiah, the Son of God.[1] But if the parallels drawn between Pharisaic tradition transmission and the transmission of the Jesus-tradition assume a parity between them that actually did not exist, if in fact, "there never was a time when the two trends were so completely separated,"[2] thus whatever comparisons made between them are attributable more to coincidence than deliberate intent, then the argument, however attractive, collapses. Yet I still have an arrow or two in my quiver, furnished me by my doctor-father. First, the creative role of the Church in handing on the Jesus-tradition, of its enhancing the tradition by supplementation or enlargement, needs radical revision.

> The time has come to demythologize the myth of a creative collectivity called *die Gemeinde*. The documents of the New Testament confirm the findings of sociology and anthropology to the effect that collectivities are receptive, not creative entities. In fact, without the authority of the apostles who counteracted the centrifugal tendencies in the congregations, the church would have disintegrated.[3]

Second, the historian needs to test the reliability of a document "by inquiring whether the *effects* of an alleged event can be found when its historicity cannot be apprehended directly,"[4] hence the reasons for believing in the historicity of a narrative, thus of a miracle, could be weightier than

---

1. Cf. Gerhardsson, Birger. *Memory and Manuscript* and *Transmission in Early Christianity* (Grand Rapids: Wm. B. Eerdmans, published jointly, 1998), e.g. 7, 11–12, 15, 27, 32, 44, 201, 258, 283, 295, 333.

2. Piper, Otto A. "Unchanging Promises: Exodus in the New Testament." *Interpretation* 11 (1957): 21; Piper, Otto A. Foreword to *Interpreting the Bible*, viii, trans. Christian Preus (Minneapolis: Augsburg, 1959).

3. Piper, Otto A. "The Origin of the Gospel Pattern," *Journal of Biblical Literature* 78, no. 2 (1959): 123.

4. Piper, Otto A. "The Virgin Birth: The Meaning of the Gospel Accounts," *Interpretation*, no. 2 (1964): 142. Italics mine. Later, in dependence on Hans-Georg Gadamer, Peter Stuhlmacher of Tübingen would cite the "consciousness of historical effects" (*Wirkungsgeschichtliches Bewusstsein*) as essential to the historical task. Cf. Stuhlmacher, Peter. *Historical Criticism and Theological Interpretation of Scripture*. Translated by Roy A. Harrisville. (Minneapolis, Augsburg, 1977), 87.

those supporting its denial. And while there is no question but that the Jesus tradition in its oral form underwent modification, in addition, that the Gospels reflect the activity of the evangelists upon the materials they inherited, I believe that tradition in its essence is faithfully preserved in the Gospels.

PART ONE

Beginnings

The Conception and Birth of Jesus

The Gospels of the New Testament vary widely in their introductions to the life and career of Jesus. Matthew begins with Jesus' genealogy, reaching back to Abraham, then follows with the holy family's flight to Egypt and its return, intersected by the massacre of the innocents. Luke opens with a series dealing with the birth of the Baptist, the prediction of Jesus' birth, the encounter of the Baptist's mother, Elizabeth, with the mother of Jesus, the song of Mary (the Magnificat), John's naming and the prophecy of Zechariah, the presentation of Jesus in the temple, the tracing of his genealogy to Adam, and the return of the family to Nazareth. John, in a radically different fashion, opens with a difficult and extended prologue concerning the *Logos* manifest in the flesh. None of these details appear in Mark, who opens his Gospel immediately with the baptism of Jesus. The result is that for the narrative of Jesus' conception and birth we are entirely dependent on Matthew and Luke.

According to these two evangelists, the parents of Jesus, Mary and Joseph, hailed from Nazareth, a town in that portion of Israel called Galilee, supposedly inhabited by the tribe of Asher in its northernmost, and by the tribes of Zebulun and Naphtali in its southernmost part. Galilee, the so-called "Northern Kingdom," was conquered by Assyria in 721 BC and from then on subjected to Babylonian, Persian, Greek and Roman rule. Unlike the Judeans, members of the so-called "Southern Kingdom," conquered by the Babylonians in 586 BC, Galileans were not subject to transmigration, removed from their homes and ultimately mixed with their foreign conquerors. In Galilee, the situation was reversed. Invasions by foreign troops led to influence in language and custom that would give to the area the name "Galilee of the Gentiles." In the Fourth Gospel, Jesus is described as "son of Joseph from Nazareth" (John 1:45). The reference need not reflect an alternative tradition to that of the virgin birth in Matthew and Luke but merely an accommodation to a principle dominant in Judaism according to which the child was named after the father, putative or no. At any rate, Matthew and Luke describe the conception of Jesus as a divine activity; an event initiated by the Spirit of God. I take the reference to contain both judgment and affirmation. Judgment insofar as the male, the active agent in human history, has no role to play in the event of Jesus' conception and birth. Joseph is in the background, and beyond the initial references to his discovery of Mary's condition, or the angel's announcement that her pregnancy has not come about by way of human initiation, he entirely disappears from the scene. According to speculation, Joseph was elderly when Jesus was conceived and born, while Mary was not yet a teenager. So be it. Further, the event denotes affirmation insofar as it indicates choice of what in that period was certainly the passive instrument of human history as the agent of revelation, as "Mother of God." An army of scholars has urged that admitting to the "biological curiosity" of the virgin conception and birth defies logic, and some feminists have suggested that the activity of the Spirit in Mary's conception hides connotations of rape. More, ancient mythology is filled with stories of the births of heroes and conquerors entirely apart from sexual activity. And while I agree that affirmation of the event as the New Testament describes it does not make me a Christian, I affirm the ancient creedal confession "that he was conceived by the Holy Spirit and born of the Virgin Mary." It is true that explicit witness to the Virgin Birth in the New Testament is extremely rare, occurring only in the Gospels of Matthew and Luke. Further, in the formula quotation of Isaiah 7:14 which Matthew uses to indicate the event as fulfilling prophecy,[1] the Hebrew term (*almah*) which he translates "virgin" (*parthenos*) can simply be translated "young woman," presumably of marriageable age. To add to the difficulty, in Judaism the text from Isaiah 7 is never interpreted messianically. But who can say whether or not the remaining Gospel witnesses assume what is explicit in Matthew and Luke, or that with his formula quotation Matthew does not intend referring to a radically new event? At any rate, however rare, according to the witness of Matthew and Luke, thus of the Church for two millennia, the event of God's taking on flesh in Jesus Christ requires the particular sign of his extraordinary birth, and, if that extraordinary birth is not the cause or condition of the event, it is nonetheless inseparably connected with it. The field of scholarship is strewn with attempts to separate the one from the other, the event from the sign. And while I do not doubt that Jesus Christ could have been born by natural means, I affirm this "biological curiosity" precisely for those intimations of judgment and affirmation cited above. Judgment on human planning

---

1. Matthew 1:22: "All this took place to fulfill what had been spoken by the Lord through the prophet: 'Look, the virgin shall conceive and bear a son, and they shall name him Emmanuel,' which means 'God is with us.'"

and proposing and initiating signaled in the relegating of any human positive activity to the fringes of saving event, and moving affirmation of the passive to its center, are a theme threading throughout the entire biblical account. There will be more than one Joseph warned away from attempting a contribution to the divine event, and to the annunciation or announcement of the coming of deliverance, more than one will only be able to answer: "Let it be with me according to your word," an answer echoed in Jesus' prayer at Gethsemane: "Remove this cup from me; yet, not what I want, but what you want" (Mark 14:36). Finally, however nuanced, Matthew and Luke cite the event of Jesus' birth as an act of God alone. As Luther writes:

> Once more the word has its way—since God promises blessing on all heathen in Christ—that Christ could not come from one man or man's work, for fleshly work (which is cursed) does not allow for what is pure blessing and blest. Therefore this blessed fruit had to be the fruit of only one female body, not of a man—even though the same female body comes from a man, and indeed from Abraham and Adam—so that this mother is a virgin and yet a truly natural mother, but not by natural ability or power, but by the Holy Spirit and God's power alone.[2]

And while I'm not insisting here that all this be taken for gospel, perhaps, when I've finished with the story, the reader may at least understand why I do so.

At any rate, Jesus was conceived in Nazareth of Galilee, a town of little consequence, as compared, say with Sepphoris to the north, a rich, deeply cosmopolitan center under Greek influence, sacked for its weapons by the rebel Judas in 4 BC. To this day the old city of Nazareth has little to commend it, with automobiles minus their wheels stacked behind fences, and the main street with a ditch in the middle to allow animal feces to spill away from the town. The birth itself occurred in Bethlehem of Judea, risen to prominence after the anointing of David, second king of Israel, and together with Hebron a capital city of the "Southern Kingdom," conquered by Babylon, and later under Hellenistic and Roman rule. According to the biblical account, Jesus' parents had traveled from Nazareth to Bethlehem, responding to a census conducted for tax purposes by the current governor of Roman Syria, Quirinius, and while there Jesus was born. Curiously, the biblical account also assigns Jesus' birth to the year of Herod the Great's death in 4. BC But however indeterminate the year of Jesus' birth, the manner, the how of it is clear. He was born in what I and my schoolmates were accused of

---

2. Luther, Martin. "Dass Jesus ein geborener Jude sei," *Weimar Ausgabe*, 11, 318, 20. http://luther.chadwyck.co.uk/ Accessed May 16, 2020.

having been born in when acting crudely—in a barn. If he had been a Julius or an Augustus room would have been made for him, whatever the cost to someone else. And, if indeed, he belonged to the Davidic line, for which reason he was at times called "Son of David," it was a line that had long petered out and been ignored. The ozone surrounding Jesus' conception and birth literally reeks with poverty and want. A pregnancy out of wedlock and birth in a spot reserved for four footed beasts scarcely trumpet the coming of a figure about to turn the world upside down. Compare these lines:

> While they were there [i.e. in Bethlehem], the time came for her to deliver her child. And she gave birth to her firstborn son and wrapped him in bands of cloth, and laid him in a manger, because there was no place for them in the inn.

with these lines, penned by the celebrated Latin poet Virgil (70–19 BC) over a noble Roman's offspring:

> ...enter upon your high honours—the hour will soon be here—dear offspring of the gods, mighty seed of a Jupiter to be! See how the world bows with its massive dome—earth and expanse of sea and heaven's depth! See how all things rejoice in the age that is at hand![3]

Tradition assigns the visit of the wise men to the manger as simultaneous with that of the shepherds, to the point where the crèche is overcrowded. Beyond referring to them as *magoi* the evangelist Matthew neither names them nor identifies their profession, though the term itself was in use since the 6th century BC to denote the devotees of Zoroaster involved in any number of pursuits including astrology, alchemy, and dream interpretation. Johann Georg Hamann, friend and later opponent of Immanuel Kant, describes the reason for the Magi's visit as an illusion „long obsolete," or as a „saga" to which they held as to a prophetic word. Adhering strictly to the narrative sequence in Matthew's Gospel (2:1–18: visit of the wise men, flight to Egypt, massacre of the infants) Hamann writes that the mothers who had to mourn the bloodbath of their children at Bethlehem would have sighed over the inconsiderateness and inquisitiveness „of these foreigners," and describes the newly born King of Israel as taking flight because he was „betrayed by his worshippers to Herod the ruling Anti-Christ, a liar and murderer from the beginning."[4]

---

3. Virgil. *Eclogues. Georgics. Aeneid: Books 1–6.* Translated by H. Rushton Fairclough. Revised by G. P. Goold. Loeb Classical Library 63, (Cambridge, MA: Harvard University Press, 1916). (The eclogue was later twisted by Christian writers to refer to Jesus).

4. Hamann, Johann Georg. „Kreuzzüge des Philologen." *Sämtliche Werke*, 2: Schriften über Philosophie/Philologie/Kritik. 1758–1763, (Vienna, 1950): 136–141.

The Prologue in John

As in Mark, the birth narratives are omitted by the Fourth Evangelist, with the exception of his reference to the Baptist, and replaced with a "Prologue," intended to describe the event of Christ from the time before time. "In the beginning was the Word, and the Word was with God, and the Word was God" (John 1:1) Any attempt to render that line 'and the Word was divine" comes a cropper on the rule that the anarthrous noun, that is, the noun absent its article, when followed by the copula, that is, the verb "to be," is to be taken qualitatively, thus "was God." That beginning was not the beginning of the creation (Genesis 1:1 "In the beginning when Goad created the heavens and the earth"), but prior to the creaction, an event come about by that Word.: "All things came to being through him, and without him not one thing came into being" (John 1:3). The view is staggering, that the babe of Bethlehem in Matthew's or Luke's account had a life, an existence before its birth, a life with God, and not merely with, but as God. ""In him was life," John continues, "and the life was the light was the light of all people" (John 1:4) Whatever existed or "came to light," could be seen, heard, tasted, smelled or touched, did so by virtue of this Word. And if there should be (as there actually was) a dispute regarding the identity of this Word, he was not a witness to the light but that very light itself: "There was a man sent from God, whose name was John. . ..He himself was not the light, but he came to testify to the light" (John 1:6, 8).

This one in whom was life and light, this Word who was with God, in fact was God, took on human existence: "And the Word became flesh and lived among us, and we have seen his glory" (John 1:14). In a terse sentence or two the evangelist records the reaction to this Word having entered the world: "The world did not know him. He came to what as his own, and his own people did not accept him." John 1:10, 11). And those who did receive him did not do so by summoning up a response from within : ("They) were born, not of blood or of the will of the flesh or of the will of man, but of God") John 1:13).

To this taking on of flesh, this Incarnation, the author is witness: "We have seen his glory as of a father's only son" (John 1:14), a "grace" and a "truth" to put the greatest figure of salvation history till then in the shade—Moses and his law—a Revealer to make known what had all the time been hidden with the hidden God: "No one has ever seen God. It is God the only Son, who is close to the Father's heart, who has made him known" (John 1:18).

If these verses are a Prologue, they are also a synopsis. They sum up, encapsulate, the life and career of Christ, how it all began, and how it ended. And perhaps to the point of controlling or harnessing the entire Gospel narrative, the signs and the discourses, the passion and its sequel in the resurrection appearances. This Prologue would raise alarm in almost every quarter of the early Church, but its author has harsh words for whomever suggests the event merely seemed to be as he describes it, that God and "flesh," God and matter cannot mix. (I John 4:2–3: "Every spirit that confesses that Jesus Christ has come in the flesh, is from God, and every spirit that does not confess Jesus is not from God. And this is the spirit of the antichrist.")

The Boyhood of Jesus

With the exception of Luke, the canonical Gospels Matthew, Mark, and John record nothing of Jesus' boyhood or growing up years. There are, however, narratives concerning Jesus' childhood which did not find their way into the canonical texts, but in one way or another answered to the Church's appetite for stories of his early life. In The Infancy Gospel of Thomas, for example, the boy Jesus is described as modeling sparrows from clay and summoning them to take flight, or is told of raising from the dead a child who had fallen from a second-story roof. One of these so-called "apocryphal" Gospels furnished the Russian composer Peter Ilyich Tchaikovsky with lyrics that describe Jesus' treatment at the hands of tormentors who saw him weaving garlands of roses:

> Do you bind roses in your hair?" They cried, in scorn, to Jesus there. The Boy said humbly: "Take, I pray, All but the naked thorns away." Then of the thorns they made a crown, And with rough fingers press'd it down, Till on his forehead fair and young, Red drops of blood, like roses sprung.[1]

The evangelist Luke furnishes the exception. In the same chapter in which he records the birth and naming of Jesus, he tells of his traveling to Jerusalem with his parents for the festival of Passover, of their concern at his disappearance, he all the while remaining behind in the temple, sitting among its teachers, listening and asking questions Virtually the same narrative appears in the apocryphal Gospel cited above. The narrative continues with the teachers' amazement at the young boy's wisdom, and with his response to his mother's irritation at his three-day absence: "Did you not know that I must be in my Father's house?" What it was about which Jesus

---

1. Shaw, Martin, and Pearcy Dearmer, *The English Carol Book, First Series*, (London: A. R. Mowbray & Co., Ltd., 1913), Carol #21.

was listening and asking questions, thus produced the teachers' amazement at his wisdom, Luke gives no clue. At the same time, his reference to the amazement of the shepherds' audience at their story of the angelic host heralding Messiah's arrival, the amazement of the child's parents at what the ancients, Simeon and Anna, had to say of the child at his presentation in the temple, the amazement of the temple academics at his wisdom, and that of his parents at finding him in the sanctuary, suggest a context calculated to accent the event of this child as removed from the ordinary and natural. Luke, concerned with setting his Jesus-story within a world-wide setting, as signaled, for example, in the reference to a decree having gone out "from Emperor Augustus that all the world should be registered," as well as in the subsequent tracing of Jesus' genealogy to Adam, may have structured his narrative in a form analogous to the ancient hierophanies and legends of Greece and Rome. I do not take this feature as pleading for dependence, since, as the French have it, "similarity does not spell identity." Further, this will be the one and only instance in which those attached to the temple will treat Jesus with deference, thus for some interpreters belonging to a "Galilean spring" supposedly marking the first portion of the third Gospel, and in stark contrast to Matthew's opening his narrative with the threat of violence against the "King of the Jews."

The Forerunner

Gospel tradition connects Jesus' first public appearance with the activity of John the Baptist, according to Luke the child of Zechariah and Elizabeth, a relative of Jesus' mother. Origins of the movement of the Baptist are subject to speculation, some suggesting that John had at one time been an adherent of the Qumran community, a sect (Essene?) located near the Dead Sea, established in the second century BC and with interruptions, continuing till Roman occupation in the early third century AD The adherents of this sect practiced ablutions or lustrations reminiscent of Old Testament washings required of persons cured of leprosy (cf. Leviticus 14: 8–9), or of personal uncleanness (Leviticus 15: 11, 13, 16, 18). In Qumran these baths, besides allowing for admittance or re-admittance to the community after a falling away, may actually have been practiced daily by the devout.[1] If John indeed belonged to the Dead Sea community, he drew from it the significance of baptism as a moral washing, but restricted it to single use.

The context into which Mark sets his narrative of the Baptist is markedly different from that of his fellow evangelists. If Matthew and the others first point to the figure and activity of the Baptist, and from that point conclude that they fulfill the prophetic word, Mark begins with the prophetic word and to it wraps the narrative of the Baptist. The result is that the Baptist's activity does not relate to the Old Testament word as fulfillment to prophecy, but rather the Old Testament word gives definition to the figure and activity of the Baptist. As to his figure, since the angel of the covenant must appear before the end (Exodus 23:20), John appears as forerunner. Because the messenger, Elijah, must prepare the way (Malachi 3:1), John preaches. Because a voice will cry (Isaiah 40:3), John is in the wilderness. Because the

---

1. Cf. The Manual of Discipline (3:4–9; 5:13–14; 6:14–23) in Vermes, Geza. *The complete Dead Sea scrolls in English* (London: Penguin Books, 2004).

last days will see a pilgrimage, an exodus of pilgrims free of sin, all Judea and all Jerusalem flock to John confessing their sins. And, because the prophet's fare and diet must be unlike that of any other (Elijah wore a leather girdle), John eats locusts and wild honey, and because the angel-Elijah-forerunner must appear before the end of days, John is the angel-Elijah-forerunner. As to function or activity, the Baptist's historical appearance is of course characterized by his baptizing with water, but the presupposition for his activity is the prophetic word. John thus does what according to the prophetic word only God can do—effect a baptism of repentance leading to forgiveness. But this gives to Mark's portrait of the Baptist a Christological cast, since it is God as author of the event which is Jesus Christ (verse 1: "The beginning of the good news of Jesus Christ, the Son of God") who gives definition to the figure and activity of the Baptist. Was this angel-Elijah-John combination Mark's invention, or had it been made before he put pen to paper? The fact that the combination appears again in Matthew 11:10 and Luke 7:27, this time in Jesus' mouth, suggests that it had a life prior to Mark. But what the "life-situation" in the Christian community may have been from out of which such a combination arose we can only speculate.

And, if Jesus first traveled in the company of the Baptist, the Gospel accounts are anxious to make clear the difference between John's and Jesus' or his disciples' baptism. In Mark, John announces that he baptizes "with water," whereas Jesus will baptize "with the Holy Spirit" (Mark 1:7). In Matthew the Baptist initially resists Jesus' request to be baptized, stating that the reverse needs doing (Matthew 3:14, and in Luke's Gospel, he will baptize "with the Holy Spirit and fire" (Luke 3:16). In John, the Baptist speaks of his being outranked by the one who follows him. The evangelist next records a dialogue between the Baptist and his questioners containing a curious reference. Priests and Levites arrive from Jerusalem and ask John "who are you?" to which he replies that he is not the Messiah. His questioners continue their interrogation, asking whether or not he is Elijah, to which he replies that he is not. Again, they ask if he is "the prophet," that unidentified figure whom Moses said God would raise up (Deuteronomy 18:15, 18–19), and which he promptly denies. The delegation then demands that John identify himself for the sake of its dispatchers. John answers in the words of Isaiah 40: "I am the voice of one crying out in the wilderness," 1:23). The evangelist then notes that the delegation had been sent by the Pharisees, the only instance in the Gospels in which priests and Levites (members of the Sanhedrin?) are at the beck and call of the Pharisees. Still not satisfied with John's answer his interrogators ask "Why then are you baptizing if you are neither the Messiah, nor Elijah, nor the prophet?" The usual interpretation of the question is that since Judaism required baptism only of proselytes whereas John baptized all and sundry, he would have required authorization from on high to engage in such a radical change, thus had to have been Elijah, or the prophet, or the Messiah himself. The syntax or shape of the question allows for a reading which assumes that when the Messiah, or Elijah, or the prophet comes, he will initiate a baptism. Such a reading is lacking in the literature of Judaism, and an argument from silence is notoriously weak, but given the emphasis on washings in the sects round about Judaism, whether or not the Fourth evangelist has allowed for it John's questioners could have entertained the idea of a radical change occurring with the advent of Messiah, Elijah, or the prophet, moreover, a change signaled in a washing or baptism.

In sight of Jesus, John declares "Here is the Lamb of God who takes away the sin of the world!" (John 1:27, 29, 36). Later, John describes Jesus as baptizing (John 3:26), a reference later corrected to read "not Jesus himself but his disciples" (John 4:2). The Baptist further distances himself from Jesus by titling himself "friend of the bridegroom," sent on ahead of the Messiah (John 3:28–29). From Mark to John something of a progression can be seen in the distinction drawn between the Baptist and Jesus, suggesting a challenge to the earliest Christian community from a sect surrounding the Baptist.[2] For example, the Gnostic sect of the Mandaeans, located in Iraq, though decimated by war, as well as in Iran, views the course of the world as a conflict between good and evil powers seeking to tempt humans through false religions—above all, through Judaism and Christianity. The sect, sometimes called "Followers of the Baptist," practices baptism in flowing water as an initiation rite and as a rite of purification.

Since the line between John and Jesus is less clearly drawn in Mark than in the other Gospels, the competition between John and Jesus may have been less keen in the period in which Mark wrote. Still, the attempt to move from a written text to its possible life prior to its being written down is an extremely hazardous business. In all four Gospels John confesses that he relates to the one who "comes after" as less than a slave to a master (Mark 1:7: "Not worthy to stoop down and untie the thong of his sandals;" cf. Matthew 3:11; Luke 3:16; John 1:27). On the other hand, set within that Christological context by Mark, he is raised to a height he will never reach again.

---

2. Acts 19:1–6 records the apostle Paul as baptizing in the name of "the Lord Jesus" disciples who had been baptized with John's baptism, and had never heard of the Holy Spirit.

The Baptism of Jesus

All the Gospels record Jesus' baptism at the hands of the Baptist, though their narratives vary widely. In Mark and Matthew Jesus alone is witness to the events connected with his baptism. Luke records that while Jesus was praying, "the heaven was opened," presumably in sight of all who had been baptized, and in John the Baptist is witness to the Spirit's descent and remaining on him. In Mark the verb used to describe what occurs at Jesus' emergence from the water is suggestive of a violent event. He writes that the heavens are "torn apart," whereas in Matthew and Luke they are merely "opened." Mark uses the same verb for the tearing of the temple curtain at Jesus' death (Mark 15:38). In view of the voice from heaven at his baptism ("You are my Son, the Beloved; with you I am well pleased," Mark 1:11: cf. Matthew 3:17; Luke 3:22), and the confession of the centurion at Jesus' breathing his last, "Truly this man was God's Son!" Mark 15:39, a revelation out of the ordinary suggests itself, as if a revelation were not such, in any case something abrupt, sudden, bursting from above and thrusting below, a rending or tearing, eliminating the distance between above and below. As noted earlier, in Matthew's account, the Baptist demurs at Jesus' coming to him to be baptized, and hears the reply, "Let it be so now; for it is proper for us in this way to fulfill all righteousness" (Matthew 3:15). The meaning is obscure, unless Matthew intends to portray Jesus as shouldering human destiny, thus "sav[ing] his people from their sins" (Matthew 1:21), and for this act gaining approval from the torn heaven. This might suit a Gospel often described as oriented toward obedience to commandment.

From earliest times, and by some of the most celebrated scholars such as Peter Abelard (1079—April 21, 1142), it has been argued that Jesus was adopted as the Son of God at his baptism, resurrection, or ascension. The view has been part of a long series of attempts at explaining the relationship between Jesus of Nazareth, Man and God, and God the Father. Some scholars see adoptionist tendencies in Mark and Paul. For example, they argue that though Mark refers to Jesus as Son of God, references occurring at 1:1 ("The beginning of the gospel about Jesus Christ, the Son of God," but not in all versions); at 5:7 ("What do you want with me, Jesus, Son of the Most High God?") and at 15:39 ("Surely this man was the Son of God!"), are adoptionist in tone. Others suggest that while some early manuscripts of Mark 1:1 do not contain the title "Son of God," neither do they contain the phrase, "Today I have begotten you," allowing for the conclusion that Mark contains less adoptionist tendencies than supposed. Notably, the *Gospel of the Hebrews*, a Jewish-Christian gospel all but equal to Matthew in size, widely known to the early Church Fathers, but preserved only in citations or summaries, and like others of its kind relegated to the periphery by the canonical Gospels, displays distinctly adoptionist tendencies. One fragment referring to Jesus' baptism as an event for which the Spirit waited in vain through all the prophets, but who now in Jesus the Son finds rest, reads:

> And it came to pass when the Lord was come out of the water, the whole fount of the Holy Spirit descended upon him and rested on him and said to him: My Son, in all the prophets was I waiting for thee that thou shouldest come and I might rest in thee. For thou art my rest; thou art my first-begotten Son that reignest for ever.[1]

Though the view has long been abandoned, of the two contesting parties in earliest Christianity which Ferdinand Christian Baur (1792–1860) thought he detected, that is, the Ebionitic, adoptionistic, legalistic Jewish Christian party, and the Pauline law-free gospel party open to the Gentiles, he regarded Matthew's Gospel as least affected by either faction and thus the best support for a life of Jesus. One thing is certain: from the historical perspective, an adoptionist interpretation of the vision and voice at Jesus' baptism represents a challenge to what may be the one and only doctrine with which all Christian communities laying claim to the name agree: the doctrine of the Trinity, implicit in the doxologies of the New Testament epistles, heralded in the Fourth Gospel's affirmation of the Word's having become flesh (1: 14), and at Nicaea (AD 325) and afterwards made touchstone of Christian confession. From this point of view it is not because the Spirit descended on Jesus like a dove or a voice was heard from heaven that

---

1 Cited by Vielhauer, Philipp; Strecker, Georg, in *New Testament Apocrypha: Gospels and Related Writings*, edited by Schneemelcher, Wilhelm and Wilson, Robert McLachlan. Vol. I (2nd ed.) (Louisville: Westminster John Knox Press, 1991), (6th German edited and translated by Georg Ogg):174–176.

he became the Son of God, but rather because he was the Son of God the Spirit descended and a voice from heaven was heard.

The Baptist's question, recorded in Matthew 11:2 ("Are you the one who is to come, or are we to wait for another?"), suggests that he expected something from Jesus he did not get. In his initial proclamation he had given his portrait of the one to come apocalyptic, end-time features: "Even now the ax is lying at the root of the trees; every tree therefore that does not bear good fruit is cut down and thrown into the fire. . .the one who is more powerful than I is coming after me. . .His winnowing fork is in his hand, and he will clear his threshing floor and will gather his wheat into the granary; but the chaff he will burn with unquenchable fire" (Matthew 3:10, 14; Luke 3:9, 17). Had the Baptist shared the idea that Messiah would come to turn Israel's enemies to ash, save the repentant remnant, and assume his place as ruler over all the earth? What else would have moved him to ask? Was Jesus ill-suited to the portrait he had drawn? Responding to John, Jesus lists his activity, hardly free of end-time intimations ("the blind receive their sight, the lame walk, the lepers are cleansed, the deaf hear, the dead are raised, and the poor have good news brought to them" (Matthew 11:4–5). According to the story line, John was in prison, and sent a delegation to put the question. Had he been in the dark respecting Jesus' activity, but if so, why does Jesus conclude with a beatitude toward whomever would take no offense at him, what with all that giving sight to the blind, and on and on to raising the dead? John had to be the candidate for that beatitude. Did he see the activity of Jesus as a string of events loosed from any serious context, say, from the context three Major and seven Minor Prophets had furnished with their heralding the "Day of the Lord," and in whose train Jesus himself had set him? (Matthew 11:11).

> Blow the trumpet in Zion; sound the alarm on my holy mountain! Let all the inhabitants of the land tremble, for the day of the Lord is coming, it is near—a day of darkness and gloom, a day of clouds and thick darkness! Like blackness spread upon the mountains a great and powerful army comes; their like has never been from of old, nor will be again after them in ages to come. (Joel 2:12)

Till now, there is little of Jesus in that.

PART TWO

The Begininings of Jesus' Ministry

Jesus' Appearing and Preaching

The Gospels record that Jesus begins his ministry with the summons to repent in view of the arrival of God's Kingdom, or as Matthew persistently refers to it, "the Kingdom of heaven," in typically Jewish fashion omitting use of the "*Shem*," the Name. As always in the New Testament, "repentance" does not denote "change of mind" as in the Greek, but "return," as in the Hebrew. As for the term "Kingdom," "Rule of God" is a happier translation, allowing for contrast with earthly powers, as well as for emphasizing God's Rule as a future as well as a present reality. In his summons and announcement of the Rule of God's arrival Jesus clearly alters the preaching of the Baptist. John's baptism is a sign of protection for those who return to a hope that threatens to be lost, hope in the future of God. More, for John this return occurs in view of the coming Judge ("His winnowing fork is in his hand, and he will clear his threshing floor and will gather his wheat into the granary; but the chaff he will burn with unquenchable fire," Matthew 3:12). On the other hand, for Jesus the Rule of God has already broken in; change in the world has already begun. God is beginning to win back the world that he made. The Rule of God is thus the constitutive event of salvation. Further, the judgment that John preaches is only the obverse side of the grace or favor of God which Jesus announces and makes explicit in his activity and mission. To the extent the Rule of God is not only a present but also a future reality, hastening toward a final consummation, to that extent, at least in a formal sense, for both John and Jesus those who receive the "good news are ranged alongside those who wait. Thus, in Jesus' proclamation of God's Rule a tension exists between its having "already" come, and its having "not yet" totally overcome what opposes it.

This Rule of God is not brought about by dint of human effort. It is not, as one noted early twentieth century theologian put it, transformed by Jesus into a "series of gifts which one is to receive by changed behavior according to the will of God," does not occur "in such fashion that one follows the leading will of God by the deed."[1] Nor did Jesus, called to establish the Kingdom, altogether detach the idea of judgment from its future conclusion,[2] totally subsuming the "not yet" aspect of the kingdom into the "now already" of an ethical action. According to the New Testament, the coming of the Rule of God Jesus brings is an event totally apart from human activity, whatever its consequences for human existence. The saving activity of God made concrete in Jesus must occur apart from human doing or willing able to taint or hinder it. One may indeed wait for it, place hope in it, long for it, as did old Simeon "for the consolation of Israel" (Luke 2:25), but, as the Reformer wrote in his Small Catechism, "the Kingdom of God comes indeed of itself without our prayer." Jesus may act in response to human need, as the stories of healing indicate, but that he is or that he acts in response to a need is his own affair. In reply to the leper's plea, "Lord, if you choose, you can make me clean," Jesus answers "I do choose. Be made clean!" Let that "I do choose" (Matthew 8:3) or "I will," as the older translation has it, serve as device over his life and career. And while there is no question that an ethical action is required in view of the Rule of God's arrival—what else could the summons to repent mean?—that ethical action is in the nature of an answer, not an accompaniment to the Rule of God. Reduction of the proclamation of the Kingdom of God to a summons to ethical action according to a series of values, current in nineteenth and early twentieth century idealism, has stood godparent for that talk of "building the Kingdom" I heard so often in my youth. In the New Testament, the call to pray in the second petition of the "Our Father" that the Kingdom or Rule of God may come "also to us" is not a call to initiate or accompany its arrival.

Writing of the beginnings of Jesus' ministry, the Fourth Gospel records two events not reported in Mark, Matthew, and Luke. The first is Jesus' conversation with Nicodemus, which may be assigned to the beginnngs of Jesus' ministry in Jerusalem. The second is his conversation with the woman at the well, in a context totally absent in the Synoptics, that is, a ministry of Jesus in Samaria. Both reports illustrate what is perhaps the greatest difference between John and his co-evangelists, that is, his recital of the language of Jesus. In John Jesus does not speak in parables, terse or brief statements, but in long, repetitive speeches which advance in spiral fashion toward a dominant theme and end in self-disclosure. Scholars tend to regard this feature as reflecting post-Easter influence on earlier Jesus-tradition. Obviously,

---

1 13 Cf. Ritschl, Albrecht. „Die Christliche Lehre von der Rechtfertigung und Versöhnung." *Der biblische Stoff der Lehre*, no 2. (Bonn: A. Marcus u. C. Weber's Verlag, 1900): 32, 40.

2. Ibid: 36.

the experience of Easter was bound to leave its mark on the Gospel tradition. Apart from that experience there would scarcely have been any gospel to record. The question is whether or not the Easter experience has so influenced the Gospel of John that it has substantially altered the memory of what Jesus actually said or did, and whether such alteration could be legitimized by invoking the Spirit who would "remind" Jesus' followers of all he had said (cf. John 14:26). Such will always be a matter of debate.

The dialogue with Nicodemus opens with the nightly visit of the Pharisee, who addresses Jesus as "Rabbi," or Teacher, as did Andrew and Peter earlier (John 1:38). Initially, the address is at considerable distance from the Baptist's heralding of Jesus as "Son of God" (John 1:34,), but then, as also occurs with Nathaniel, it is heightened to the acknowledgement of Jesus' unique relation to God. In Nathaniels' case the acknowledgement ("You are the Son of God!" John 1:49) is occasioned by Jesus' foreknowledge ("I saw you under the fig tree before Philip called you," John 1:48), and in that of Nicodemus ("We know that you are a teacher who has come from God," John 3:2a), by a conclusion drawn from Jesus' activity ("No one can do these signs that you do apart from the presence of God," John 3:2b). To this Jesus responds that none can enter the kingdom of God without being born "from above." Nicodemus takes the adverb to mean "again," and in utter confusion asks, "How can anyone be born after having grown old? Can one enter a second time into the mother's womb and be born?" Actually, in the Greek the adverb may be taken to mean either "from above" or "again." The same is true of the adverb in the Aramaic, the language of the dialogue. Nicodemus tripped over the double entendre, conceived the "birth" as a repetition. Jesus had in mind a "birth" distinct from human activity, a birth beyond and in contrast to the earrthly or fleshly: "What is born of the flesh is flesh, and what is born of the Spirit is spirit" (John 3:6). But if this "birth" is in contrast to what is earthly or fleshly, it occurs *by way of what is earthly*, by *"water* and Spriti." Not a scintilla of the Gnostic's hatred of the earthly here. Further, this birth is undiscoverble by those who have not undergone it. In a sentence reminiscent of the Jewish wisdom teacher, Jesus says, "The wind blows where it chooses, and you hear the sound of it, but you do not know where it comes from or where it goes. So it is with everyone who is born of the Spirit" (John 3:8). To all of which Nicodemus responds: "How can these things be?" only to be reprimnded for an obtuseness suggestive of deficient learning: "Are you a teacher of Israel, and yet you do not understand these things?" (John 3:10). Continuing his reprimand, Jesus appeals to the testimony of witnesses which Nicodemus should have allowed: "We speak of what we know and testify to what we have seen, yet you do not receive our testimony." According to Mosaic law, two witnesses sufficed to sustain a charge,³ and to whom would that "we" refer, if not "the one who descended from heaven" (John 3:13) and the one from whom he descended? The inability to understand hides a refusal to receive. Then, curiously, Jesus says: "If I have told you about earthly things and you do not believe, how can you believe if I tell you about heavenly things?" (John 3:12). The refusal to receive has become a refusal to believe. But how could that "birth from above. . .by water and Spirit" be taken to be "earthly things"? Nicodemus has been conceded some grasp of the situation. The Pharisee has at least understood that the "birth" of which Jesus speaks has to do with being, with existence. He has tumbled to the ontological aspect of the event, though he construes it entirely in terms of an earthly, human activity, entrance into the womb a second time, an event he rejects, disbelieves. Then follows the first passion prediction in the Fourth Gospel, prefaced by the statement that "no one has ascended into heaven except the one who descended from heaven, the Son of Man." Whether a post-Easter titular use or no, "Son of Man" here is a self-reference, and the word of his ascent is a prolepsis, the anticipation of an event yet to occur, the hour of his "going to the Father" (John 14:12), the "hour" of his glorification, for this evangelist synonymous with his crucifixion (John 17:1). Faith in this "Son of Man," not the apocalyptic figure of Jewish hope, masked, incognito, suspected of being this one or that, but the one "lifted up," crucified, gives eternal life. "For," Jesus continues (use of the indeclinable particle is argumentative, gives the reason for the statement preceding), it was love of the world that God gave his only Son, "gave" being another prolepsis, another anticipation of an event yet to occur. The term used for that event ("gave" = *edoken* in the Greek), willed by both Father and Son, would reflect the Old Testament concept of sacrifice as atonement. And if the evangelist was not only at odds with members of the synagogue whio refused Jesus as Messiah, but also with Gnostics and their notion of earth as evil, and the body as a prison, this was one more shot across their bow. Nor was this "sending" of the Son a condemnation of the world, but a salvation through faith in him. Faith, then, would decide the issue whether the world would return the love it had been shown in the "lifting up" or the "giving" or the "sending" of the Son of Man. And that lifting up, that giving or sending was a "light" to which those would come who "do what is true," or as the original reads, "who do the truth." This curious phrase appears nowhere else in the New Testament, and however construed it leaves no room for truth as an abstraction, a mere correspondence of thought and reality pursued with the mind, but a coherence realized in action, in something done, in

---

3. Cf. Deuteronomy 19:15 and its echo in Sotah 6, 2 in Danby, Herbert. *The Mishnah* (MA: Peabody, 2012), 299.

a coming to "the light." On the other hand, those who would not come to "the light" loved "darkness" because their evil risked exposure. "Light" and "dark" make up a pair used to illustrate every fundamental theological idea of the Old Testament. None better contrasts chaos and creation; none more adequately reveals glimpses of the holiness of God, expresses the experience of the Creator, or conveys the prophecy of the revelation of the Being of God and his judgment. The pair is forerunner of some of the greatest New Testament utterances. And so they appear here in a context which for many is the most signal utterance in the Gospel of John: "For God so loved the world that he gave his only Son, so that everyone who believes in him may not perish but may have eternal life" (John 3:16). Ultimately, Nicodemus will have negotiated the hurdle, will have come to "the light." With Joseph of Arimathea he brought myrrh and aloes with which to wrap the body of Jesus (John 19:39-40).

Jesus' conversation with the woman at the well occurs at Sychar, near Shechem, chief city of the Samaritans. The inhabitants of the region, the "Northern Kingdom," originally comprised the tribes of Ephraim, Manasseh, Issachar, Asher, and Zebulun. Led by their reading of II Kings, historians have traditionally described the Samaritans as a mixed race, resulting from a massive transmigration during the Assyrian occupation in approximately 721 BC Taking its lead from II Chronicles, current research tends to regard the inhabitants as retaining their Jewish identity, despite the Assyrian military campaigns. For example, in II Chronicles 30, King Hezekiah of Judah issues an invitation to "all Israel and Judah. . .also to Ephraim and Manasseh," to come to Jerusalem to keep the Passover. The division between Judaeans and Samaritans may not have occurred till the third century BC when the Israelites of Samaria built their sanctuary to Yahweh at Mt. Gerizim. From that point the Samaritan religion as we know it began to harden, with its sole appeal to the Pentateuch as scripture mediated by Moses, appeal to the altar at Gerizim as built by Joshua at Moses' command, and its prospect of a final day of vengeance and recompense initiated by the Messiah or *Taheb*. The New Testament as well as the Mishnah reflect ambivalence toward the Samaritans. For instance, the New Testament records that Jesus encountered resistance in the Samaritan villages (Luke 9:52-53), and instructed the disciples not to go there (Matthew 10:5-6), but it also notes that Jesus healed a Samaritan (Luke 17:11-19), and that a Samaritan figured large in his most famous parable (the Good Samaritan in Luke 10:29-37). The Book of Acts, chapter 8, refers to Samaria as an early mission field. Likewise, the Mishnah allows the Samaritan to share the Common Grace, to pronounce the "Amen" after the Benediction, to care for produce and sell wine designated for tithing.⁴ But it also records the saying of Rabbi Eleazar ben Hyrcanus, one of the most prominent scholars of the first and second centures AD, and the sixth most frequently mentioned in the Mishnah, that "He that eats the bread of the Samaritans is like to one that eats the flesh of swine."⁵ Jesus encountered the Samaritan woman on his way from Judea through Samaria to Galilee. Seeing her at the well he asked her to give him a drink, to which she replied "How is it that you, a Jew, ask a drink of me, a woman of Samaria?" (John 4:9), to which the evangelist adds his note that the one has nothing to do with the other, reflecting one of the coontradictories noted above. Then follows an extended exchange about water in which the woman, just as Nicodemus, trips over the double entrendre, construes Jesus' reference to the "living water" he will give as one part hydrogen and two parts oxygen, and he without a bucket and the well deep. To Jesus' correction, but this time without tracing the error to a lack of learning, the woman asks for a water that will never again need drawing from Jacob's well. The woman has tripped again, but, just as Nicodemus, has caught at least a glimpse of Jesus' intent. She acknowledges him as the one able to furnish such an uncommon element: "Sir," she says, or "Lord" (*Kyrie* in the Greek), "give me this water" (4:15). Then Jesus abruptly breaks off the dialogue to tell the woman to go, call her husband. She replies that she has none, Jesus agrees, notes she has had five, and is not married to number six. Addressing Jesus as "Lord" for the second time, the woman in astonishment says, "I see that you are a prophet" (4:19), and proceeds to engage in a theological conversation reflecting the competition between Jews and Samaritans over the central sanctuary: "Our ancestors worshiped on this mountain, but you say that the place where people must worship is in Jerusalem" (4:20). Then, majestically ("Woman, believe me"), Jesus gives worship a character sufficient to render site irrelevant: "The hour is coming when you will worship the Father neither on this mountain nor in Jerusalem. . .when the true worshipers will worship the Father in spirit and truth" (4:21, 23). Curiously, between those two phrases, Jesus denies that to the Samaritan and asserts that only the Jew has a worship aware of its object: "You worship what you do not know; we worship what we know, for salvation is from the Jews" (4:22). Having just rendered worship sites irrelevant, it cannot mean that Judaism is an exception, but rather that despite its clinging to geography the reltivizing of site has its origin in Judaism, and God for its author: "For the Father seeks such as these to worship him" (4:23b). To

---

4. Cf. Berakoth 7, 1: 8, 8; Demai 2, 4: 5, 9: 6, 4; Teremoth 2, 9, in Danby, Herbert. *Mishnah*. (MA: Peabody, 2012), 7, 9, 23, 25, 27, 55.

5. Shebith 8, 10, in *Ibid.*, 49.

this the woman responds, "I know that Messiah is coming" (4:25). There is nothing askew in her response. Just as true worshp of the Father "in spirit and truth" is an event for the end-time ("the hour is coming"), so also is the coming of the Messiah. But that Messiah is not the Taheb or the Moses of Samaritan religion. In the sovereign predication originating in the revelation to Moses,[6] and threading throughout the discourses in John, Jesus says "I am he" (4:26a). The narrative ends with the woman's return to her city with news of the encounter, with the disciples' tripping over yet another double entendre,[7] and with the Samaritans' independently coming to faith in "the Savior of the world" (4:42).

According to the first three Gospels, following a forty-day fast, Jesus was tempted of the devil. First of all, Mark's account is extremely abbreviated when compared with that of Matthew and Luke. He merely notes that the Spirit "immediately drove" Jesus into the wilderness, the verb suggestive of a having been "thrown," the very same as used in Mark's exorcism narratives. In Matthew and Luke the solicitations of Satan begin with the temptation to turn stones to bread, an obvious opener in view of the forty-day and night fast, after which Jesus was "famished" (Matthew 4:2; Luke 4:2). In Matthew the second temptation consists of the devil's taking Jesus to the pinnacle of the temple and urging him to prove his sonship with God by throwing himself down, and the third of the devil's showing him all the kingdoms of the world, promising to give it all away on the condition of Jesus' worship. In Luke the sequence of the second and third temptations is reversed, with the promise to give Jesus all the world's kingdoms in second place. For Luke and Matthew the temptation to turn stones to bread logically follows Jesus' exhaustion at the forty day fast, but Luke's assigning the temptation to assume the glory and authority of all the kingdoms of earth to the next position might match his interest in accenting the story of Jesus within a world-historical context.

Attempts on the part of scholars to wrest meaning from this narrative as "in some measure" corresponding to real experience, as symbolic, denoting a "conflict of soul," or as an encounter and a conquest of ideas unworthy of Messiahship in Jesus' own mind, only indicate anguish at having to deal with the narrative. Naturally, questions arise. If there were no witnesses to the event of the struggle, how did the news of it get out? Is it at all reasonable to suppose that Jesus told his disciples of it? Or, is the entire scene to be put down as legend, to which each of the evangelists adds his nuance?

6. Hebrew: *Eh/ye asher eh/yeh*: "I am who I am," Exodus 3:14.

7. "Rabbi, eat something." But he said to them, "I have food to eat that you do not know about." So the disciples said to one another, "Surely no one has brought him something to eat?" 4:31–33.

As will soon be shown, in Mark, for all its brevity, the narrative serves as engine for an activity threading through his Gospel. In Luke the event ends with the devil's departure till "an opportune time," (4:13), the time when "Satan entered into Judas called Iscariot" (22:3). If Luke does not intend that those comments serve as an "inclusion," bracketing his Gospel as an extended passion narrative, then at least as omen of the passion to come. In addition, if the evangelists did not compose their writings simply to furnish their readers with factual knowledge, but to invoke faith, then the dialogue between Jesus and Satan, in each instance concluding with a Deuteronomic text, is calculated to remind the reader about the one from whom strength to endure in the hour of temptation derives. Thus Matthew and Luke 4:4 read: "One does not live by bread alone, but by every word that comes from the mouth of God;"[8] Matthew 4:7 and Luke 4:12 read: Do not put the Lord your God to the test,"[9] and finally Matthew 4:10 and Luke 4:8 read: "Worship the Lord your God, and serve only him."[10]

Fyodor Dostoevsky's great novel, *The Brothers Karamazov*, with its story-poem entitled "The Grand Inquisitor," may be among the most thoughtful of expositions on the temptations. The story is told by Ivan, suspected atheist, to his brother Alyosha, a novice monk, with its setting in Seville, the city to which Jesus comes down after almost a hundred heretics have been burned at the stake. Everyone recognizes him. An old man blind from childhood cries out for healing, and the scales fall from his eyes. At the cathedral steps weeping mourners bring in a little white coffin containing a child of seven. The child's mother throws herself at his feet, and at Jesus' word the little girl rises and sits up. At that moment the Grand Inquisitor arrives, sees everything, orders the guards to take him, and shuts him up in prison. In the darkness the prison door suddenly opens, the Inquisitor enters, and proceeds to list his prisoner's errors at the temptation. Only three powers, says the cardinal, are able to conquer and hold captive—miracle, mystery, and authority—but his prisoner rejected them all, and gave a freedom no one understands, only fears and dreads. If he had given men bread, they would have run after him like a flock of sheep. Next, refusing to throw himself down from the pinnacle of the temple, he had rejected miracle, and finally, spurning the royal purple with which he could have founded a universal state, he had asked only for the free verdict of the human heart. Admitting he had once prized that freedom, the Inquisitor confesses he had awakened,

---

8. Cf. Deuteronomy 8:13 (and or Exodus 23:25 in Luke 4:4).
9. Cf. Deuteronomy 6:16.
10. Cf. Deuteronomy 6:13.

and joined with those who had corrected Christ's work.[11] This story-poem, to say nothing of the interpretation of the evangelists from which it takes its origin, deserves hurling against the suspected historicity of the event. In the last century, and well into the present, we have witnessed what can only have been transcendent, from hell, not simply from an aggregate of human error. As for Jesus, the temptation never left him: "Let the Messiah, the King of Israel, come down from the cross now, so that we may see and believe" (Mark 15:32; cf. Matthew 27:42–43).

---

11. Dostoyevsky, Fyodor. *The Brothers Karamazov*, trans. Constance Garnett. (NY: Dover, 2001), (originally published London: Heinemann, 1914).

Calling of the Disciples

Similarities and differences exist in the Gospel narratives of the calling of the disciples. In Mark and Matthew, Simon and Andrew, James and John, in Luke, Simon, James and John are first to be summoned. All three Synoptists record Jesus' calling of Levi (Matthew), all three give a list of the twelve, including Thaddaeus in Mark and Matthew, Judas of James in Luke, and end with Judas Iscariot. The same list as appears in Luke's Gospel appears also in his second volume (Acts 1:13). While Mark and Matthew describe the other Simon as a Galilean or Canaanite, Luke describes him as the zealot. In John, the calling of the disciples is more complicated. First, Peter and Andrew are introduced to Jesus by the Baptist, and in the same phrase he had used earlier to announce him to the crowd ("Here is the Lamb of God"). But only Simon, "son of John. . .to be called Cephas (translated Peter),"[1] and Philip, both of Bethsaida in Galilee, are summoned to follow. Nathanael, the hardest to convince, ultimately acknowledges Jesus as Son of God, King of Israel, following their dialogue. In Mark, Matthew and Luke the lists of the disciples are virtually alike, whereas in the Fourth Gospel the number is drastically reduced to two, Simon Peter and Philip.

Could the slight differences existing between the three Synoptists derive from later remembrance of the number of the Twelve, a remembrance absent or deliberately erased by the time the Fourth Gospel was composed? Or, are the listings simply trajections into the record of traditions that took on life in the communities from which they derived? In view of the four evangelists' agreement, as well as the priority they give to the one they first name, whatever may have been the role of the others, Simon Peter must surely have belonged to the first company of Jesus' followers, and, if the

---

1. Note the Fourth Evangelist's translation of the name from Aramaic to Greek.

Synoptists are to be credited, Andrew, and the Zebedees, James and John, together with the tax-collector Levi or Matthew, belonged to it as well.

The appellation "zealot," attached to the second Simon named by Luke in his Gospel and Acts, has suggested to some that among Jesus' followers at least one disciple belonged to a group involved in resistance to Rome. The conclusion drawn is that the revolt by Judas of Galilee gave birth to a Jewish freedom movement which developed into the Zealots by the time Jesus lived and worked, and that "*Simon Zelotes*" belonged to this movement. The suggestion that the title "Iscariot" naming Jesus' betrayer is a transliteration of the Latin *sicarius,* that is, "dagger man," thus that Judas was also a guerrilla whose betrayal was actually a move intended to force Jesus to assume power, puts a considerable strain on the imagination. The most plausible explanation is that "Iscariot" is a Greek transliteration of a Hebrew name, consisting of two elements, the first a common noun meaning "man," and the second denoting provenance, the place from whence, hence "the man from *Kirioth*," that is, from a town in south Judea. Of all those called to follow, Matthew (Levi) was the most despised. His ilk put in bids with the local governor for the opportunity to collect taxes among their own kind, notoriously bilking them in excess of the amount bid along with their expenses. For all intents and purposes the "publican" was a minion of the hated conqueror. The assortment of disciples was thus a "mixed bag," comprised of Galilean fisherfolk, one, if not two. possibly resistance or protest types, and a hated lackey of the Roman rule. But it would not do to set the aggregate down as simple, unlearned country bumpkins, particularly in light of what they later accomplished.

In contrast to his fellow evangelists, Mark writes that the response of Simon and Andrew to Jesus' call to follow was absolutely without hesitation: "Jesus said to them, 'Follow me. . .'" And immediately they left their nets and followed him" (Mark 1:18). Use of the same temporal adverb together with the tenses of the verbs used in connection with the summons to James and John indicate a like reaction: "Immediately he called them; and they left their father Zebedee in the boat with the hired men, and followed him" (Mark 1:20). There is nothing in the way of preparation for the summons or the response, nothing to be compared with the Baptist's witness, with Jesus' invitation to potential disciples to "come and see," or with the miracle of "second sight" resulting in an acknowledgement of Jesus' identity, as in the Fourth Gospel. The response is sudden, instantaneous, devoid of choice or reflection; the four abandon their occupation and family responsibility in a trice. "The Gospel of St. Matthew," a 1964 film in memory of Pope John XXIII, directed by the Marxist Pier Paolo Pasolini, and described by the Vatican as the best film on Christ ever made, while assigning the disciples' immediate response to Matthew, rather than to Mark, nonetheless gives a stunning recital of the event. In one minute Peter and Andrew are putting in their nets, in the next they are out of their boats trailing off after Jesus, followed by James and John running to have a look. If indeed the evangelists are not interested in simply supplying information but in engaging their readers on behalf of faith in Christ, then Mark's expectation is that the reader's or hearer's reaction to this event of the disciple's calling and response requires as sudden and as uncalculated a reaction as theirs. But aside from whether or not the account in Mark or in the others, for that matter, is nuanced for the hearer or reader's sake, whatever power emanated from that Man to effect such response as is recorded in all the Gospels deserves paying mind if not pure wonder. Not for nothing Mark uses the same verb for Jesus' appointment of the Twelve as the Septuagint uses for God's creation of the world: "He made (Greek: *epoiesin*) twelve. . .to be with him" (Mark 3:13; cf. Genesis 1:1).

The Exorcisms

The form or structure of the exorcisms is simple and uncomplicated: Each event is comprised of four and often five "constants" or ingredients. The first sets the scene for the activity to be described. The scene or venue of the first exorcism is the Capernaum synagogue (Mark 1:21); of the second, the house of Simon and Andrew (Mark 1:32, 34); of the third Jesus' departure to the sea of Galilee (3:7); of the fourth Jesus' and his disciples' arrival at the country of the Gerasenes (5:1), and the scene or venue of the fifth is the crowd's encounter with Jesus and the disciples following the Transfiguration (9:14). The second constant or ingredient is the evangelist's statement of the problem or dilemma, and not always in terse fashion. The first exorcism involves the man with an "unclean spirit" (Mark 1:23–24); the second involves those who were sick or possessed with demons (Mark 1:32, 34); the third has to do with "unclean spirits" (Mark 3:11); the fourth with the "unclean spirit" living among the tombs (Mark 5:2–7), and the fifth involves the boy with a "spirit" (Mark 9:17–18). The third constant or ingredient marks Jesus' advance to the problem. In the first instance he rebukes the unclean spirit: "Be silent, and come out of him!" (Mark 1:25); in the second it is merely stated that he cast out many demons (Mark 1:34); in the third it is repeated that he cured many, among them the unclean spirits (3:10). In the fourth instance Jesus commands, "come out of the man, you unclean spirit!" (Mark 5:8), and in the fifth he says, "You spirit that keeps this boy from speaking and hearing, I command you, come out of him, and never enter him again!" (Mark 9:25). The fourth ingredient marks the result of Jesus' action. In the first exorcism narrative, the unclean spirit, convulsing the man and crying with a loud voice, comes out of him (Mark 1:25). In the second, it is simply stated that many were cured (Mark 1:34); in the third, the unclean spirits fall down before him and shout, 'You are the Son of God!" (Mark 3:11); in the fourth, the Gerasene demoniac, Legion, enters the herd of swine (Mark 5:13), and in the fifth, the spirit cries out, convulses the boy, and comes out (Mark 9:26). The fifth ingredient may be described as "the chorus," indicating the response of the witnesses to the act. In the first instance, the synagogue members are amazed, herald the newness of Jesus' teaching, coupled with his command over the spirits, and his fame spreads throughout Galilee (Mark 1:27–28). In the second, absent the "chorus," the narrative concludes with Jesus' ordering the demons to be silent because they know him (Mark 1:34). In the third, the "chorus" consists of the Phariseers' conspiring with the Herodians to kill Jesus (Mark 3:6). In the fourth, the demoniac proclaims in the Decapolis what Jesus did for him, and all are amazed (Mark 5:20: In the fifth and last, the disciples ask Jesus why they could not heal the boy with the spirit, to which he replies, "this kind can come out only through prayer" (Mark 9:28–29).

Clearly, the references to the persons involved do not yield a medical diagnosis, but denote a condition that renders impossible genuine participation in the religious community. The persons involved have "unclean" spirits. These references, together with the Baptist's description of the one to come as "more powerful" (1:7, in Greek the comparative adjective" strong-er" is used), and Jesus' parable in response to the charge that he is in league with the devil ("no one can enter a strong man's house and plunder his property without first tying up the strong man") all take their force from the temptation event in which the "strong man," Beelzebul, or Satan, is tied and bound.

Jesus as exorcist, or more precisely, Jesus as victor over the demonic powers, is the portrait yielded by the exorcism narratives of Mark's Gospel, a role suited to the Messiah in the ancient Jewish literature, rife with parallels to Mark 1:21–28. For example, in the pseudepigraphical *Book of Enoch* 55:4 (written under an alias), an apocalypse dating from ca. 160 BC, the author writes:

> Ye mighty kings who dwell on the earth, ye shall have. To behold Mine Elect One, how he sits on the throne of glory and judges Azazel, and all his associates, and all his hosts in the name of the Lord of Spirits.[1]

The Testament of Levi 18, another pseudepigrapical book, written before AD 70, perhaps before 70 BC, reads:

> And Beliar shall be bound by him (the high priest of the Messianic age), And he (the high priest) shall give power to His children to tread upon the evil spirits.[2]

---

1. R. H. Charles, *The Apocrypha and Pseudepigrepha of the Old Testament* (Oxford: Clarendon Press, 1913), vol. 2, 221.

2. R. H. Charles, Ibid, vol. 2, 314.

The Testament of Zebulun 9 reads:

> He shall redeem all the captivity of the sons of men From Beliar;
> And every spirit of deceit shall be trodden down.[3]

The Assumption of Moses 10:1, still another pseudepigraphical work, written before AD 30, reads:

> And then (in the blessed age of consummation) His Kingdom shall appear throughout all His creation, And then Satan shall be no more.[4]

It has been argued that the whole of the story of Jesus is regarded by Mark as the continuation of the climactic struggle between the Spirit and Satan begun at the temptation, a struggle relived in the story of the Christian Church. Jesus thus opens the battle and carries it on as the "Son of God" equipped with the Spirit. His exorcism of the demons manifests his struggle and victory. It is the "beginning of miracles" at Capernaum, the commission of the Twelve (3:15), and proof of supreme power at the transfiguration (9:14–29). Power over the demons is the assurance that Jesus is "the Holy One of God" (1:24, 34; 3:11–12; 5:7), the basis on which the Twelve are brought to this conviction (4:39–41). As Benjamin W. Bacon of Yale put it years ago, "exorcism. . .is the nucleus and core of Markan Christology."[5] Matthew and Luke give much less attention to exorcisms. Matthew repeats the narrative of the Gerasene demoniac (8:28), as well as Jesus' response to his enemies' charge that he is an agent of Beelzebul, though altering the occasion to the exorcism of a deaf and mute (Matthew 12:22), to which he then adds Jesus' parable of the return of the unclean spirit (Matthew 12:43–45). The second evangelist includes only one other exorcism, that of the epileptic boy following the Transfiguration (Matthew 17:14–21). In Luke references to exorcisms are drastically reduced. The charge against Jesus is repeated, and as in Matthew its occasion is altered to the exorcism of a mute, not deaf, demon (Luke 11:14). This is the one lone reference in Luke, aside from an earlier general note regarding Jesus' healing those troubled with "unclean spirits" (Luke 6:18). Exorcisms are totally absent from the Fourth Gospel.

If this gradual elimination of exorcisms indicates that Matthew, Luke, and John were wary of casting Jesus in the role of a wonder-worker, of the "divine man" of pagan or even Jewish tradition, Mark was not in danger of it. Framing the exorcism with references to the crowd's astonishment (Mark

---

3. R. H. Charles, Ibid, vol. 2, 130.
4. R. H. Charles, Ibid, vol 2, 420.
5. Bacon, Benjamin Wisner. *Is Mark a Roman Gospel* (MA: Harvard University Press, 1919), 3.

1:22, 27), he clearly coupled Jesus' teaching with the exorcism as evoking the crowd's fear and amazement. The reference to the crowd's reaction to Jesus' teaching (Mark 1:22: "They were astounded at his teaching, for he taught them as one having authority, and not as the scribes"), has its proper exposition in the narrative of the exorcism. Likewise, the reference to the crowd's reaction following the exorcism (Mark 1:27, as I prefer to translate: "What is this? A new teaching! With authority He commands even the unclean spirits, and they obey him"), makes clear that what is involved is more than something heard. It is something seen, a revelation, an epiphany. This same conjunction of amazement at Jesus' teaching and his deeds occurs at his appearance in Nazareth: "Where did this man get all this? What is this wisdom that has been given to him? What deeds of power are being done by his hands!" (Mark 6:2). For both events at Capernaum and Nazareth Mark uses the same verb to describe the crowd's reaction.

A significant number of interpreters has argued that whereas the healing narratives and miracle stories reported of Jesus are almost without exception legendary, all of them transferred to Jesus since the Son of God in the first century could only be considered a wonder-worker, Jesus nevertheless healed the possessed, and in the earliest Christian communities exorcisms were among the signs of an apostle.[6] In response, I believe that restricting belief to Jesus' performance of exorcisms reflects influence from the side of psychology, the assumption being that his casting out of demons may be explained in terms of the treatment of psychic disorders, whereas his miracles of healing cannot. However, attempts to explain the exorcisms in this fashion comes a cropper over the fact that in each instance of an exorcism, the result is sudden and instantaneous, whereas the treatment of such psychic disturbances as are assumed for these narratives is not, but requires time for their resolution. We are left with the alternative that the exorcisms are to be set down to the legendary or mythical, or are to be believed as having actually occurred.

---

6. Cf. Käsemann, Ernst. *Kirchliche Konflikte* (Gottingen: Vandenhoeck & Ruprecht: 1981), 205–206.

Miracles of Healing

Of all the healing miracles recorded in the four Gospels, the first three in tandem record seven.[1] Mark and Matthew together record two healing miracles[2]; Matthew and Luke together record two[3], Mark alone records one[4], Matthew alone records three[5], and Luke alone records five.[6] The Gospel of John records only one miracle in tandem with the first three Gospels,[7] one in tandem with Matthew and Luke,[8] and two healing miracles independently of them.[9]

Each of the seven healing miracles recorded by the first three evangelists contains the same number of "constants" as the exorcism narratives.

---

1. Simon's mother in law healed: Mark 1:29 (Matt. 8:14; Lk 4:38); the leper cleansed: Mark 1:40 (Matt. 8:1; Lk 5:12); the paralytic healed: Mark 2:1 (Matt. 9:2; Lk 5:17); man with withered hand healed: Mark 3:1 (Matt. 12:9; Lk 6:65); the synagogue leader's daughter raised, and the woman suffering from hemorrhages healed: Mark 5:21 (Matt. 9:18; Lk 8:40); 5,000 fed: Mark 6:30 (Matt. 14:13; Lk 9:10); deaf man healed: Mark 7:31 (Matt. 9:32; Lk 11:14).

2. Healing the sick at Gennesaret: Mark 6:53 (Matt. 14:34). 4,000 fed: Mark 8:8 (Matt. 15:32).

3. Healing the centurion's servant: Matthew 8:5 (Lk 7:1); healing the Canaanite woman's daughter: Matthew 15:21 (Lk 8:40);

4. Healing the blind man of Bethsaida: Mark 8:22.

5. Two blind men healed: Matthew 9:27; many cured: 15:29; two blind men healed: 20:29.

6. Raising the widow of Nain's son: Luke 7:11; healing the crippled woman: 13:10; healing the man with dropsy: 14:1; healing the ten lepers: 17:11; healing the blind beggar near Jericho: 18:35.

7. 5,000 fed: John 6:1.

8. The healing of the Centurion's son: John 4:36b-54; Matt. 8:5-13; Luke 7:1-10.

9. Healing of the lame man at the pool of Bethesda (John 5:2-9), and the man blind from birth (John 9:1-12).

The scene set for the healing of Simon's mother-in-law is Jesus' departure from the synagogue and entry into the house of Simon and Andrew (Mark 1:21); for the healing of the leper the man's begging and kneeling before Jesus (Mark 1:40); for the healing of the paralytic the report that Jesus is at home in Capernaum (2:1); for the healing of the man with the withered hand that Jesus has re-entered the Capernaum synagogue (Mark 3:1). The scene set for the healing of the woman with hemorrhages and the raising of the synagogue leader's daughter is Jesus' encounter with the leader after leaving the country of the Gerasenes (5:21); the scene for the feeding of the 5,000 is Jesus' and the disciples' departure to a deserted place (Mark 6:30–31), and for the healing of the deaf man Jesus' return from the region of Tyre (Mark 7:31). The second constant, indicating the problem or dilemma, involves the fever of Simon's mother-in-law (Mark 1:30); the leprosy of the man who begs and kneels before Jesus (Mark 1:40); the paralysis of the man lowered through the roof (2:33–34); the withered hand of the man met in the synagogue (3:1b); the death of the synagogue leader's daughter, the hemorrhages of the woman who touches Jesus' cloak (Mark 5:21–43); the hunger of the 5,000 (Mark 6:33–37), and the deafness and speech impediment of the man brought to Jesus (Mark 7: 32). As for the third constant, Jesus may utter a word, or may touch the afflicted person. He takes Simon's mother-in-law by the hand (Mark 1:31); he touches the leper and says "be healed" (Mark 1:41); to the paralytic he says "my son, your sins are forgiven," then "stand up, take your mat and go to your home" (2:5, 11). To the man with the withered hand he says, "come here," then, "stretch out your hand" (Mark 3:3, 5b); to the woman suffering from hemorrhages he says, "Daughter, your faith has made you well," and to the synagogue leader's daughter he says, "little girl, get up!" Before the 5,000 he takes the five loaves and two fish, looks up to heaven, blesses and breaks the loaves, and gives them to the disciples to set before the crowd (6:41), and he puts his fingers into the deaf man's ears, spits and touches his tongue, and says "Be opened" (7:34). The fourth ingredient denoting the result of Jesus' action is, in the majority of instances, sudden, dramatic, marked either by the temporal adverb "immediately" or by a description making clear the instant cure or solution. Simon's mother-in-law rises to serve her guests (Mark 1:13); "immediately" the leper is cleansed (Mark 1:42); the paralytic stands up, and "immediately" takes his mat and leaves; the hand of the man with the withered hand is restored (Mark 3:5); the woman's hemorrhages "immediately" stop, and "immediately" the synagogue leader's daughter gets up and begins to walk about; the 5,00 all eat, with twelve baskets of broken pieces and fish taken up (Mark 6:42–43), and the deaf man's ears are "immediately" opened, his tongue is released, and he speaks plainly (Mark 7:35). A chorus as the fifth ingredient puts the period to four of the seven healings in the first three Gospels. In Mark 1:27 and parallels, the crowd in the synagogue asks, "what is this? A new teaching! With authority he commands even the unclean spirits." In Mark 1:45, the man healed of dropsy spreads the news so that Jesus cannot openly enter a town. In Mark 2:6–7 and parallels, when hearing Jesus' word to the paralytic, the scribes exclaim, "Why does this fellow speak in this way? It is blasphemy! Who can forgive sins but God alone?" Following the healing of the man with the withered hand, the Pharisees hold counsel, how to destroy Jesus. In Mark 5:42 and parallels, following Jesus' raising the synagogue leader's daughter, the onlookers are "overcome with amazement." In Mark 7:37 and parallels, witnesses to the healing of the deaf mute are "astounded beyond measure, saying, "He has done everything well; he even makes the deaf to hear and the mute to speak."

Of the pair shared by Matthew and Luke, Matthew contains four and Luke five ingredients. The one independent narrative of Mark contains four ingredients. Of Matthew's independent narratives the first contains five, the second four, and the third four. Of Luke's independent narratives the first contains five, the second five, the third four, the fourth five, and the sixth five ingredients. The first "constant" or ingredient might well be Mark's own editorial additions or "seams," simply repeated in the parallel narratives of Matthew and Luke. Next, in a goodly number of instances, the word uttered by Jesus or joined to an action is exorcistic in nature. In 1:41 Jesus commands the leper, "be made clean!" In 1:43 he is angered at the leper and sends him away at once. In 5:13 the same verb is used for the herd's entering the swine as for the exorcism in 1:25. Use of the Aramaic ("Talitha cum") in 5:41, "Ephphatha" in 7:34 are suggestive of a secret formula or incantation, and in 9:26 the same verb appears as is used in 1:25 and 5:13.

Obviously, not all the stories recorded by Mark and repeated in Matthew and Luke deal with demon possession, but the repetition of the constants adhering to the exorcism narratives and repeated in the healing stories suggests that Mark used the mould of the exorcism for the majority of those healing narratives, with Matthew and Luke following suit where their stories are in parallel. This would square with the observation that Mark records the story of Jesus as a continuation of the struggle between the Spirit and Satan begun at his temptation.

In John's "Book of the Seven Signs," the same constants appear. The scene of the first sign (John 2:1–11) is a wedding in Cana of Galilee. Jesus' mother states the problem: the wine has given out. The narrrative is interrupted with Jesus' retort that it is of no matter to him since his "hour" has not yet come.

Surprisingly, at this his mother summons the servants to do whatever he commands. Jesus makes multiple application to the problem. He instructs the servants to fill the six water jars intended for Jewish rites of purification, then summons them to fill them, next to draw some out, and bring it to the steward, who performs the role of chorus by exclaiming that good wine is always served first, but in this instance has been reserved for last. There is dual choral response with the evangelist's note that at this first of Jesus' signs, his disciples believed in him. Cana is also the scene of the second sign (John 4:36b–54). The problem: A royal official arrives to plead with Jesus to come down and heal his son, ill and near death at Capernaum. Again the narrative is interrupted with Jesus' comment that his audience will not believe unless it sees signs and wonders. Jesus advances to the problem by summoning the official to go, stating that his son lives. The result is announced by the official's servant who tells him that his child is alive, that he began to recover the moment Jesus said he would live. The chorus consists of the official's coming to faith together with his entire household. Scene of the third sign is the Pool of Bethesda, at which lies a man with a thirty-eight year illness (John 5:2–47). Again the sequence is interrupted with a dialogue between Jesus and the invalid. Jesus then advances to the problem with the word that the man "stand up, take your mat and walk," the result of which is that the man is immediately cured. The chorus is a compound: The Jews' complain that the deed was done on the Sabbath, then ask who was responsible for the cure; the erstwhile invalid admits his ignorance of Jesus' identity; Jesus encounters the fellow in the temple and enjoins him to sin no more, lest worse befall; the man informs the Jews that it was Jesus who healed him, following which they commence their persecution for his sabbath breaking, and at his word that he and his Father are at work, plan to kill him. The scene for the feeding of the five thousand (John 6:1–15) is variegated. At the Sea of Tiberias a crowd follows Jesus due to his "signs. . .for the sick." Near to Passover, Jesus goes up the mountain with his disciples, and himself describes the problem. With the crowd coming toward him, he asks Philip where they are to buy bread for the crowd to eat. The sequence is interrupted with the evangelist's note that Jesus was testing Philip. The problem is accented with Philip's response that six month's wages would not buy enough for each to get a little, and with Andrew's information about a boy with a mere five loaves and two fish. Finally, Jesus advances to the problem with a command that the people sit down. He takes theloaves, gives thanks, and distributes them along with the fish. The result is initially downplayed with the simple statement that "they were satisfied," then emphasized with the gathering of the remnants in twelve baskets, at the sight of which the people chorus with the word that "this is indeed the prophet who is to come into the world," rush to make Jesus king, while he withdraws to the mountain. The same constants or ingredients are present in sign number five, Jesus' walking on the water, shared with his co-evangelists (John 6:16–21) as noted above. The scene is set near the sea where the disciples board a boat for Capernaum in the dark. The problem involves a rough sea, hard rowing, and terror at the sight of Jesus walking near the boat. Jesus advances to the problem, says: "It is I; do not be afraid." The result: the boat immediately reaches the shore toward which the disciples were first headed. The chorus follows the people's search for Jesus after discovering the disciples had taken to the sea without him, and finding him on the other side ask: "Rabbi, when did you come here?" The scene for the sixth sign, the healing of the man blind from birth (John 9:1–41), is set with a mere two words (*kai paragon*), translated "as he walked along," presumably in sight of the temple where Jesus had just engaged in dialogue with the Jews over Abraham (John 8:39–59). The problem is that of the man born blind. Jesus' application to the problem, interrupted by his remonstrating with the disciples respecting the cause of the man's condition ("Neither this man nor his parents sinned; he was born blind to that God's works might be revealed in him," 9:3), involves spitting on the ground, making mud with the saliva, spreading it on the man's eyes and ordering him to wash in the pool of Siloam. The result: The man returns from the pool able to see. The chorus consists of a dialogue between the man and the Pharisees respecting Jesus' breach of the Sabbath with his healing, their interrogation of his parents who allow he can speak for himself, and after a second dialogue with the Jews, ends with the man's confession, "Never since the world began has it been heard that anyone opened the eyes of a person born blind. If this man were not from God, he could do nothing," in response to which his interrogators drive him out of the synagogue. The seventh and final sign is that of the raising of Lazarus, like the sixth, consuming the entire chapter (John 11:1–57). The scene is set in Bethany, home of Mary, Martha, and their brother Lazarus. The sisters inform Jesus of the problem: their brother is ill. Solution to the problem is interrupted by Jesus' diagnosis ("this illness does not lead to death; rather it is for God's glory," 11:4b), and by the protracting of his visit to Bethany, following which the narrative is strewn with dialogue, first with Jesus' conversation with the disciples who warn him against another visit to Judea, next with his announcement of Lazarus' death and of his plan to return to Bethany, on the way toward which he meets Martha who tells him her brother has died, then with a dialogue with her over the resurrection and her confession of him as Messiah, Son of God, then with Martha's informing her sister of the "Teacher's" arrival, and Mary's reproach ("Lord, if you had been here, my brother would not have died," 11:32b), and finally, with the Jews' query concerning Jesus' power ("Could not he who opened the eyes of the blind man have kept this man from dying?" 11:37). At last, Jesus makes advance to the problem, but not before another dialogue with Martha at his order to remove the stone to the tomb. He looks upward, says "Father, I thank you for having heard me," an aside uttered for the sake of those standing by,[10] cries with a loud voice, "Lazarus, come out!" And the result: the dead man comes out with bound hands and feet, his face wrapped in a cloth. In what has come to be a typically Johannine device, the chorus is divided between those who believe in Jesus and the chief priests and Pharisees who call a meeting, at which the high priest Caiaphas prophesies Jesus' death "for the nation," and the crowd at Jerusalem before Passover in doubt over Jesus' showing himself in public.

Now the question arises as to whether or not these miracles of healing are to be set down as legendary, at best containing a smidgin of historical fact blown out of all proportion through multiplication. What urges toward this assessment is the fact that stories such as are told of Jesus' healing abound in pagan literature. First and foremost among the divine men of the period was the first century wandering Pythagorean Apollonius of Tyana (ca. 15—ca. AD 100) a figure much discussed by the fourth century Church fathers. A current introduction to a textbook on the New Testament teases the reader with a description of Appollonius as if it were of Jesus:

> . . ..a supernatural being informed his mother the child she was to conceive would not be a mere mortal but would be divine. He was born miraculously. . ...As an adult he left home and went on an itinerant preaching ministry, urging his listeners to live. . .for what is spiritual. He gathered a number of disciples. . .who became convinced that his teachings were divinely inspired. . .in no small part because he himself was divine. He proved it to them by doing many miracles, healing the sick, casting out demons, and raising the dead. But at the end of his life he roused opposition, and his enemies delivered him over to the Roman authorities for judgment. Still, after he left this world, he returned to meet his followers in order to convince them that he was not really dead but lived on in the heavenly realm. Later some of his followers wrote books about him.[11]

---

10. Cf. the same device in 6:5b-6: "'Where are we to buy bread for these people to eat?" He said this to test [Philip], for he himself knew what he was going to do."

11 Ehrman, Bart D. *Did Jesus Exist?: The Historical Argument for Jesus of Nazareth* (New York: Harper Collins, 2012), 208–209.

First of all, the historicity of the life and career of the Appollonius depends upon the amount of trust placed in his principal biographer, Philostratus the Elder (ca.170—c.247). According to recent research, the discourses which Philostratus professes to copy from Damis, an acolyte and companion of Appollonius, may or may not be genuine. Second, though the possibility that the Jesus-tradition is dependent on that of Appollonius is out of the question, the reverse is not. In such a society as Rome, which had abandoned its traditional gods for deities of the east, assigning divinity with all its trappings to a celebrated figure from Cappadocia, whether or not in competition with Jesus of Nazareth, would scarcely represent a departure from usual habit. Lastly, to cite G. K. Chesterton, in contrast to the great thinkers of antiquity who had very little to do except to walk and talk,

> . . .the life of Jesus went as swift and straight as a thunderbolt. . ... Something had to be done. It emphatically would not have been done, if Jesus had walked about the world forever doing nothing except tell the truth. . . .The primary thing that he was going to do was to die. . ...He may be met as if straying in strange places, or stopped on the way for discussion or dispute; but his face is set towards the mountain city."[12]

It is no secret that for over a hundred and fifty years the majority of Bible interpreters has denied the genuineness of the healing miracles reported of Jesus, to the point that anyone with an opposite view risks a *sacrificium intelligentiae*. To great extent what has largely motivated the great chorus of scholars is the contention that the space-time continuum to which we are all subject does not allow for interruption on the part of the transcendent, that if God is at work in creation, it is through the means available in ordinary, everyday life. In the last century, this view was given large space in the interpretation of the so-called mythical world-view of the Bible. That is, the view that the biblical understanding of the universe as comprised of the heavenly, earthly, and nether worlds, with humans subject to sorties from one or the other, had not been "baptized," but represented a relic of antiquity, not to be jettisoned, as per the nineteenth century liberal understanding, but as "cradle" of the New Testament message to be reinterpreted in terms of human self-understanding. The reinterpretation was ingenious, and the influence of its principal adherents extended throughout Europe and the United States. Now, this so-called "existential" understanding has more or less given way to an earlier wholesale dismissal of the miraculous, "cradle" or no. But however liberal or "existential" the persuasion reveals

---

12. Chesterton, G. K. *The Everlasting Man* (Oxford: Oxford City Press, 2011), Book 2, Chapter 3.

two flaws. The first is that the miracles of healing and related narratives are treated as isolatable data, strung together at the whim of the evangelists, and whose purpose may or may not be to indicate the principal's magical and therapeutic powers. If we do not submit to this notion, there must be some factor imposed on the narratives which yields a unity beyond, if not counter to that of historical sequence. Luke, for one, gives the clue. In his account of Jesus' exorcism of the mute demon, he writes that some said "He casts out demons by Beelzebul, the ruler of the demons," to which Jesus replies: "If it is by the finger of God that I cast out the demons, then the kingdom of God has come to you (Luke 11:15, 20). It is the kingdom of God brought by Jesus which serves the Gospel writers their organizing principle, their "paradigm" respecting material which without it appears disjointed and unconnected. To this paradigm of the kingdom all the narratives of exorcism and healing are bent and warped. In response to the philosopher David Hume, in the New Testament the miraculous is not made "the foundation of a system of religion."[13] Rather, it is in the service of the kingdom brought by Jesus by which its authors intend to evoke faith in their hearers/readers. Clearly, from the lists above, in themselves those narratives have little unity, but when seen in relation to the kingdom as organizing principle they become an integrated whole. The failure to distinguish the historical data from the proclamation they are meant to serve has led to regarding the miracle narratives as evidence of the Christian community's attempt to meet the demands of its hearers for material at any cost. Only by its service to the kingdom brought by Jesus does Hume's dictum regarding the miraculous apply:

> the Christian Religion not only was at first attended with miracles, but even at this day cannot be believed by any reasonable person without them. Mere reason is insufficient to convince us of its veracity: and whoever is moved by Faith to assent to it, is conscious of a continued miracle in his own person, which subverts all the principles of his understanding, and gives him a determination to believe what is most contrary to custom and experience.[14]

We are used to listing and interpreting events in historical sequence. In fact, we demand it in the name of reason. The Gospel writers themselves give some, albeit modest, attention to historical sequence. Mark, despite gathering his material in "blocks," for example, clustering his narratives of the exorcisms within the so-called "Galilean" period, and, with only one

---

13. Hume, David. *An Enquiry into Human Understanding*,

14. Hume, David. *An Enquiry Concerning Human Understanding*, *The Harvard Classics*, ed. Charles W. Eliot. (New York: P.F. Collier & Son, 1909–1914), vol. 37, part 3 of 3.

exception (the healing of blind Bartimaeus, Mark 10:46) listing all his healing narratives ahead of Jesus' triumphal entry, thus giving Papias of Hierapolis (AD 70–163) occasion to write in his *Exposition of the Sayings of the Lord* that he did not compose his Gospel "in order" (*ouch en taxei*) nevertheless strictly adheres to days and hours in his narrative of the passion. But the Gospel writers saw an alternative beyond the linear (or the cyclic) in the paradigmatic. In this purely formal respect they were not unlike their pagan counterparts. What gave to their paradigm its power to embrace what was disparate was the kingdom of God, whose bringer and guarantor they confessed as Messiah and Son of God.

The second flaw in current irritation over the miraculous is that of the rigid conservatism on the part of biblical scholarship which resists the arrival of the new, of change and alteration, in favor of the status quo. Clearly, toward the end of the Old Testament the miraculous retreats in favor of the mighty word, finally in favor of that word at second hand, in Judaism called the *Bat Qol*, "daughter of the voice." The words of the later prophets are substituted for the mighty acts of the former prophets, of Moses and Elijah. But with the coming of Jesus a new time phase has begun, a phase in which the redemptive activity of God breaking into human history is made both visible and audible. Mighty acts reappear, harnessed to his proclamation that in him God has drawn near in a way never to be supplanted or surpassed. Conservatism, love for the status quo, resistance to the new, to the affirmation that in Jesus of Nazareth the coming Kingdom of God has broken in, may lurk behind relegating the miracle narratives of the New Testament to the mythical and legendary, allowing a shred for the exorcisms.

The Gospels, to say nothing of the remainder of the New Testament, are strewn with references to the new, to the "new teaching," the "new covenant," "new tongues," the "new commandment," etc. The evangelists are convinced that the nature of the world would have remained essentially unchanged if Christ had not brought in the kingdom. Through his proclamation the powers formerly holding the world in thrall must give way, and what was once shrouded in obscurity can now be grasped and understood. Let an atheist thinker put period to the argument:

> What is peculiarly new in the Christian mythos is this, that there is no imitation of resurrection gods from ancient time, rather that the resurrection and the life, as the totally novum of history, should have emerged just now. Only the dead-living Jesus disclosed to his followers the renewal of the inner man from day to day (2 Cor. 2:16), and sustained the Christians with the words of the new heaven and the new earth (Is. 26). Only the star that never appeared before, and showed the Magi the way to

an event that never happened before, shed light on the novum of the apocalypticist regarding the new Jerusalem, and the totally revolutionary word of its capitol city: "Behold, I make all things new (Rev. 22:5). Finally, only through the Bible did such a public and pivotally emerging idea of the Incipit vita nova come into the world. The youthful source of the fable did not spring up since time out of mind in some distant space or remembered age-old legend of Osiris or Attis. Rather, it emerged quite by itself, a novum in time, as if there had been nothing really new before Jesus, only a yearning for it, only signs, only expectation. As a later mystic formulated it: "The unbegotten God becomes in time/ what he never was in all eternity" (Silesius, Cherubinische Wandersmann, TV 1).[15]

---

15. Bloch, Ernst. *Religion im Erbe, Eine Auswahl aus seinen religionsphilosophischen Schriften*, Siebenstern-Taschenbuch 103, ed. Jürgen Moltmann (Suhrkamp: Frankfurt am Main, 1959, 1961, 1964, 1966), 63.

The Nature Miracles

The Synoptists record Jesus' stilling of the storm (Mark 4:35–41; Matt. 8:23–27, and Luke 8:22–25), and all four evangelists record the feeding of the five thousand (Mark 6:30–44; Matt. 14:13–21; Luke 9:10–17; John 6:1–15). Mark, Matthew and John record the narrative of Jesus' walking on the water (Mark 6:45–53; Matthew 11:22–34; John 6:15–21). Mark and Matthew record the feeding of the four thousand (Mark 8:1–10; Matt. 15:32–50, and Jesus' cursing the fig tree (Mark 11:12–14; Matt. 21:18–22). Matthew alone records the miracle of the fish and the temple tax (Matt. 17:24–27), and John alone records the miracle at Cana (John 2:1–12). These seven nature miracles are outnumbered by the exorcisms and miracles of healing, to the effect that the Gospel writers appear hesitant to lard their records with reports of events contradicting the course of nature, Matthew and Luke having already done so to a maximum with their accounts of Jesus' conception and birth. Hence the question as to whether these miracles can be legitimated as serving the same "paradigm" of the kingdom as do the exorcisms and healing narratives, or are to be jettisoned as reflecting the influence of pagan, Hellenistic legend on the Jesus-tradition and its transmission. Perhaps Jesus' cursing the fig tree requires symbolic interpretation, urging the question whether the Messiah will find fruit among a people given a half millennium since the Exile to get ready for him, and perhaps his guiding a single fish out of multiple schools to Peter's hook with the precise amount in its mouth of the tax from which he was exempt can be construed as metaphor.

The narrative of Jesus' stilling the storm (Mark 4: 35–41; Matthew 8:24–27; Luke 8:22–25) may appear to some as absurd as a purple cow.[1] Others

---

1. "I never saw a Purple Cow, I never hope to see one; But I can tell you, anyhow, I'd rather see than be one" (Gelett Burgess, 1866-1951).

may believe the story is true simply because it appears in the Bible. Still others may view it as needing demythologizing, rescue from the context of a three-storied-universe with heaven above, hell below, earth between, and humans the object of sorties from each, for the sake of an interpretation of existence:

> Where can I go from your spirit? Or where can I flee. From your presence? If I ascend to heaven, you are there; if I make my bed in Sheol, you are there. (Psalm 139:7–8)

There are Greco-Roman and Jewish parallels a-plenty. Here are four which have often been cited. Let Homer's hymn to Castor and Pollux be first in line:

> glorious children of neat-ankled Leda. . .deliverers of men on earth and of swift-going ships when stormy gales rage over the ruthless sea. Then the shipmen call upon the sons of great Zeus. . .until suddenly these two are seen darting through the air on tawny wings. Forthwith they allay the blasts of the cruel winds and still the waves upon the surface of the white sea.[2]

The legend is repeated in Thomas Babington Macaulay's (1800–1859) ode to The Battle of Lake Regillus in his *Lays of Ancient Rome*:

> Back comes the chief in triumph Who in the hour of Fight Hath seen the great Twin Brethren In harness On his right. Safe comes the ship to haven Through Billows and through gales, If once the great Twin Brethren Sit shining on the sails.[3]

Next, in his history of Rome, Dio Cassius (AD ca. 165–235) records an episode involving Julius Caesar during a storm at Lacus Curtius:

> Wishing, therefore, to sail to Italy in person and unattended, he embarked on a small boat in disguise, saying that he had been sent by Caesar; and forced the captain to set sail, although there was a wind. When, however, they had got away from land, and the gale swept violently down upon them and the waves buffeted them terribly, so that the captain did not longer dare even under compulsion to sail farther, but undertook to return even without his passenger's consent, then Caesar revealed himself, as if by this act he could stop the storm, and said, "Be of good cheer: you carry Caesar."[4]

---

2. *Homeric Hymns*, trans. Hugh G. Evelyn-White (Cambridge: Harvard University Press, 1914).

3. Macaulay, Thomas Babington. "The Battle of the Lake Regillus," *Lays of Ancient Rome*, XL (London: Longmans, Green, Reader, & Dyer, 1867): 138.

4. Dio Cassius, *Roman History*, trans. Earnest Cary, *Loeb Classical Library* (Cambridge: Harvard University Press, 1916), IV.

Third, the Babylonian Talmud contains a story of Rabban Gamaliel aboard ship during a storm that almost drowned him. The Rabban pleads with God that it was not for his honor he had exiled Eleazar ben Hyrcanus who brought ruin wherever he directed his eyes, but solely for the honor of God, "in order that disagreements do not multiply in Israel." The plea was accepted, "the sea immediately rested from its anger."[5]

Fourth and finally, the Jerusalem Talmud contains the story of a Jewish lad on a heathen ship during a great storm. After praying in vain to their gods, the heathen order the boy to pray to his, adding that Israel's God hears his own and is mighty. The lad prays with all his might and the sea becomes silent. The story ends with quoting Deuteronomy 4:7: "For what other great nation has a god so near to it as the Lord our God is whenever we call to him?"[6]

The differences between at least these four parallels and the narrative in Mark, Matthew, and John need little space. Macaulay's words, "The gods who live forever Have fought for Rome to-day! These be the Great Twin Brethren To whom the Dorians pray," hardly apply to the One who abhorred violence. As for Dio Cassius' story, despite Caesar's bidding, the storm did not cease, and the ship had to ply toward land. Again, none of the exorcisms, miracles of healing, or nature miracles reflect the *quid pro quo* behind Rabban Gamaiel's plea, and as for the Jewish lad, he had to pray to achieve his end, whereas the wind and sea are suddenly quiet at Jesus' *summons*. In the New Testament, the raising of Lazarus is the only event at which the miracle follows a prayer, but the prayer is not for the miracle:

> Father, I thank you for having heard me. I knew that You always hear me, but I have said this for the sake Of the crowd standing here, so that they may believe That you sent me (John 11:41b-42).

Here, at least, no continuum of cause and effect.

While all four evangelists record the feeding of the five thousand Mark and Matthew record a second feeding of four thousand, Mark setting the scene in a foreign country, "the region of the Decapolis" (7:31), and Matthew setting it in Galilee (Matthew 15:29), just as his co-authors the first feeding. The two feeding narratives are so strikingly similar that they appear to be two records of the same event. For example in Mark's narratives the site is a desert place (cf. Mark 6:31 and 8:4); in both there is reference to the crowd's confusion and hunger (cf. Mark 6:34 and 8:2–3); in both the disciples are in a quandry (cf. Mark 6:35 and 8:4), and in both Jesus asks

---

5. Baba Mezia 59b.
6. Berachah 9.13b, 22, line 12.

the disciples what is at hand to feed the crowd (Mark 6:38 and 8:5). In John, the question is addressed to Philip (John 6:5), but then, as if to forestall any suggestion of limited knowledge on the part of Jesus, John immediately adds: "He said this to test him, for he himself knew what he was going to do" (John 6:6), a reprise of the refrain in chapter two ("he knew all people and needed no one to testify about anyone; for he himself knew what was in everyone, John 2:25), and echoed by Jesus at Lazarus' tomb ("I knew that you always hear me, but I have said this for the sake of the crowd standing here," John 11:42).

In the accounts of the feedings, each segment appears to reflect earliest Christianity's celebration of the Lord's Supper. In Mark 6:39 and 8:6 Jesus functions as presiding officer. The disciples' distribution of the loaves and fish in Mark 6:41 and 8:6 as well as their gathering up of the frarments (Mark 6:43 and 8:8) corresponds to the duties assigned the "deacons" in primitive celebration. The blessing or thanksgiving (Mark 6:41; 8:6) and the breaking of the bread (Mark 6:41 and 8:6), in which verbs are used from which the ancient church derived its technical terms for the thanksgiving and breaking of bread (*eulogeo* and *klao*), reflect practices that have continued till the present. Even the references to the hour of the day and the arrangement of the crowds into companies of fifty and one hundred (Mark 6:35, 39–40) reflect ancient Christian practice. Mark's reference to the "green grass" on which Jesus commands the crowds to sit (Mark 6:39) could allude to Western, Roman practice of celebrating the Supper at Passover, a springtime, April festival. Could the ancient church's celebration have fathered the feeding narrative? Or, is the assumption of a community creation trajected back into the life and career of Jesus too heavy a burden for that community to bear? There is more: Mark 8:17–21 and Matthew 16:7–10 record the disciples' neglecting bread for their trip to the other side of Gailee, and Jesus' remonstrance at their having tripped over a dietary minim when infinitely more was at stake. Jesus says, "when I broke the five loaves for the five thousand how many baskets full of broken pieces did you collect...and the seven for the four thousand, how many baskets full of broken pieces did you collect?" (Mark 8:19–20), and to their answers replies, "do you not yet understand?" (Mark 8:21). Is this scene intended to furnish an allegorical interpretation of the feedings? To these questions John would respond with a robust denial. For this evangelist the feeding is a "sign," the third after Cana (John 2:1–11), and the healing of the official's son (John 4:46–54). That is, it is a tangible, palpable event calculated to point beyond itself to Jesus' significance and power. Without that tangibility, there would be no sign, and nothing beyond it to which to point. Of course, whatever it was to which that tangible event was intended to point could be skewed, misinterpreted.

And the crowd missed the point. It hailed Jesus as "the prophet who is to come into the world" and rushed to make him king (John 6:14–15). But the sign, the tangible event needed to be there for the point to be missed.

The narrative of Jesus' walking on the water (Mark 6:45–52; Matt. 14:22–33; John 6:16–21) has led to innumerable contortions on the part of interpreters. One reckons on a wooden plank on which Jesus was balancing; another on an optical illusion of the disciples who imagined Jesus walking on the water when he was actually walking along the shore; still another opines that in ancient times Palestine experienced periods of cold which would have frozen the water close to the shore of Gennesaret, so that Jesus was walking on ice floes. Or again, another attempts to explain the event against the background of altered states of consciousness on the part of the eyewitnesses. For those who spurn such notions as hostile to the intention of the texts, there is always the expedient of appealing to Graeco-Roman parallels, according to which divine men walk by foot on the sea, a scene allegedly replicated by the evangelists intent on accenting the epiphany.[7] The scene is especially vulnerable with those who oppose the transcendent or the religious, among whom naturalists and biologists may be the most ardent. Since the Enlightenment scientists have been wary of assigning to the divine what cannot be grasped by reason, since the reasonable or rational as essence of the human is taken to be the essence of the divine as well. Whether or not in appeal to Augustine's insistence on curbing biblical answers to cosmological questions, or to Galileo's notion of God's "two books," one of faith, and the other of nature, a host of interpreters, many with scientific backgrounds, have opted for a *separation* of the structures of the observable world and the interpretation of those structures from the perspective of faith. In other words, while the meteorologist could assign Jesus' quieting of the storm to the prevailing winds round and about Galilee, the believer could acknowledge the event as a divine interference, with neither invading the other's territory. The truce achieved by this separation is uneasy. "Enthralled" by the "luminous figure of the Nazarene," a figure "too colossal for the pen of phrasemongers,"[8] Albert Einstein stated that conflict between science and religion occurred when religion insisted on the absolute truthfulness of everything recorded in the Bible, or when science attempted to arrive at fundamental judgments with respect to values and ends. And since he believed the principal source of the conflict lay in the concept of a personal God, obviously that concept had to be abandoned for the conflict to

---

7 Cited in *Jesus Handbuch*, ed. Jens Schröter und Christine Jacobi (Tübingen: Mohr Siebeck, 2017), 325.

8 "What Life Means to Einstein: An Interview by George Sylvester Viereck," *The Saturday Evening Post*, October 26, 1929, 17.

be resolved. And there's the rub. For, *this person*, this Nazarene is confessed as God, the one by whom the worlds all came to be, with power to turn the structures of the observable world on their head, to perform what to reason is a violation of the natural and rational, to do the impossible, the unbelievable. And as for reason, hailed as essence of the divine as well as of the human, as for that insistence on the superiority of scientific rationality with its claim to objective reality, it is as pious and "religious" a view as insistence on the existence of a personal God. All of which means that there is as much warrant for faith as for that of scientific rationality. William Blake's argument respecting art may be stretched to apply also to science or faith:

> If perceptive Organs vary; Objects of Perception seem to vary;
> If the Perceptive Organs close: their Objects seem to close also.[9]

In the face of inevitable resistance, *the expectations and preconceptions on which all seeing depends* and which I bring to this narrative have to do with Christ's lordship over creation, readily admitting the story's judgment on that much vaunted "objectivity," its challenge to any current or prevailing world-view, and its announcement of the new over against what has given thousands comfort and ease: the impenetrable and unassailable continuum of cause and effect.

In Matthew 17:24–27, after the disciples have reached Capernaum, Peter is met by temple tax collectors who ask whether or not his teacher pays the tax (Greek: *didrachma*). Peter acknowledges that he does. At home, Jesus asks him from whom the kings of the earth receive tribute, from their children or from others. Peter answers, "from others." "Then," Jesus responds, "the children are free," but adds that to avoid offence Peter should go to the sea, and in the mouth of the first fish he catches find a stater, enough to satisfy the payment for the two of them. The text raises questions. First, the English versions wrongly translate Peter's interrogators as "collectors of the temple tax." The original simply refers to tax collectors, either to those who collect the poll tax required of everyone, Jew or Gentile, or to collectors of the temple tax. But if the latter, the analogy to the "others" from whom the "kings of the earth take toll or tribute" breaks down, since the temple tax was required only of Jews. Second, the *didrachma* was a foreign, Greek silver coin. The stater, equal to two *didrachmas*, and which Peter was to retrieve from the fish's mouth, had to be exchanged for the equivalent silver half shekel since foreign coin was tabu in the temple. Taken alone, the narrative seems haphazard, that is, until linked to the passion prediction

---

9. Blake, William. "Jerusalem" in David V. Erdman, *The Poetry and Prose of William Blake*, (Garden City, New York: Doubleday, 1970), 175.

which immediately precedes. There, Jesus predicts that the Son of Man will be betrayed, killed, and rise again on the third day. Thus, interpreted in the light of what precedes, our narrative reads that Jesus, Son of Man (the self-reference is obvious), is free of legal obligation but nevertheless takes it on to prevent giving offense.[10]

Initiators and followers of the School of the History of Religions have rushed to accent the similarity between pagan myuthology and the Cana miracle in John 2:1–11; seen it as a "parade example of the penetration of hellenistic miracle tradition into the Jesus tradition."[11] One recalls the temple of Dionysus the wine-god, located not too far distant from Cana, at which the priests on the eve of the god's yearly festival, roughly corresponding to Christian celebration of Epiphany, locked three empty crocks in a sealed building and presented them on the next day full of wine. Another comments that in Judaism wine serves as metaphor for the joys of the time of salvation. Still another suggests that Jesus' participation in a wedding at Cana developed into the narrative of a miracle, in this case, outdoing the feat of Dionysus, or Bacchus, his Roman counterpart, with twice as many crocks, each holding twenty to thirty gallons. But all this may be missing the subtelties for tripping on the obvious. Why, for example, does the evangelist first note Jesus' mother's invitation to the wedding, and that of Jesus and the disciples as if an afterthought: "Jesus and his disciples had *also* been invited" (John 2:2)? What to make of Jesus' seemingly coarse rebuff to his mother's announcement that the supply of wine is exhausted: "Woman, what concern is that to you and to me?" (John 2:4) , together with the remark that his "hour" has not yet come? Incidentally or no, this is the first of seven instances in which I reference is made to Jesus' "hour." In 7:30 the Evangelist writes of Jesus' enemies inability to lay hands on him because "his hour had not yet come." In 8:20, following Jesus' teaching in the temple, the Evangelist writes again that no one arrested him, because his hour had not yet come." In 12:23, Greeks who have come to Jerusalem for the festival, approach Philip and ask to see Jesus, who after being informed of it, says "the hour has come for the Son of Man to be glorified." In 12:27 Jesus is recorded as saving, "Now is my soul troubled. And what should I say—Father, save me from this hour? No, it is for this reason that I have come to this hour." In 13:1 the evangelist records that at the festival of Passover Jesus knew that his hour had come to depart from this world and go to the Father. Finally, in 17:1, following his high priestly prayer, Jesus looked up to heaven and said, "Father, the hour has come; glorify your

---

10 Cf. Jesus' exchange with the Baptist in Matthew 11:6: "Blessed is anyone who takes no offense at me."

11 Cf. *Jesus Handbuch*, ed. Jens Schröter und Christine Jacobi (Tübingen: Mohr Siebeck, 2017), 321.

Son that yo ur Son may glorify you." This "hour," described as an hour of glorification, and identified with an event Jesus might pray to avoid ("What should I say—Father, save me from this hour?") , or, as per the evangelist, with "going to the Father," can only mean his death. It is an "hour," the coming of which Jesus is aware, as for example at the arrival of the Greeks, and for which he prays ("Father, the hour has come; glorify your Son") but which he does not own or bring about. Reference to it as "his" simply describes him as its subject. More, since this "hour," this "glorification" will be the glorification of the Father, the death of Jesus is an event initiated by the Father. It will be"an"hour," a death he takes on himself.

To return to the Cana miracle, what to make of his mother's reposte that the servants do whatever he commands? Doesen't she hear, or understand what he said, or does she pay no mind to it? And what of Jesus' reversal of his earlier demurrer in favor of his mother's plea with the order to fill with water six stone jars designated for purification, jars, as it turned out, about to be defiled? Had his "hour" come in that moment, and if so, why is that term later reserved for his crucifixion? (cf. John 8:20; 12:23, 27; 13:1; 17:1). And, prior to the servants' drawing it out and bringing it to the steward, why not a simple statement to the effect that the water had been changed to wine, the servants cognizant of the entire affair but the steward totally unaware? Finally, what to make of the evangelist's conclusion that at Cana Jesus "revealed his glory" (shades of the Prologue, 1:17), "and his disciples believed in him" (John 2:11)? If we agree that the evangelist is pursuing a specific goal with his work, what provokes our questions may not be due to lapses, or a haphazard "go" at the event. Then, beneath the servant's knowledge of the source of the miracle, or the disciples' belief in the revelation of his "glory," *and* beneath the order of Jesus' mother in face of her son's rebuff, or the steward's surprise at the water's being changed to wine, may lie the intent to distinguish a faith dependent on the "sign" as sheer fact, and a faith that grasps what it is to which that "sign" is meant to point. In either case what is "signed" is the same: Jesus' power over nature, a power to leave an Olympian god leagues behind, though the one faith is given superiority over the other, as at the end of the Gospel in Jesus' word to Thomas: "Have you believed because you have seen me? Blessed are those who have not seen and yet have come to believe" (John 20:28). Then, by way of parallel, there may be two "hours," and two revelations of his "glory," one at Cana matched by a seeing, and the other, an "hour" of glorification-crucifixion matched by a believing absent the seeing, the latter the greater of the two, and at Cana, at the least signaled in Mary's antecedent appearance at the event, and her summons, if not in the steward's surprise.

The Parables

Whether to the crowds or his disciples, Jesus' teaching made generous use of the parable, a device parallel to the Hebrew *masal*, and broad enough to include everything from narrative to similitude and allegory, from proverb to riddle and symbol. In fact this habit of speaking was so characteristic of Jesus that the Gospels can describe his entire teaching as "parabolic speech" (Mark 4:34: "He did not speak to them except in parables"). According to recent estimate, the New Testament contains more than one hundred parables.[1] Of those discussed here, Matthew, Mark, and Luke share eight, Matthew and Luke share five, Mark has one alone, Matthew has nine alone, and Luke fifteen alone. Whereas the three synoptists use the term *parabolai* (pl.) to denote this type speech, the Fourth Gospel uses the term *paroimiai* (John 16:25: "I have said these things to you in figures of speech."). The parable may be introduced by the simple conjunction "as" (Greek: *hos, hosper;* cf. Mark 4:26-29; Matt. 25:14-30), the comparative adjective "like" (*homoios, homoia;* cf. Matt. 13:45-46; 25:1-13, and Luke 6:46-49), the verb "to compare" (Greek: *homoioo;* cf. Luke 13:20-21), or by the noun "parable" (Greek: *parabole;* cf. Matthew 13:31-32), prefixed by the verb "to tell" (Greek: *lalein, legein;* cf. Matthew 13: 3-9; Luke 14:7-14), to "put" (Greek: *tithesthai;* cf. Matthew 13:24-30), or by the summons to "learn" (Greek: *mimneskein;* cf. Mark 13:28-31, and Matthew 13:3-9, 24-30). Traditionally, the Fourth Gospel has been described as lacking in parables, and in fact, what initially appears to introduce a parable in that Gospel is actually absorbed by the argument that precedes or follows (cf. the figure in John 3:8a "The wind blows where it chooses," absorbed in the argument that follows in vss.8b, 9-10, and the figure In John 16:25: "For here the

---

[1] *Jesus Handbuch*, ed. Jens Schröter und Christine Jacobi (Tübingen: Mohr Siebeck, 2017), 384.

saying, 'One sows and another reaps,'" absorbed in the argument that precedes in vss.16–24). Currently, the view that the Fourth Gospel is lacking in parables has been challenged. Attention has been given such reminiscences as that of the shepherd who leads his sheep (John 10:1–5); the seed sown (John 12:24), or the woman in labor (John 16:21). Additionally, there are instances in which material in John intersects with synoptic tradition (cf. John 9–21 with Matthew 11:27; John 13:16 with Matthew 10:24–26).[2]

The "paradigm" served by the parables is exactly the same served by the exorcisms, miracles of healing and nature miracles: The kingdom of God. As if to accent this fact, seven times Matthew records Jesus' introducing his parable with the phrase "the kingdom of heaven may be compared to" (cf. Matthew 13:24–30, and 18:23–35), or "is. . ." (cf. Matthew 13:44; 13:45–46; 13:47–50; 20:1–16,), or "will be, like. . ." (cf. Matthew 25:1–13).

Mark and Matthew differ regarding the purpose of the parables. In Mark 4 Jesus tells the disciples they have been given the secret of the kingdom of God, but to those outside, everything is in parables (i.e. riddles), *in order that* (in Greek: *hina*), then follows the quotation from Isaiah 6:9: ". . .they may indeed look, but not perceive, and may indeed listen, but not understand; so that they may not turn again and be forgiven." In Matthew 13:13, Jesus says that he speaks in parables *for the reason that* or *because* (in Greek: *dia touto. . .hoti*), "seeing they do not perceive, and hearing they do not listen, nor do they understand." Mark's construction clearly matches his theme of the Messianic secret threading throughout his Gospel, according to which Jesus' identity is unknown to his disciples, family, and adversaries, is known only to the demons whom he commands to be silent, then is finally acknowledged by the centurion at the cross. In Matthew, Jesus' identity is clearly acknowledged, as is clear from the titles assigned him by those petitioning him for help (cf. the centurion's plea in Matthew 8:6; that of the blind men in 9:28; the plea of the Canaanite woman in 15:21, and that of the father of the epileptic boy in 17:15). If Luke had a choice between Mark's and Matthew's versions, he clearly preferred that of Mark, without sharing Mark's over-all theme of the Messianic secret (cf. Luke 8:9).

In John 9:35–41 the Isaiah quote is set in an entirely different context. Finding the blind man he had healed expelled from the synagogue, Jesus asks if he believes in the Son of Man. The man responds that if he knew him he would believe him. Upon Jesus' declaration that he is the Son of Man the once blind land beggar worships him. Jesus then says "I came into this world for judgment so that those who do not see may see, and those who do

---

2 Cf. *Jesus Handbuch*, ed. Jens Schröter und Christine Jacobi (Tübingen: Mohr Siebeck, 2017), 384.

see may become blind." The Isaiah passage is nuanced to serve the dialogue between Jesus and the Pharisees that follows. Inserting themselves into the conversation they deny their blindness and are told that if they ere they would have no sin, but now that they see their sin remains. There is more than nuance here. In the Synoptics the parables are cause of the listening and not perceiving, hearing but not understanding, as though Jesus were once removed from the judgment. In John, Jesus declares outright that he is the one who brings the judgment.

The grouping of Jesus' parables far and away equals the number of interpreters assaying to group them. What follows here is yet another, mayhap aesthetic, attempt. Rather than treating the parables in each Gospel separately, they are grouped here according to theme. The similitude, opening with "the kingdom is as if," or "is like," or "may be compared to," is obvious in the parables of the self-growing seed (Mark 4:24–30), the sower (Mark 4:3–9; Matthew 13:3–9; Luke 8:5–8), the mustard seed (Mark 4:30–32; Matthew 13:31–32; Luke 13:18–19), and the leaven (Matthew 13:32–33; Luke 13:20–21). Customarily, these parables are read as emphasizing the kingdom's growth from the lesser to the greater, as though Jesus were assuring his listeners that despite its humble origins the kingdom would end in a world-wide embrace. This is a reading subordinate to the parable's main emphasis. In typical oriental fashion, Jesus does not bother with enumerating the various stages of growth from blastula to bloom, but describes *the kingdom or rule of God as possessing an intrinsic force which determines its progress and hurries it onward toward its goal.* Thus, the kingdom is like seed that is sown and sprouts and grows, the earth producing "of itself" (Mark 4:27–28), or its fate may be like that of a seed eaten by birds, fallen on rocky ground, or choked by thorns, but where there is good soil will yield a hundredfold (Mark 4:8), or again, it is like the mustard seed which "becomes the greatest of all shrubs" (Mark 4:32); and finally it is like yeast when mixed with flour till "all of it is leavened" (Matthew 13:33). The dynamic intrinsic to this kingdom may be hidden—"the seed would spread and grow, *he does not know how*"—but its progress is inevitable.

The similitude is also obvious in the parables of the hidden treasure (Matthew 13:44), and the pearl (Matthew 13:45–46). In these Jesus makes clear that *the kingdom is worth abandoning everything to gain it,* each ending with the refrain: "he goes and sells all that he has and buys that field," and, "he went and sold all that he had and bought it." In Luke 14:7–14, the theme of abandonment is contained in Jesus' parable addressed to the crowds. Here, since family, and life itself are worth abandoning for the sake of discipleship, whoever attempts it must reckon with the cost, as, for example, a person who intends to build a tower must determine whether or not he has the funds to complete it, or, again, as a king going to war needs to consider whether his army is sufficient in strength to engage the enemy. Miscalculation leads to ridicule in the one instance, and in the other to a stacking of arms. The surprisingly harsh word precedes the parable ("whoever comes to me and does not hate father and mother, wife and children, brothers and sisters," vs. 26) has its proper interpretation in the word that follows ("Whoever does not carry the cross and follow me cannot be my disciple," vs. 27), as well as in the word at the parable's conclusion: "None of you can become my disciple if you do not give up all your possessions" (vs. 33).

The parable of the talents in Matthew 25:14-30, and Luke 19:12-27 indicate *the risk attached to the kingdom.* The two accounts differ in several respects. In Matthew the parable opens with a man going on a journey, in Luke with a nobleman off to a distant country to gain royal power. Entrusted with their master's property, in Matthew one slave is given five talents, another two, and another one talent. In Luke ten slaves are summoned and given ten pounds. Luke adds that the citizens of the nobleman's country hated him, and sent a delegation stating they would not be ruled by him. Matthew adds that the slaves proceed to trade, the one with five talents earns five more, the one with two doubles his, and the one with the single talent digs a hole in the ground, burying the money. On the master's return to settle accounts, in Matthew the first two slaves are commended for their trustworthiness in a few things, and are promised charge over many things. In Luke the first slave is given charge of ten cities, and the second charge of two. In Matthew the slave who buried his talent surrenders it to the one with ten, and is cast into the outer darkness, where, according to the Matthean refrain, "there will be weeping and gnashing of teeth." In Luke the wicked slave surrenders his pound to the one with ten; then the line in Matthew is repeated that to those who have, more will be given, and the parable comes to a jarring finish: no further punishment for the wicked slave, but the slaughter of those who refused to hail the nobleman as king. Despite these differences the similarity in substance between Matthew and Luke is too great to suggest that, in this instance at least, Luke had access to an exemplar independent of Matthew. As with much of the material shared by Matthew and Luke, there is nothing to forbid supposing that Jesus uttered similar sayings on more than one occasion, but lacking a clue from the evangelists, we have little support for our imaginings. At any rate, the "moral" of the story is that in face of the looming encounter, to "trade" on what is given determines destiny. But it also involves risk. "See" (Greek: *ide* = "behold!!") says the slave who doubled his five talents, "I have made five more," and "see," says the one with two who doubled his, "I have made two more," as if the result were somehow out of their hands, left with the bankers, an inference drawn from the master's reproach of the single talent slave ("you ought to have invested my money with the bankers . . ." Matthew 25:27). But whatever the risk, the refusal to venture has vast consequences. In Matthew: "Throw him into the outer darkness. . ." (25: 30). In Luke, the initial reference to the citizens' hatred of the nobleman, and to their delegation with its refusal to have him rule over them, seems erratic, an interruption of the parable, but it furnishes the nobleman now become king with a power and authority to enact his bloody sentence, a feature lacking in Matthew's version: "bring them here and slaughter them in my presence" (Luke 19:27). At any rate, whether spoken by Jesus in precisely this form, or embroidered on by Matthew or Luke, the violence that ends this parable yields a perspective held by Jesus most would rather ignore: "You are a harsh man; you take what you did not deposit, and reap what you did not sow" (Luke 19: 26).

In Luke 15, the parables of the lost sheep, lost coin, and the two sons allow classification under many themes, including that of repentance. The comparison of finding the lost sheep and lost coin with the "joy in heaven" or "joy in the presence of the angels of God over one sinner who repents," together with the celebration of the return of the younger son who "was dead and has come to life. . .was lost and has been found" (vs. 32) *indicates the transformation requisite for existence in the rule or kingdom of God.* According to Luke's account, prior to his parable of the barren fig tree (Luke 13:6–9), Jesus had summoned those present to repent or perish (Luke 13:5). If Luke intended a connection between the summons and the parable, patience could well be the link. The fig tree has not yielded figs for three years, and the owner says "cut it down!" But the servant persuades him to wait, to allow him to pamper it for a year, then, if it does not yield, to put an end to it. The lord yields to his gardener. He will wait, he'll not rush to act and cut the tree down. Later, in the parable of the two sons, the younger demands his inheritance before his father is dead, goes off, loses his money whoring around, ends up with the pigs—a revolting development for any Jew with a modicum of morality—and after coming to himself, pleads with his father to take him in, if only as a servant. And all the while the father has been waiting. In the one instance the summons to repent is softened by the parable that follows. The lord will allow digging to go on around the old tree, allow dung to be spread around it till it produces the yield he wants. In the other instance the father bides his time. With all Jesus' summons to repent, *the kingdom emerges as a waiting, patient thing.*

But if the kingdom is a waiting, patient thing, the parables of the friend at night and the unjust judge (Luke 11:5–8; 18:1–8) indicate that patience and perseverance are needed to receive the kingdom's benefits. As usual, there is nothing of the everyday attached to the first parable. Everything happens at midnight. There is an arrival at midnight; the man playing host goes to his friend to beg bread at midnight, no doubt intending to serve his guest at midnight. His friend shouts back, says his whole family is in bed with him, meaning he would have to crawl over the entire family to get to the door. And all this at midnight. But because of his friend's "importunity," as the King James translates, not his "impudence" as in the modern English version—the fellow is, after all, carrying on in a fashion likely to wake the neighbors—his friend will open up and give him what he wants. In view of Luke's attaching the parable to the disciple's request that Jesus teach them to pray (Luke 11:1-4), its point must be the manner in which the "Our Father" is to be prayed. Importunity is the requisite, like that of a Jacob struggling with the angel.

In the parable of the judge and the widow (Luke 18:1-8) the data are as odd as in its twin. In Judaism, a judge advertised as having arrived at the bench without fearing God or man, would be an anomaly, to say the least. In the words of Jethro, priest of Midian and Moses' father-in-law, those qualified for judgeship were to be "able men among all the people men who fear God, are trustworthy, and hate dishonest gain" (Exodus 18:21). In the period of the Second Temple judges had to be ordained and authorized by the Sanhedrin, and distinguished for seven qualities: wisdom, humility, fear of God, hatred of money, love of truth, amiability, and a good reputation.[3] Further, judges could not listen to the arguments of one lone litigant in the absence of the other, nor could they assist either litigant in argument, but had to listen to the case presented by both parties. In Jesus' parable, only one litigant is involved, the widow. The parable's oddity is heightened by the fact that according to Jewish law cases of theft and personal injury, claims for damages and half-damages, double (Exodus 22:3), quadruple or quintuple restitution of stolen goods (cf. Exodus 21:37), had to be judged by three ordained judges.[4] Only one judge figures in the parable. Finally, the absurdity is raised to the maximum by the judge's decision to give the widow what she wants solely for the sake of his physical relief. Jesus' purpose with this congeries of oddities can only be to hammer home once more the contrast between what a human would do, in this case not a caring parent, but an unbelieving judge oblivious to the law (though from the word in 11:13, "if you then, who are evil," both are at bottom alike) and what God would do: "Will not God grant justice to his chosen ones who cry to him day and night? Will he delay long in helping them? I tell you, he will quickly grant justice to them" (Luke 18:7-8a). And, once more, what this contrast is meant to serve is Jesus' summons to "pray

---

3. *Tractate Sanhedrin, Mishnah and Tosefta*, trans. Herbert Danby (London: Society For Promoting Christian Knowledge, 1919), 112. https://www.toseftaonline.org/seforim/tractate_sanhedrin_mishna_and_tosefta_1919.pdf.

4. Ibid, 23.

always and not to lose heart" (Luke 18:1). The benefits of the kingdom ("give us each day our daily bread," "forgive us our sins," "do not bring us to the time of trial") require persistence, perseverance in petition.

Matthew records Jesus as recounting parables dealing with contrasts, the one between king and slave (Matthew 18:23–25), the other between the two sons (Matthew 21:28–32). Luke records Jesus' recounting such parables of contrast, between the two debtors (Luke 7:41–43), the rich man and Lazarus (Luke 16:19–31), master and servant (Luke 17:7–10), the Pharisee and the publican (Luke 18:9–14). Let the characteristic opening in the first parable in Matthew "the kingdom of heaven may be compared to. . .." serve as opening for the others. In the first, a king remits a slave's staggering debt and the slave turns around and throws a fellow slave into prison for a debt minuscule by comparison, only to end in torture till he has paid the last penny. Again, the data are absurd. Reckoning the talent equal to twenty years of a day laborer's wages, no slave on earth could have gone into debt for the unimaginable sum of the ten thousand which Jesus describes, and roughly equal to two hundred thousand years' wages. And a fellow slave who in turn owed him one hundred silver coins (Greek: *denarii*), equal to one hundred daily wages, would have been an employer, not a laborer. Or again, no wicked slave could serve time in prison till he had paid off the unbelievable amount described. Or what torture could he endure till he had paid the debt? What lies behind this welter of absurdities? The contrast between the cancellation of the wicked slave's debt, and the mercy he should have shown his debtor, is immense. The contrast between what is owed "my" heavenly Father (an implication demanded by the comparison), and the forgiveness to be shown a brother or sister is equally immense. On that incalculable contrast between what is owed the One and owed the other, hangs the warning to allow for the contrast: "So my heavenly Father will also do to every one of you, if you do not forgive your brother or sister from your heart."

While in the temple, flocked by chief priests and elders (Matthew 21:23), Jesus tells the parable of the two sons, in which the one tells his father he'll not work in his vineyard, then changes his mind and does so, while the other agrees to work, then changes his mind and does not. When asked which of the two did the will of his father the religious authorities answer, "the first," to which Jesus replies that tax collectors and prostitutes will enter the kingdom of heaven before them. For that entry a change was needed, a change comparable to that undergone by the first, not by the second son. Significantly, the appearance and message of the Baptist is described as the occasion for that change, a surprising feature in a Gospel otherwise intent on drawing a radical distinction between the Baptist and Jesus (cf. John's question at Jesus' baptism in Matthew 3:14: "I need to be baptized by you, and you come to me?"). The religious authorities refuse to undergo change and believe John. More, they persist in their unbelief even after witnessing the change in the dregs of society. "Even after you saw it," says Jesus, "you did not change your minds and believe him." With this feature Jesus "threatens" the parable, makes it wobble, renders the unbelief of the religious authorities greater than the disobedience of the second son, since the parable gives no hint of the second son's witness to his brother's change and by it worsening his refusal.

Luke's account of the parable of the two debtors is set within a scene of considerable length. The occasion is Jesus' invitation to the home of a Pharisee, into which a woman, "a sinner," enters, bathes his feet with ointment from an alabaster jar, and dries them with her hair. The host says to himself that if Jesus were a prophet he would have known what kind of woman was handling him. Jesus speaks up, tells his host he has something to say to him, and proceeds with the parable of the debtors. The one is in debt to the amount of five hundred daily wages (five hundred *denarii*), and the other to the amount of fifty (fifty *denarii*). Unable to pay, their creditor cancels the debts. "Now," Jesus asks, "which of them will love him most?" His host replies, no doubt the one for whom the greater debt was cancelled. Jesus commends him for his judgment, then proceeds to draw the contrast between what the woman and his host had done for him. She had bathed his feet, dried them with her tears, kissed them and anointed them, whereas he had done none of this. For this reason, Jesus concludes, the woman's many sins were forgiven since she loved much, adding "but the one to whom little is forgiven, loves little," leaving his host to consider whether the contrast between him and the woman earned him the axiom. The scene ends with Jesus' telling the woman her sins are forgiven, while the others at table mutter over his presumption.

The parable of the rich man (named *Dives* in the Vulgate) and Lazarus is without an occasion, but preceded by Jesus' reflections on the law and the kingdom, and followed by various sayings regarding causes for stumbling, forgiveness, faith, and service. The contrast described in the parable is as great as between heaven and hell. The rich man, who according to the King James "fared" sumptuously, lands in hell, while the beggar Lazarus who lay at his gate, and ate the crumbs that fell from his table, his sores licked by the dogs, lies in the bosom of Abraham. In Ethiopic Enoch, believers are allowed a look-see into the place of torment.[5] Here, the situation is reversed, and the rich man in torment looks up from hades at "father" Abraham and Lazarus. The sight prompts him to call to Abraham to slake his thirst with

---

5 Ethiopic *Enoch*.

the tip of his finger, only to hear that a chasm exists between them which neither can bridge. *Dives* then begs Abraham to send "him," presumably Lazarus, to his five brothers, to spare them torment, is rebuffed by the word that they have Moses and the prophets. The parable concludes with the rich man's response that if someone goes to them from the dead they will listen, only to be told that if they do not hear Moses and the prophets, they'll not hear even if someone rises from the dead. Did Jesus have it in mind to say this of himself?

In a brief parable near the opening of Luke, chapter 17, and threaded in with sayings regarding repentance, forgiveness, and faith, Jesus rather harshly deals with the disciples respecting their obligation. Without the customary conjunction "as" or "like," or verbal construction, he shapes the parable in the form of a question: Which of the disciples would allow his slave to sit with him at table, rather than ordering him to serve before feeding himself, and then would proceed to commend the slave for doing what was commanded. Then follows the application: "So you also, when you have done all that you were ordered to do, say, 'We are worthless slaves; we have done only what we ought to have done!'" The application makes clear the meaning of the parable: The slave cannot boast of reward. A similar saying appears in the so-called Avoth, "The Fathers:" Be not like slaves that minister to the master for the sake of receiving a bounty, but be like slaves that minister to the master not for the sake of receiving a bounty and let the fear of Heaven be upon you."[6] The disciples could hardly have missed the implication: Their status was that of slaves in thrall to a master, a contrast heightened by the summons to admit that after having done all they were "worthless," not worth getting what the slave in the parable could conceivably have gotten—a commendation. A certain absurdity attaches to the parable, as if any disciple had the wherewithal to employ a servant or slave. A certain harshness attaches to it as well. Apart from assuming a practice rife in the Graeco-Roman world, that of holding thousands of conquered peoples in bondage, many among them more cultured and educated than their captors, by law masters had the right to command, but refusing the slave commendation for his service, however customary, would have been abrupt, heavy handed. The role cast here is scarcely that of "Gentle Jesus, meek and mild."

A further parable dealing with contrast is that of the Pharisee and the publican in Luke 18. Immediately following the parable of the unjust judge (verses 1–8), and preceding Jesus' blessing of the children (verses 15–17), no occasion is recorded beyond the statement that it was told to "some who

---

6. Danby, Herbert. *Mishna*, Aboth ("The Fathers'), I, 3, 466.

trusted in themselves that they were righteous and regarded others with contempt" (Luke 18:9). Here again, Luke has set the parable within sayings of Jesus without concern for a common theme. The principals include a Pharisee, member of the group intent on reform within Judaism, and a Jew, allowed by the empire to bid for the opportunity to collect taxes from his fellow-citizens, hated for acting hand-in-glove with a despised conqueror, and for extortion, exacting more than required to feather his own nest. The Mishnah, rabbinic exposition of Jewish oral tradition, records that tax-collectors need not be told the truth, nor may change for money or alms be taken from them, and the Talmud, the authoritative body of Jewish tradition comprising both Mishnah and Gemara,cites biblical law as disqualifying them from serving as arbitrators.[7] These two go up to the temple to pray, the puritan and the low-life, first set at odds by their posture. The one is standing "by himself," savoring his God-given distance from "thieves, rogues, adulterers," enumerating his fasts beyond the two major and four minor, and his tithing after the pattern of the great patriarch (cf. Jacob's vow in Gen. 28:20–22). Then, with an eye to the tax-collector, and within a space of approximately one hundred eighty feet long, ninety wide, and fifty high[8], suggestive of a hyperopia beyond the natural (again, the absurdity!), adds, "or even like this tax-collector." The other, standing "far off," a league from the Holy Place and the High Altar, does not dare look up to heaven but beating his breast cries "God, be merciful to me, a sinner!"—words loaned by Bach for a cantata based on a sixteenth century hymn: "*Herr, sei mir armem Sünder gnädig.*" "I tell you," Jesus says: "This man went down to his home justified rather than the other," and in a reprisal of his mother's *Magnificat* ("he has scattered the proud in the thoughts of their hearts, He has brought down the powerful from their thrones, and lifted up the lowly," Luke 1:51b–52), lays down the axiom that those who exalt themselves will be humbled, and those who humble themselves will be exalted. And, what

---

7. Cf. "Nedarim" ("Vows") 3.4: "Men may vow to murderers, robbers, or tax-gatherers that what they have is Heave-offering even though it is not Heave-offering," and "Babba Kamma" ("The First Gate") 10.1; "None may take change for money from the counter of excisemen or from the wallet of tax-gatherers, or take any alms from them," in *The Mishnah*. Translated From The Hebrew With Introduction And Brief Explanatory Notes by Herbert Danby, Oxford University Press, 1933, 267, 346, and Tractate "Sanhedrin," Folio 25b: „At first they though that they coollected no more than the legally imposed tax. But when it was seen that they overcharged, they were disqualified," in *Sanhedrin*, Translated Into English With Notes, Glossary, And Indices, Chapters I-VI by Jacob Schechter, Chapters VII-XI by H. Freedman, Under the Editorship of Rabbi Dr. I. Epstein, Chapter III, p. 25, n.d.

8. That is, if the temple assumed in the parable was approximately the same as that of the First.

else could that exaltation mean but the man's going down to his home "justified," put right with God?

Of the eschatological parables dealt with here, Mark, Matthew, and Luke have three, in common, Matthew and Luke two, Matthew alone has five, and Luke alone three. The first parable common to all three (Mark 4:21–25; Matthew 5:14–15; Luke 8:16–18) is in two parts. In the first, Jesus refers to a lamp's belonging on a lampstand, not under a bushel or a bed. This piece of seemingly common sense is made to serve the word that follows, to the effect that nothing is secret except to come to light, and ends with the repeated command to listen, separating the two parts. The second contains the word that the measure one gives will be the measure one gets, that even more will be given than one gave, and ends with the statement that those who have will receive more, and those who have nothing will lose whatever they have. The parable is opaque. Each evangelists attempts his own interpretation, Mark uses the parable to relax the tension in Jesus' earlier statement regarding the intent of the parables to obscure, Matthew sets the parable within the context of the Sermon on the Mount, in which Jesus describes those who are his as lights, but omits the saying dealing with giving and having, and Luke sets the parable between the interpretation of the sower and the narrative of Jesus' family, ending with the saying regarding his mother and brothers as those who hear the word of God and do it (Luke 8:32). Attempting to get beyond the evangelists' interpretation to the original occasion for the parable would be an enterprise many have abandoned, but at least this much can be said: Jesus is speaking of a future event, of a revelation ("nor is anything secret, except to come to light") and a reward those who have, more will be given") yet to come, and that what is to occur in future depends on an attitude assumed in the here and now ("let anyone with ears to hear listen!"). And since it is Jesus, and no one else, who demands that this attitude be assumed, what is to be revealed or rewarded can only have to do with him.

The next two eschatological parables dealt with here occur in Mark's "Lttle Apocalypse" (13:28–31, 34–37) and its counterparts in Matthew (24:32–35, 42–51) and Luke (21:29–33). Here, the occasion is clear. Both parables appear in the context of Jesus' words to his disciples regarding the coming of the Son of Man. In the first, in Mark and Matthew following the description of his advent to gather those who are his, and in Luke following the prediction of the destruction of Jerusalem, Jesus urges the disciples to read the signs of the coming of the Son of Man as they would the signs of a ripening fig tree. The parable ends with Jesus' prediction that "this generation" will not pass away till all is fulfilled. To begin with, the identity of that "Son of Man" has been the object of dispute. Is it possible that Jesus is referring to someone other than himself? Or, is the phrase a manufacture of Mark intended to enhance his view of Jesus' life and career as a mystery, and in which, in this instance at least, his co-evangelists follow suit? Or again, is the phrase from Jesus' own lips? In any case, the phrase cannot help conjuring up associations with that apocalyptic figure celebrated between the Testaments as hidden till the day of judgment:

> And there I saw One who had a head of days, And His head was white like wool, And with Him was another being whose countenance had the appearance of a man, And his face was full of graciousness, like one of the holy angels.2. And I asked the angel who went with me and showed me all the hidden things, concerning that Son of Man, who he was, and whence he was, (and) why he went with the Head of Days? And he answered and said unto me: This is the son of Man who hath righteousness ,With whom dwelleth righteousness, And who revealeth all the treasures of that which is hidden, Because the Lord of Spirits hath chosen him, And whose lot hath the pre-eminence before the Lord of Spirits in uprightness for ever.4, And this Son of Man whom thou hast seen Shall raise up the kings and the mighty from their seats. And the strong from their thrones And shall loosen the reins of the strong, And break the teeth of the sinners.5. And he shall put down the kings from their thrones and kingdoms Because they do not extol and praise Him ,Nor humbly acknowledge whence the kingdom was bestowed upon them. 6. And he shall put down the countenance of the strong, And shall fill them with shame.[9]

The argument that the phrase "Son of Man"[10] is Jesus' own self-reference, and that he identified himself with that apocalyptic figure come to judgment, is as legitimate as any other. More troubling is the statement that "this generation will not pass away until all these things have taken place" (Mark 13:30; Matthew 24:34; Luke 21:32). If "all these things" include the entire sequence of events preceding and following the advent of the "Son of Man"—the destruction of the temple, the "woes," wars and rumors of wars, persecutions. Divisions within households, the "desolating sacrilege," the flight to the mountains, the rising of false Messiahs and false prophets— they did not occur within the lifetime of Jesus' contemporaries. Attempts to solve the problem such as taking the reference to "this generation"[11] to mean

---

9. Charles, R.H. *The Book of Enoch*. Santa Cruz, Internet Sacred Text Archive, 1917, XLVI, 63–64. https://www.sacred-texts.com/.

10. Adam, Ben. *Ben Enosch* = Hebrew; *Bar Nasha* = Aramaic.

11. Greek = *he genea aute*.

"this kind of person" have not been convincing. Was Jesus wrong? Was his prediction unfulfilled? Such was the opinion of at least one noted scholar of my generation.[12] But, as if to temper the prediction, in what immediately follows Mark (13:32) records Jesus as saying, "about that day or hour no one knows, neither the angels in heaven, nor the Son, but only the Father." The saying is repeated in Matthew (24:36). Jesus may not have been an apocalypticist, but the prediction that the end is near enough to be experienced by those now living harnessed to the acknowledgement that no one, not even the Son knows the hour or day of its coming, is nothing if not a reprise of the apocalyptic mood. Contrary to majority opinion, apocalyptic was not preoccupied with the exact time of the visible manifestation of the deity for judgment and salvation. The two ideas could live together: He is coming soon, and, no one knows the day or the hour. Further, Mark's and Matthew's immediate attachment of the tinier parable of the man going on a journey, leaving his slaves in charge, and commanding the doorkeeper to keep watch, since he does not know wether the master will come in the evening, at midnight, at cock crow, or at dawn (at one of the four Roman watgchs of the night, Mark13:34–37; Matthew 24:42–51) is calculated to give priority to the feature that "no one knows, neither the angels in heaven, nor the Son. . . ." In his parables of the watchful, and the faithful and unfaithful slaves (Luke 12:35–48), Luke nuances the theme of ignorance of the hour by transferring it to the owner of the house who would not have allowed his home to be broken into had he known the hour of the thief's coming. In the second parable, the unfaithful slave who uses his master's delay to abuse his fellow slaves and carouse, is cut in pieces at the master's arrival, while the slave who knew what his master wanted but did not do it, and the one who did not know it but did what deserved a beating, will receive sentences equivalent to their behavior. What will become clear as a characteristic feature in Luke, both parables conclude with a "moral," the first addressed to the disciples: "You also must be ready, for the Son of Man is coming at an unexpected hour" (Luke 12:39), and the second to Peter who inquires after the audience intended: "From everyone to whom much has been given, much will be required; and from the one to whom much has been entrusted, even more will be demanded" (Luke 12:49).

Matthew and Luke share two of the eschatological parables dealt with here, one of the wise and foolish builders (Matthew 7:24–27; Luke 6:46–49), the other of the great banquet (Matthew 22:1–14; Luke 14:15–24). In Matthew the first parable concludes the Sermon on the Mount, and in it Jesus

12. Kümmel, Werner Georg. *Verheißung und Erfüllung. Untersuchungen zur eschatologischen Verkündigung Jesu*; AThAT 6; Basel 1945 (Zürich: Zwingli Verlag, 1953², 1956³).

declares that whoever hears his words and acts on them is like the wise man who builds his house on a rock, whereas the one who hears his words but does not act on them is like the fool who builds his house on sand, a prey to ruin by rain, flood, and wind. In Luke the parable concludes the "Sermon on the Plain," begun at 6:17, a variant of the Matthaean account. Differences between the two are minor, Luke merely adding the feature of the wise man's digging a deep foundation inured to flood, while the other builds his house without a foundation. As indicated above, because the parables of Jesus, like the Hebrew *masal*, are broad enough to include a variety of types, not every parable will have a single point, in scholarly jargon, the *tertium comparationis* or point of comparison. This parable, however, does have a single point: Escape from the future cataclysm, denoted by rain, flood, and wind, depends on making concrete and visible what is heard from Jesus. What gives "bite" to the parable is its contrast between the two builders, the one called wise, the other a fool, the inevitability of the doom to come, and limiting escape from it to making concrete what is heard from Jesus, and from him alone. And, presumably, for the two evangelists what is heard and needs "acting on" are the words beginning with the Sermon on the Mount or on the Plain, nothing short of a Herculean effort on the part of the crowds and disciples gathered to hear him (cf. Matthew 5:1; Luke 6:17).

The second parable shared by Matthew and Luke is that of the great banquet. In Matthew the occasion is Jesus' appearance in the temple, in sight of the chief priests and elders; in Luke he is invited to dine at the home of a Pharisee. I am tempted to treat the parable allegorically, taking the banquet to represent the divine offer of redemption, those invited and offering regrets (embroidered on in Luke's version "I have bought a piece of land;" "I have bought five yoke of oxen;" "I have just been married," 14:18–20) as representing Israel; the seizure and murder of the second group of messengers (Matthew 22:4, 6) as representing Israel's treatment of its prophets; the king's destruction of the murderers and the burning of their city as Israel's ultimate fate, and the invitation to "both good and bad," or as in Luke, to "the poor, the crippled, the blind, and the lame," in other words to those for one reason or another unable to fulfil the requirements of the law, as foreigners or Gentiles, and finally construe the one in whose honor the banquet is held and the oxen and fat calves slaughtered (Matthew 22:4), that is, the king's son (Matthew 22:2), as representing Jesus himself. Treating this parable allegorically might be a dubious venture if not for the fact that in the parable of the wicked tenants which immediately precedes, the chief priests and Pharisees perceive that Jesus is talking about them. Matthew's connection of the two parables at least suggests that he construed them in this way.

Unlike Luke, who ends the parable with the banquet hall filled with the flotsam and jetsam, Matthew appends the parable of the man who appears at the feast without a wedding garment, for which he is bound hand and foot, and thrown into the "outer darkness," where, in the evangelist's refrain, "there will be weeping and gnashing of teeth" (cf. 8:12; 13:42; 22:13; 24:51; 25:30). Interpretations of the parable are legion, from taking the wedding garment to mean the righteousness of Christ, to construing the man's appearing without it as Matthew's attack on the universal law-free gospel of the apostle Paul. Further, the last line reading "many are called, but few are chosen" (22:14) appears misplaced, since the scene ends with the king's command to his slaves to invite "everyone you find" (22:9-10), resulting in the wedding hall's being filled with guests. These interpretations may be too literalistic, whereas the accent lies on the right of the king to invite and separate. It is this right that calls forth his annoyance at the refusals of his invitation, his rage at the slaughter of his slaves, his destruction of their murderers and their city, his renewed invitation to all and sundry, and finally his judgment on the hapless fellow minus the wedding garment. Whatever occurs, all the way from determining what is to come, to the summons to welcome it, and finally to make of it an occasion for division and judgment, is in the king's hands.

With one exception: In the five eschatological parables dealt with here and appearing only in Matthew Jesus deals with the theme of separation. In 13:24-30 at night an enemy sows weeds in a man's field, good and bad seed are allowed to grow till harvest when the weeds are bound up to be burned, and the wheat gathered into the barn. In 13:47-50 the net thrown into the sea catches fish of every kind, the good put in baskets and the bad thrown out. In 25:1-13 five foolish virgins take no oil for their lamps, at the announcement of the bridegroom's arrival go to buy oil and on their return find the door to the banquet hall shut, the five wise virgins entering with the bridegroom. In 25:31-46 the nations are gathered and separated as sheep from goats, those on the king's right hand who served "the least" are invited to "inherit the kingdom," while those on the left are dispatched to eternal fire. In 20:1-16 the emphasis is not on separation but on the landowner's assertion of his right to pay the same wage to every laborer, despite the complaint over the disparity in time and energy. The parable thus accents a feature less developed in the other four parables, first, the role of the master and his directive to allow the weeds to grow along with the wheat; next that of the angels who arrive to separate the evil from the righteous as one separates good fish from bad; then the role of the lord who enjoins the five foolish virgins to keep awake, since they know "neither the day nor the hour," and finally that of the Son of Man, the king (25:34), and Lord (25:37,

44) who arrives to separate the nations, the righteous from those destined for eternal punishment.

The eschatological parables dealt with here and appearing in Luke alone lack a unifying theme. Two, however, have settings. In the first, someone asks Jesus to serve as arbiter in a dispute with a brother over their inheritance, hears Jesus' refusal to act as judge in such affairs, and his warning against greed. Then follows the parable of the man who plans a future in which his soul can take its ease, only to be called a fool whose life will be taken in midst of his imaginings, and his possessions left without inheritors (Luke 12:16–21). The setting for the second parable, (more an admonition than a parable, thus a *masal* in the wide sense) is Jesus' appearance at a meal in the home of a Pharisee, at which he observes the guests choosing the places of honor, enjoins the guests to avoid disgrace with taking the highest seats and being called to take the lower (Luke 14:7–11). The third parable lacks a setting, merely follows the three parables of the lost sheep, coin, and the two sons in chapter 15. Here Jesus tells of an unjust steward who, about to lose his post as manager, subtracts the amounts owed his employer by his debtors, hoping to reap benefits from them after his dismissal, and is commended by Jesus for his shrewdness (Luke 16:1–9). Characteristically, to all three parables a "moral" is attached. To the first, that the plight of the fool is that of "those who store up treasures for themselves but are not rich toward God" (Luke 12:21); to the second, that "all who exalt themselves will be humbled, and those who humble themselves will be exalted" (Luke 14:11), and to the third that Jesus' hearers "make friends for yourselves by means of dishonest wealth so that when it is gone, they may welcome you into the eternal homes" (Luke 16:9), the pronoun ("they") left undefined.

Finally. there are parables of which Jesus is subject. Of those dealt with here, five are shared by all three Synoptists, two are shared by Matthew and Luke, and two by Luke alone. The first of the five shared by all three is the parable of the bridegroom, followed by the double parable of the cloth, and the wine and wineskins in Mark 2:18–22 (Matthew 9:14–17, and Luke 5:33–39). Rhetorical criticism would describe this parable as a sayings *chreia*, which opens with the *narrative* of John's disciples' and the Pharisees' custom of fasting, and their question to Jesus regarding his disciples' refraining. In *response* Jesus asks, "The wedding guests cannot fast while the bridegroom is with them, can they?" Then Jesus gives the *explanation* for the response: "As long as they have the bridegroom with them, they cannot fast." Next follows his *argument from the opposite:* "The days will come when tahe bridegroom is taken away from them, and then they will fast in that day." Finally, two arguments *from analogy* follow, in the double-parable of the cloth and the patch, the wine and the wine skins.[13]

First of all, fasting in Judaism signaled mourning over the separation of God from his people. In Matthew's parallel Jesus asks, "the wedding guests cannot mourn as long as the bridegroom is with them, can they?" (Matthew 9:15). Iesus thus states that the reason for fasting no longer exists, the appearance of the bridegroom has put an end to the separation. Next, the allusion to Jahve the bridegroom of Hosea 2 is unmistakable. There, Jahve declares to Israel, "in that day, says the Lord, you will call me, 'My husband'. . ..I will take you for my wife for ever; I will take you for my wife in righteousness and in justice, in steadfast love and in mercy, I will take you for my wife in faithfulness, and you shall know the Lord." By his self-identification as bridegroom Jesus makes as august a claim as is found anywhere in Gospel tradition. Then follows the double-parable making clear that the attempt to combine Jesus' way of life with that of the Baptist or the Pharisees would be similar to sewing on an old cloth a new patch, or putting new wine in old wine skins. There is an energy at work in Jesus which is absent in the old traditions, and would destroy the entire edifice of the old. Finally, the eschatological thrust of the parable cannot be missed. By identifying himself as the bridegroom, and the disciples as the sons of the bridegroom, Jesus makes clear that his relationship to them is determined by what still lies in the future, that is, the marriage consumation, which nevertheless conditions all of their activity in the present. This energy at work in Jesus and his relationship with his disciples to the theme of the marriage produces a total discontinuity between the three groups, and renders any attempt to unite them absurd.

The third parable shared by the Synoptists is that of the strong man in Mark 3:27; Matthew 12:29, and Luke 11:21–22. In Mark the parable follows the attempt of Jesus' family to restrain him, and the scribes' accusation that he is possessed by Beelzebul and by him casts out demons. In Matthew the parable follows Jesus' healing of a demoniac born blind and mute, the Pharisees' accusation that he is possessed, and Jesus' response that every kingdom , city or house divided against itself is laid waste, or will not stand, that if Satan casts out Satan, he is divided, and his kingdom will not stand. Luke records that "some of them" say that Jesus casts out demons by Beelzebul, then adds to Jesus' response regarding the kingdom, house, and Satan divided the question, by whom their exorcists cast out demons, concluding that if it is by the finger of God that he does so, then the kingdom has come

---

13 Cf. the discussion by Vernon K. Robbins, "The Chreia," *Greco-Romn Literature And The New Testament*, ed. David E. Aune, (Atlanta: Scholars Press, 1988).

to them. In Mark's and Matthew's record of Jesus' saying about the one who cannot enter a strong man's house without tying him up, then plundering his house, and in Luke his reference to the strong one guarding his castle who is attacked and overpowered by one stronger, there is clear reminiscence of the Baptist's announcement of the one coming after who is "more powerful" than he (Mark 1:7; Matthew 3:11; Luke 3:16). In the immediate context of the charge that Jesus casts out demons by the power of Beelzebul, as well as of his exorcism of the demoniac, Jesus himself emerges as subject of the parable. He is the "more powerful" or stronger one who plunders the "house" or "castle" of Satan, proof that the rule of God over his beleaguered creation has begun with him.

Respecting the kingdom parable of the sower discussed above (Mark 3: 3-9; Matthew 13:9) Luke 8:5-8), Jesus emerges again as subject. Mark 3:11 reads: "When he was alone, those who were around him along with the twelve asked him about the parables. And he said to them, 'To you has been given the secret of the kingdom of God, but for those outside, everything comes in parables. . ..'" The parable need not be stretched to the point of comparing Jesus with that "someone" in Mark 4:27 who is ignorant of the how of the seed's spread, but the obvious inference to be drawn from the passage is that Jesus is the sower.

Once again, the feature of the absurd looms up in the parable of the wicked tenants (Mark 12:1-9; Matthew 21:33-41, and Luke 20:9-16). After a man planted a vineyard he leased it to tenants who beat three of the slaves sent to collect the owner's share of the produce, and finally sent his son on the same errand, saying "they will respect my son." In Matthew the parable is embroidered to read that one slave was beaten, another killed, another stoned, and that others, more than the first, were treated in the same fashion. The absurdity is registered in the imaginings of the wicked tenants that the inheritance will fall into their lap once they have done away with the heir. Numbers 27:6-11 limits inheritance strictly to members of the family. If a man dies without male or female heir, his inheritance goes to his brother; lacking a brother, the inheritance goes to his uncles; lacking uncles, the inheritance goes to the nearest kinsman of his clan. Proverbs 17:2 reads that a slave who deals wisely with an unruly child will share the inheritance as one of the family, and Ezekiel 46:16 reads that a prince may make a gift out of his inheritance to one of his servants. A proverb, however, can scarcely be read as anything but, and as for the servant of the prince, he may not keep the gift but must surrender it on the "year of liberty." Nothing of this applies to those murderers in the parable. The absurdity remains. But the comment in Mark that the chief priests, scribes, and elders (or in Matthew the chief priests and the Pharisees, or in Luke the scribes and chief priests) realized he had told the parable against them (Mark 12:12; Matthew 21:45; Luke 20:19) demands the inference of Jesus as subject, of the fate of the slaves sent to collect the owner's share as that of Israel's prophets, and, possibly, of the destruction of the wicked tenants and leasing of the vineyard to others as the rejection of Israel in favor of the Gentiles.

The parable of the good Samaritan in Luke 10:25–37 follows a dialogue between Jesus and a lawyer who, according to the evangelist, "stood up to test him." The initial verb does not denote purpose or intent, but simply posture. Where he stood up, Luke does not tell. The dialogue follows woes on unrepentant cities, the return of the seventy from their mission, and Jesus' rejoicing over the Father's having hidden "these things" from the wide and prudent, and revealed them to babes. Matthew is usually described as taken with describing Jesus in dialogue, but here Luke give as interesting a back-and-forth as his co-evangelist. The lawyer rises to put Jesus to the test. He puts the question respecting the way to eternal life. Jesus answers his question with a question: "What is written in the law? What do you read there?" The lawyer responds with Israel's creed, the *Shema Yisroel* ("Hear, O Israel!!"), with its command to love God with all one's heart, soul, and strength (Deuteronomy 6:4–5), adding "and your neighbor as yourself," a summary of the injunctions regarding strangers and sojourners (cf. Deuteronomy 10:18–19). Jesus commends the lawyer for his answer, tells him he will live if he practices what he preaches, only to hear the lawyer ask "who is my neighbor?" to which Jesus responds with the parable of the Good Samaritan, of his rescue of a man, obviously a Jew, "going down from Jerusalem to Jericho," who is robbed and left to die, ignored by priest and Levite. When, concluding the parable Jesus asks, which of the three was neighbor to the man who fell among thieves, once again he has turned the argument on its head. Now the question reads "to whom or for whom am I a neighbor?" Whatever the challenges to interpretation, it is tempting to ask whether or not Jesus sat for the portrait of that that Samaritan. Clearly, the status of a Galilean was not rungs above that of a Samaritan. Both were a people known to be of mixed blood, of questionable religious bent, and were shunned by the elite from Jerusalem. In the Fourth Gospel the Jews' reply to Jesus' accusation that they are "far from God," reads, "Are we not right in saying that you are a Samaritan and have a demon?" (John 8:48).[14] Next, Jesus states that the man who fell among thieves was left "half dead" (vs. 30). Aid to such a person could involve violation of a fundamental law of ritual purity, that is, contact with a dead body (cf. Numbers 19:11–22).

---

14. The accusation is repeated in a recent article titled "John 8 and the Birth of Jesus" by Asif Iqbal and published by *Bismika Allahuma* on October 15, 2005, in an attempt to undermine the legitimacy of Jesus' birth.

Imaginings aside, the religious and cultural distinctions between Samaritans and such a victim as was aided in this parable were as wide as heaven from earth, whatever the ritual strictures. One thing is certain, Jesus violated one established law of cleanliness after another, and with a will. No doubt, for his adversaries, his most egregious violation would have been his contact with the haemorrhaging woman (Mark 5:25-34; Matthew 9:20-22; Luke 8:43-48). The Old Testament, Mishnah and Talmud are replete with injunctions against contact with bloody discharges. Lastly, the innumerable instances of Jesus' exorcisms, healings, and acts of mercy urge the suggestion that after Jesus himself that man is modelled who bandaged the victim's wounds, set him on his beast, brought him to an inn, took care of him, gave two denarii to the innkeeper to tend him in his absence, and promised to return to repay whatever more was spent. But if so, then Jesus' word to the lawyer, "go and do likewise" (vs. 37) was nothing if not a call to discipleship.

The parables of the lost sheep, lost coin, and the two sons in Luke 15, perhaps the greatest and most moving of all those told by Jesus, deserve a second look. At the opening of the chapter, Luke records that tax collectors and sinners came to listen to Jesus. As already noted, the tax collector was a lackey of Rome and the Herods, classed with thieves and robbers, to whom one could lie with impunity,and who rendered whatever house he entered unclean. As for "sinners," the term used here occurs almost fifty times in the New Testament, and as any dictionary indicates, ranges in definition from devotion to or being captive to sin, to being pre-eminently sinful, or wicked, and is used specifically of those tainted by particular vices or crimes, such as tax-gatherers and heathen. On the arrival of this rabble, the Pharisees and scribes grumble, "this fellow welcomes sinners and eats with them" (vs.2). The demonstrative (Greek: *houtos*) translated "this fellow," is deliberately indefinite, as if Jesus were of indeterminate origin, any bloke off the street. To the charge respecting his dining habits Jesus responds with the three parables, all of which accent the feature of celebration. The shepherd leaves the ninety-and-nine for the one lost sheep, finds it, lays it on his shoulder and rejoices, then calls his friends and neighbours to join in; the woman loses one of her ten silver coins, lights a lamp, sweeps the house, searches till she finds it, then gathers friends and neighbours to celebrate with her; the father whose profligate son has returned home calls for a robe, a ring, and sandals for the returnee, and to the remonstrance of the elder son says "we had to celebrate and rejoice, because this brother of yours was dead and has come to life; he was lost and has been found' " (vs. 32), a variation on the theme following the first two parables: "there will be more joy in heaven over one sinner who repents than over ninety-nine righteous persons who need no repentance (vs. 7), and, "there is joy in the presence of the angels of

God over one sinner who repents" (vs. 10). The accusation to which Jesus replies in these three parables demands the inference that his welcoming and dining with the "lost" or dregs of society, is a celebration, like that of the shepherd who has found his lost sheep, the woman who has found her lost coin, and, at the climax of the three *mesalim*, that he stands in the stead of the father who welcomes home his lost son. Who else would take it upon himself to speak of the joy of heaven or of joy in the presence of the angels at the rescue of "one sinner who repents"? Jesus himself is subject of the triple-parable. And as for the "ninety-and-nine righteous persons who need no repentance" (15:7), the phrase is accommodation to popular parlance or opinion, nothing more, and by association demands that here, at least as used in the Pharisees' and scribes' complaint, the term "sinner" be taken in precisely the same way.

The Hard Sayings

The Demon Possessed Child

Returning from the Transfiguration mount, Jesus is meet by a father whose son is possessed by a demon the disciples are unable to cast out. To the father's plea, "if you are able to do anything, have pity on us and help us," Jesus replies, "If you are able!—All things can be done for the one who believes" (Mark 9:22–23). In Matthew's parallel account the boy is described as an epileptic, and in response to the father's statement that the disciples were unable to cure him, Jesus first upbraids the disciples ("You faithless and perverse generation, how much longer must I be with you?" Matthew 17:17), then demands that the boy be brought to him and heals him. When the disciples ask why they could not perform the deed, Jesus replies: "Truly I tell you, if you have faith the size of a mustard seed, you will say to this mountain, 'Move from here to there,' and it will move; and nothing will be impossible for you" (Matthew 17:20–21). In Luke's account the context is altered to a petition put by the disciples that Jesus teach them to pray. Jesus replies, "Truly I tell you, if you have faith the size of a mustard seed, you could say to this mulberry tree, 'Be uprooted and planted in the sea,' and it would obey you," Luke 17:5–6).

In Matthew and Luke Jesus makes clear that the effects of this faith for which everything is possible, or which can move mountains or mulberry bushes, has nothing to do with its size. It may be as small as to render it invisible, small as a mustard seed, a faith which the father in Mark's account admits is compounded with unbelief, and for lack of which, in Matthew, the disciples are unbraided. It would not be uncharacteristic of Jesus to engage in hyperbole here. But that introductory "Truly I tell you" recorded in Matthew and Luke, which comes only from Jesus' mouth, and by which he lays claim to authority, gives a seriousness to his statement beyond the use of hyperbole. Jesus is assigning such power to faith as is able to remove mountains. But this requires inferring from the father's plea ("I believe; help my unbelief!" Mark 9:24), or from the disciples' earlier petition ("increase our faith!" Luke 17:5) that such faith cannot be simply summoned up, but originates elsewhere, in Jesus alone, and made explicit in his word in the original account: "All things can be done for the one who believes "(Mark 9:23).[1]

The Rich Man

The same thought is present in the accounts of Jesus' encounter with the rich man. Following the man's grief at Jesus' invitation to sell all and follow him, Jesus looks around and says to the disciples, "How hard it will be for those who have wealth to enter the kingdom of God!" (Mark 10:23). At this the disciples are perplexed, but they are astounded when Jesus "ups the ante," giving his word universal application: "Children, how hard it is to enter the kingdom of God!" reinforcing it with that metaphor of the camel and the needle's eye. The disciples do not miss the application. In astonishment they exclaim, "then who can be saved?" Jesus replies, "for mortals it is impossible, but not for God; for God all things are possible" (Mark 9:22-27).

The Fig Tree

Mark and Matthew share Jesus' cursing of the fig tree (Mark 11:12-14; Matthew 21:18-22). On the day following the temple cleansing, Jesus is hungry, sees a fig tree in leaf, finds nothing on it but leaves, and curses it: "May no one ever eat fruit from you again." To all of which Mark adds: "It was not the season for figs," an aside avoided by Matthew, and for which a majority of interpreters might have devoutly wished. How to interpret the scene? Many see the event set within a context of conflict (in Mark preceding the cleansing of the temple; in Matthew following the cleansing and preceding the priests' and elders' questioning of Jesus' authority), but are forced to view it as parable or metaphor for the intransigence of Jesus' opponents. But only a few verses later both Mark and Matthew register the disciples' amazement at the withering of the tree, so that whatever parabolic or metaphorical significance the story may have seems eliminated by the miracle. "Rabbi, look!"

---

1. This translaton of *panta dunatai to pisteuonti*, typically reflects a theological position, here one with which I agree.

cries Peter, "the fig tree that you cursed has withered" (Mark 11:21; Matthew 21:20). But the aside in Mark remains, and if the word for "season" he uses denotes a time "out of our hands," a period or season that cannot be lengthened or recalled, but with a specific beginning and end, something spelling destiny, then he has given leave to interpret the event symbolically, however inconsistent it might appear alongside the event construed as miracle, together with Jesus' use of it to indicate the power of prayer (Mark 11:23: "If you do not doubt in your heart, but believe that what you say will come to pass, it will be done for you"). Certainly, it will not be the first or last time Mark has refused to put asunder what with his pen he has joined together. By omitting the aside, Matthew has avoided the irritation.

Ask, Seek, and Knock

In Mark 11:22–24, immediately following Peter's exclamation at the withering of the fig tree, Jesus says, "have faith in God. Truly I tell you, if you say to this mountain, 'Be taken up and thrown into the sea,' and if you do not doubt in your heart, but believe that what you say will come to pass, it will be done for you. So, I tell you, whatever you ask for in prayer, believe that you have received it, and it will be yours" (Mark 11:22–24). The more familiar parallel occurs in Matthew's account of the Sermon on the Mount: "Ask, and it will be given you; search, and you will find; knock, and the door will be opened for you. For everyone who asks receives, and everyone who searches finds, and for everyone who knocks, the door will be opened" (Matthew 7:7–8).

In Luke's parallel account Jesus says, " Is there anyone among you who, if your child asks for a fish, will give a snake instead of a fish? Or if the child asks for an egg, will give a scorpion? If you then, who are evil, know how to give good gifts to your children, how much more will the heavenly Father give the Holy Spirit to those who ask him?" (Luke 11:9–13). The contrast between what God would do and what a caring, loving parent would do is as great as the difference between good and evil. And, what God would do would be to give the Spirit to those who ask. This word puzzled the Church to the point where it offered alternatives. One ancient tradition reads that whoever asks would get a good gift, another that he would get good gifts, plural, or another that he would get a good spirit. But, for a disciple, the promise of the Holy Spirit could mean the world and all. The summons is echoed in the Fourth Gospel: "If you abide in me, and my words abide in you, ask for whatever you wish, and it will be done for you" (John 15:7). The summons is echoed also in the Epistle of James: "If any of you is lacking in wisdom, ask God, who gives to all generously and ungrudgingly, and it will be given ou. But ask in faith, never doubting. . .." (James 1:5). In the same epistle, the case is put negatively: "You do not have, because you don't ask. You ask and do not receive, because you ask wrongly. . .." (James 4:3). The Gnostic Gospel of Thomas 2 and 92 likewise contain echoes of the summons: "Jesus said: He who seeks must not stop seeking until he finds; and when (*'otan*) he finds, he will be bewildered; and if he is bewildered, he will marvel, and will be king over the All. . ..Jesus said: Seek and you will find. But (*alla*) those things about which you asked me during these days, I did not tell you on that day. Now I am willing to tell them, and you do not inquire about them."[2]

In Luke and James the breadth of he summons to ask, search, and knock is clearly narrowed. In Luke it is restricted to the giving of the Holy Spirit. In James the case is put negatively. In the first passage the doubter will not receive; in the second, the one who asks "wrongly" will not receive, "wrongly" (*kakoos*), unspecified. In the Gospel of Thomas, chapter two one will get more than one asked for, presumably control of the universe. In chapter 92 there is contrast between receiving what is asked for in future, and what is asked of Jesus what once was hidden, and is now available, but leading to no inquiry.

The question to be put is where the accent in these texts belongs, on the petitioner, or on the one able to satisfy the petition. In Luke the accent is clearly on the provider, on God: on the other hand, the petitioner is challenged, whether by doubt or as the Gospel of Thomas has it, by lack of curiosity. If the accent is on the provider, then the basis for all this asking, searching, and knocking must be the power of God, admittedly able to be countered, resisted, ignored, but by one "like a wave of the sea, driven and tossed by the wind" (James 1:6). But what of the one who asks in faith, does not doubt, and still does not receive? To that question, that odd piece from a movement bidding to overwhelm the nascent Christian community, may give the answer. "He who seeks must not stop seeking until he finds."

David's Son

Mark writes that while Jesus was teaching in the temple he said, "How can the scribes say that the Messiah is the son of David? David himself, by the Holy Spirit, declared, 'The Lord said to my lord, "Sit at my right hand, until I put your enemies under your feet." 'David himself calls him Lord; so how

---

2. *The Gospel of Thomas*, trans. B. M. Metzger, *Synopsis Quattuor Evangeliorum*, ed. Kurt Aland, (Stuttgart: Deutsche Bibelgesellschaft, 1985), 517, 528.

can he be his son?"(Mark 12:35–37). In Luke's parallel account, the question is put to the Sadducees; the Psalms are cited in support of the disclaimer, and Mark's comment to the effect that "the large crowd was listening to him with delight" is omitted (Luke 21:41–44).

Only in the Synoptics is Jesus addressed as "son of David," and chiefly in Matthew's Gospel. Further, the title is never used of the exalted Christ, only of the earthly Jesus. It is certainly possible that those who witnessed Jesus' healings and exorcisms addressed him as son of David. The question is whether use of the title originated with Jesus himself, or whether Matthew and Luke undertook a revision by assigning the title to him. One thing is sure: in Mark's Gospel Jesus is not indulging in banter or wordplay, but actually rafting what in Judaism had become a traditional messianic title, and in support gone to "the sweet singer of Israel" himself. As for Jesus, there were other titles to which he would lay explicit claim:

> Again the high priest asked Him, "Are you the Messiah,[3] the Son of The Blessed One?" Jesus said, "I am; and you will see the Son of Man seated at the right hand of the Power; and coming with the clouds of heaven." (Mark 14:61–62)

Hating Father and Mother

In Luke 14:26 Jesus says, "whoever comes to me and does not hate father and mother, wife and children, brothers and sisters, yes, and even life itself, cannot be my disciple." In Matthew's accent the saying is softened to read, ""whoever loves father or mother more than me is not worthy of me; and whoever loves son or daughter more than me is not worthy of me": (Matthew 10:37). Interpreters suggest that for Jesus' early followers, discipleship spelled a breach of tabu. That is, eliminating filial relations, relegating family conditions to a secondary position.[4] The question is whether or not reference to eliminating the familial or to relegating it to second place can substitute for or replace the mood or the emotion conjured up by use of the term "hate." But how can Jesus, who urges love of parent, and excoriates those who refuse them financial support, speak of hating them? To the rich man he holds up the requirement to honor father and mother (Mark 10:19), and to the Pharisees and scribes says, "Moses said, 'Honor your father and your mother. . ..' "But you say, that if anyone tells father or mother, 'Whatever support you might have had from me is Corban' (that is, an offering to

---

3. In Hebrew, "The anointed one;" in Greek, "the Christ."
4. Cf. *The Jesus Handbuch*, 452–453.

God)—"then you no longer permit doing anything for a father or mother, thus making void the word of God through your tradition that you have handed on" (Mark 7:10-13; Matthew 15:4-6). Jesus is either involved in an inconsistency or that word "hate" in his mouth deserves another definition. But that definition would have to oppose the forty instances of its use elsewhere and with the usual connotation. Whatever the solution, the term must somehow retain its original sense. The elimination of filial piety, the relegating of it to the periphery spells an act normally resulting from or accompanied by a mood or emotion we call "hate." Of course, it could be the same with the term "hate" as with the term "love" in the New Testament, that it denotes an act not needing coupling with an emotion. Still, with whatever connotation Jesus may have loaded the term, to his audience "hate" had to carry the full weight of its everyday use, and in the end demand a response that was total, absolutely total.

Conflict

The Gospels give considerable space to the opposition to Jesus. Till now his three principal adversaries, the scribes, Pharisees, and Sadducees, have merely been named by name. Space is given here to their origins and views.

The first, the party of scribes, derived from earlier prophetic or seer-priests, were intent on preserving the ruins of the theocracy existing prior to the Babylonian exile (BC 586). For this group, all of life was concentrated in the Torah and its six hundred and thirteen commandments. In fact, the summons to obedience to Torah bid fair to equal that of obedience to Jahve, to God himself. For example, in the Talmud, Rabbi Akiba, one of Judaism's greatest scholars (AD 50-135), interpreted the Hebrew conjunction *eth* in the word of Deuteronomy 10:20 reading "fear the Lord your God," as applying also to the scribes.[5] It was to this party that the Pharisees belonged, hence the frequent mention of the two in tandem. When, due to foreign rule, the influence of the Sanhedrin began to wane, that of the scribes with their repristination of the ancient traditions, began to rise. "Chairmanship" of the scribes was bequeathed through the family of Hillel (BC 110-AD 10), associated with giving codification to the oral tradition in the Talmud and Mishnah. According to Matthew, it was in part the scribes' and their colleagues' application of commandments to every aspect of human life that aroused Jesus' ire: "They tie up heavy burdens. . .but they themselves are

---

5. Pesharim 229, cited in Wellhausen, Julius. *Pharisäer und die Sadducaer* (Bamberg: Greifswald, 1871), 17.

unwilling to lift a finger to move them" (Matthew 23:4). The enormity of commands left little room for the function of conscience.

The Pharisees emerged from a group called the Hasidim, participants in the Maccabean revolt against the rule of the Seleucids, one of the dynasties following the breakup of Alexander's Macedonian empire. The party was known for giving strictest application to the requirements of the scribes, and introducing innovations rivalling the Torah itself. The Pharisees were few in number in the high Jewish court of the Sanhedrin, and their influence, unlike that of the scribes and Sadducees, was not political but religious in nature, its site the religious life. Hatred of the eighty-year-old Hasmonean dynasty, birthed by the Maccabees, but grown independent with the collapse of Seleucid rule, and ultimately a Roman client state, was similarly religious in nature. Differences between the Pharisees and the average Israelite lay in the degree of their zeal for the Torah, giving them an inquisitorial and controlling nature, leading to disdain for the rabble. As is clear from the New Testament, the Pharisees affirmed faith in a personal Messiah whose advent they awaited toward the end of the reign of Herod the Great. In contrast to the Sadducees, they also affirmed faith in the resurrection. Ultimately, Pharisaic reaction to the Hasmonean usurper gave the people a taste for power, estranging them from their original rescuers. Over a century ago, the noted German scholar, Julius Wellhausen, insisted that the term "hypocrite" as applied to the Pharisee should not be construed as an analytic judgment, that is, as a predicate already contained in the subject "Pharisee."[6] Clearly, the term as used in Matthew 23:13, 25, 27, 29, or in Luke 12:1, does not merely denote those who do not practice what they preach, but those who exclude from the mercy of God those who are unable to satisfy the innumerable rites and observances.

The Sadducees were a sect that drew its name from Zadok, priest during David's reign, who was ninth in descendance from Eleazar the son of Aaron, aided David during Absalom's revolt, and was the first high priest to serve in the temple built by Solomon.[7] Like the Pharisees, the Sadducees emerged from the Maccabean revolt, rose to become representatives of the new state, and enjoyed the highest offices in the land. These aristocrats, more than the Pharisees, were able to maintain their authority even after the ruin of the old temple. Though of priestly caste, the priesthood as such meant less to them than as a path to political power. Care for the sanctuary thus took second seat to concern for the secular or worldly. They were at home dealing with affairs of state, participating in the Sanhedrin, mediating

---

6 Cf. Wellhausen, 127.

7. Cf. II Samuel 8:17; I Chronicles 6: 4–8; 24:3.

domestic grievances, and treating with the Roman conquerors.[8] However they may have held to the ancient usages initially, their support in the scriptures came loose from practice and turned abstract. They rejected the oral law proposed by the Pharisees, regarded the written Torah as sole source of divine authority, rejected belief in the resurrection of the dead, and retained the traditional belief in *Sheol* for those who had died. The Sadducees disputed with the Pharisees over matters of purity, inheritance, slavery, and perjury. Matthew records an instance in which representatives of both groups set a trap for Jesus.[9]

At least ten narratives record encounters with his adversaries and their plans to be rid of him. Following the outline of Mark, the Synoptists record opposition to Jesus' breaking the Sabbath.[10] Mark alone records the opinion held of him by his family.[11] The three Synoptists record his rejection at Nazareth.[12] Mark and Luke alone record the conspiracy of the high priests and scribes against Jesus.[13] All four evangelists record the questioning of Jesus' authority,[14] and the question concerning taxes.[15] The three evangelists record the question concerning the resurrection,[16] and the dialogue over the first commandment.[17] Finally, all four evangelists record the plot to kill Jesus.[18]

Respecting the first encounter, Matthew and Luke record that while Jesus was going through the grainfields on the sabbath, his disciples were hungry, began to pluck heads of grain and eat, Luke adding that they were rubbing the kernels in their hands. Mark simply records that they were making their way plucking heads of grain. How could they be accused of breaking the Sabbath, when Mosaic law allowed a traveller to pluck and eat grain that grew alongside a path?[19] According to the Mishnah, thirty-nine activities were prohibited on the Sabbath, among them sowing, ploughing, reaping, binding sheaves, threshing, winnowing, cleansing crops, grinding,

---

8. Wellhausen, *op. cit.*, p. 44.
9. Matthew 16:1.
10. Mark 2:23–28; Matthew 12:1–8; Luke 6:1–5.
11. Mark 3:2–21.
12. Mark 6:1–6; Matthew 13:53–58; Luke 4:16–20.
13. Mark 11:18–19; Luke 19:47–48.
14 64 Mark 11:27–33; Matthew 21:23–27; Luke 20:1–8; John 2:18–22.
15. Mark 12:13–17; Matthew 22:15–22; Luke 20:20–26; John 3:2.
16. Mark 12:18–27; Matthew 22:23–38; Luke 20:27–40.
17. Mark 12:28–34; Matthew 22:34–40; Luke 10:25–28.
18. Mark 14:1–2; Matthew 26:1–5; Luke 22:1–2; John 11:47–53.
19. Cf. Deut. 23:25.

sifting, and kneading.[20] According to the members of that singular reform movement of Judaism called Pharisaism, the disciples were reaping, harvesting. So, according to Mark they ask Jesus why the disciples are doing *what is not lawful* on the Sabbath, according to Matthew why they are doing what is not lawful *to do* on the sabbath, and in Luke they put the question directly to Jesus: "Why are *you* doing what is not lawful on the sabbath?" To this Jesus answers with a counter-question containing a historical reference to David and his company. Emerging hungry from his place of hiding from King Saul, he encountered the priest Ahimelech at Nob,[21] site of the ever-traveling tabernacle, begged for bread, and for lack of the ordinary variety was given the "shewbread" ("bread of the presence") designated for the priests alone, and on the assurance that his company had kept themselves from women.[22] The answer is stunning. It assumes an analogy between the activity of Israel's soon-to-be greatest king together with his company, and that of Jesus and his group. More, from his reference Jesus draws the conclusion that necessity has priority over law, at least of the liturgical variety. Thus, he states, "the sabbath was made for humankind, and not humankind for the sabbath" (Mark 2:27). More yet, if the indeclinable particle immediately following (Greek: *hoste*) may be translated "so that," "wherefore," "insomuch that," or "therefore," then for this very reason "the Son of man is lord even of the sabbath." Step by step Jesus shreds the analogy, turns it into an argument leading from the lesser to the greater. If the right to give priority to necessity over law applied to David, how much more does it apply to the Son of Man, lord of the Sabbath? The title, "Son of Man," is enigmatic. It can denote the human as such,[23] it can refer to that figure come for judgment and deliverance celebrated in the intertestamental, apocalyptic literature,[24] or it can be taken as a self-reference, as is the case here. The context demands that it be taken as a self-designation, for to whom would the lordship over the sabbath apply, if not to Jesus, to the one who has just assigned priority to necessity over law?

Following the description of Jesus' appointment of the twelve, Mark records the attempt to restrain him for having lost his senses (3:21). Both the RSV and the NRSV read that his family went out to seize him because "people were saying" he had lost his mind. The NIV reads that "his family,"

20. Danby, Herbert. "Shabbath" 7.2, *The Mishnah*, 106.

21. Mark 2:26 records that the event took place when Abiathar was high priest.

22. Cf. I Samuel 21:1–6.

23. Cf. Psalm 8:4

24. Cf. "The Similitudes of I Enoch," chapters 37–71, in Charles, R. H. *The Apocrypha and Psendepigrapha of the Old Testament in English*, (Oxford: The Clarendon Press, 1913), Vol. II, pp.

"or his associates," went to take charge of him, for they said, "He is out of his mind." The Vulgate detours around the problem, simply furnishing the verbs needed for the narrative in the third person plural ("they. . .they. . .they, etc."). The Greek phrase (*hoi par' autou*), the exegete's "cross" in this instance, allows for any one of the above translations. But the context makes clear, that the reference is to Jesus' own family. The scribes' charge that Jesus is possessed by Beelzebul; his explicit reference to his "mother and his brothers," and his response to their inquiries about him, to say nothing of the suitability to Mark's concept of the "Messianic Secret" and its obverse side, the disciples' and the crowds' unknowing, all require translating the phrase in question as denoting the members of Jesus' own kith and kin.

The three Synoptists introduce the narrative of Jesus' rejection at Nazareth with his arrival at his hometown, Luke adding "where he had been brought up" (Luke 4:6). While Mark and Matthew simply refer to Jesus' teaching in the (or "their" = Matthew 13:54) synagogue, Luke refers to Jesus' habit of attending worship on the sabbath, to his standing for the reading of the Servant Song in Isaiah 42, returning the book to the synagogue leader, and with all eyes on him announcing "today this scripture has been fulfilled in your hearing" (Luke 4:21). All three evangelists record the crowd's amazement at his wisdom and deeds of power, the reference to his occupation ("is this not the carpenter"? (Mark 6:3; "the carpenter's son?" Matthew 13:55), the members of his family present at the event, and finally the crowd's taking offense. In Luke's account, following the axiom ("prophets are not without honor, except in their hometown" (Luke 4:24; cf. Mark 6:4, and Matthew 13:57), and the evidence given for it from the time of Elijah and Elisha, the enraged crowd drives him out of town, planning to hurl him from a cliff (Luke 4:28–29). Mark concludes his narrative with the contradictory, almost humorous note that Jesus was unable to do a deed of power there, except that he laid his hands on a few sick and healed them, then adds that Jesus was amazed at their unbelief. Mark's co-evangelists seem puzzled at the suggestion that Jesus' deeds of power were somehow dependent on geography or audience attitude. Luke omits the comment, ends his narrative with Jesus' disappearance through the crowd (Luke 4:30), while Matthew writes that *because* of their unbelief Jesus did no mighty work there, and as Luke, omits the reference to his having been taken aback at their unbelief (Matthew 13:58). Mark's terse, and contradictory comment suggests a consciousness of the relation between divine power and the movement of faith, a relation Matthew and Luke were not eager to explore. It suggests that in the concrete instance, say at Nazareth, neither Jesus' divine power nor Nazareth's belief could do without the other, though the initiative lay with the divine ("except that he laid his hands on a few sick people and cured them"), still for all that a divine vulnerable to unbelief ("and he was amazed at their unbelief"). If Mark was conscious of the relation, that little verse initiated a reflection that has never come to an end.

In Mark and Luke, following Jesus' cleansing of the temple the chief priests, scribes, and, according to Luke, "leaders of the people" (19:47b) look for a way to do away with him. A certain robustness attaches to Mark's report which Luke appears to soften. According to the usual translation, Mark writes that the conspirators were looking for an opening "for they were afraid of him, because the wholecrowd was spellbound by his teaching." The subordinating causal particle translated "for," then "because," is thus used to indicate that the crowd's astonishment at Jesus' teaching was the reason for his conspirators' fear of him. But that little particle could be rendered in such fashion as to allow that the conspirators were afraid of Jesus, and, secondarily, of the crowd amazed at his teaching, Mark's purpose being to double the risk of plotting his death. What gives weight to the suggestion is that the initial phrase contains the same combination of verb and particle as appears in the narrative of the resurrection: "They [the women at the tomb] said nothing to anyone, *for they were afraid*" (Mark 16:8). In that case, Luke's record of the conspirators' inability to find a way to eliminate him due to the people's being spellbound at his teaching, would be a softening.

John's report differs vastly from that of his co-evangelists. First of all, he sets the cleansing of the temple at the outset of Jesus' ministry, and not at the end, as do his co-evangelists. There is merit in the view that in John the temple cleansing is positioned at the beginning of Jesus' ministry to render it the opening volley of his attack on "the Jews," an attack which persists throughout the Gospel. Second, in his report of the incident, John makes no mention of Jesus' enemies plotting to kill him, merely that Jesus charges them with rapacity, having changed the temple into a den of thieves (John 2:16–17). It is only after raising Lazarus that Jesus' enemies plot his death (John 11:38–53). Here, he merely adds the note that many believed him because of the signs he was doing. Assuming two temple cleansings, one at the beginning and the other at the end of Jesus' ministry, might strain credulity, but so would the assumption that the Fourth Evangelist's purpose was merely "dramaturgical," Jesus totally unconcerned with temple purification. One thing is certain: The "sign" Jesus' enemies demand for authorizing his act has the accent: "Destroy this temple, and in three days I will raise it up" (John 2:19). Tripping over the double entendre, his adversaries boggle at the promise of a raising in three days against the time required for the Herodian temple construction: "This temple has been under construction for forty-six years, and will you raise it up in three days?" (John 2:20).[25] In an aside to the reader, John reports that "he was speaking of the temple of his body" (John 2:21). Apparently the disciples tripped over the same entrendre, since it took a resurrection to pry Jesus' meaning loose: "After he was raised from the dead, his disciples remembered that he had said this; and they believed the scripture and the word that Jesus had spoken" (John 2:22).

Following their report of Jesus' sole entry into Jerusalem, his cleansing of the temple, the plot to kill him, and the lesson of the fig tree, the Synoptists record the question put to Jesus by the chief priests, scribes, and elders (in Matthew the chief priests and elders) respecting his authority, its agency ("by what authority are you doing these things?) and its source ("who gave you this authority. . ..?").

As already indicated in Mark and Luke, this question had already been answered for those who witnessed the exorcism in the synagogue at Capernaum: there the crowd is astounded and asks, "What is this? A new teaching—with authority! He commands even the unclean spirits, and they obey him." (Mark 1:27; cf. Luke 4:36-38). The crowd instinctively feels who Jesus is. It recognizes his teaching as an activity rooted in authority, not in the strangeness of its doctrine. That is, it regards that activity as existing by virtue of a divine gift, however ignorant it may be of its full implication. In the scene immediately preceding, Jesus' audience is astounded at his teaching because he teaches with authority, "and not as the scribes" (Mark 1:22). In other words, his teaching differs radically from rabbinic exposition with its reliance on precedent or its search for new expression. As is clear from the Gospels throughout, Jesus' teaching is strikingly lacking in those characteristics common to rabbinic teaching, contradicting the notion prevalent in his time that the prophetic office had ceased to function.

The fourth evangelist records the Jews' demand for a sign immediately following the temple cleansing, the first of Jesus' four appearances in Jerusalem (John 2:18-22). Despite interruptions in the record, and their distance from the Fourth Gospel, the Synoptists no doubt draw the same connection, Jesus' questioners' adverting to "these things" and his authority to do them (Mark 11: 28; Matthew 21:23; Luke 20:2) thus referring to the temple cleansing. In the Synoptics Jesus counters his critics' question with his own: "Did the baptism of John come from heaven, or was it of human origin?" (Mark 11:30; Matthew 21:25; Luke 20:4). The question cannot have been put haphazardly, as if Jesus were merely after teasing his attackers. It forges a link between John's and Jesus' careers. If the baptism of John came

---

25. Scholarly affirmation of the correctness of John's dating suggests a pat on the head, cf. *Jesus Handbuch*.

from heaven, then Jesus' authority derived from there. If it was of human origin the same held true of Jesus' authority. What applied to the one had to apply to the other. There is a sovereignty in Jesus' linking the career of the Baptist with his own, in assigning to John and his baptizing activity a similarity with his "doing these things." Scarcely anywhere else is that link so intimately forged, and the Baptist given such status, not by way of the intimation of an evangelist, as, for example, in the record of Jesus' ministry initiated by John's arrest (Mark 1:14), or even by Jesus' own words concerning the Baptist as the "Elijah who is to come" (Matthew 11:14), but here, in his response to his attackers following the cleansing of the temple. The link is absent in the Fourth Gospel, replaced by the demand for a sign, by Jesus' response, by his enemies' confusion, and by his disciples' post-Easter recollection. If John had the accounts of his co-evangelists in hand, then the replacement was deliberate, perhaps for apologetic reasons, since with some the Baptist was more than Elijah, had come to enjoy a status above that of Jesus. That notion has had long life. In an attempt at recovering the original relation between Jesus and the Baptist, one Chicago scholar concluded that John was the apparent master, a fact later reinterpreted by the Christian community in light of its conviction concerning Jesus' supremacy.[26]

The first in a series of four so-called "conflict speeches" in Mark 12, Matthew 22, and Luke 20,[27] records the attempt of Jesus' enemies to entrap him "in what he said" (Mark 12:13; Matthew 22:15; Luke 20:20). In Mark and Matthew the conspirators are a contingent of Pharisees and Herodians,[28] ostensibly a political party friendly to Herod the Great, and often paired with the Pharisaic party of reform.[29] The differences between those two groups had to have been vast. Their cooperation thus signalled a hatred of Jesus that reduced whatever differences in theology and practice existed between them subordinate, the lesser of two evils. At any rate, the plan of entrapment begins with what the old rhetoricians called a *captatio benevolentiae*, a device intended to capture the good will of the hearer: "Teacher, we know that you are sincere, and show deference to no one; for you do not regard people with partiality, but teach the way of God in accordance with truth" (Mark 12:14). Then the trap is set: "Is it lawful to pay taxes to the emperor, or not?" Jesus, seeing behind the *captatio*, stigmatizes his attackers ("you hypocrites," Matthew 22:18), calls for a coin, is handed a small silver coin (denarius),

---

26. Case, Shirley Jackson. *Jesus, a New Biography*, (Chicago: University of Chicago Press, 1927), 215–216.

27. Mark 12:13–17; Matthew 22:15–22; Luke 20:20–26.

28. Luke 20:20 simply describes them as "spies who pretended to be honest."

29. Cf. Mark 3:6; 12:13; Matthew 22:15–16.

and asks whose image and superscription it bears. When his would-be captors answer, "the emperor's," he responds, "give to the emperor the things that are the emperor's, and to God the things that are God's" (Mark 12:17). The hypocrisy of Jesus' interrogators lay in having about them a "graven image," worse, in the holiest place on earth, in the temple. Further, in Matthew's account the call was for a coin "used for the tax" (Matthew 22:19), in other words, for the infamous poll tax (Greek = *kensos*), which in Jesus' own time sparked the uprisings of Judas the Galilean (Acts 5:37), and may even have given rise to the Zealot movement. That such a tax was anathema to strict Pharisaic teaching only doubled the hypocrisy of Jesus' interrogators.

Interpretations of Jesus' response are legion, most often used to buttress arguments for the separation of Church and state, or for the Lutheran teaching regarding the "two kingdoms," the one ruled by law, and decree, the other by the gospel of Christ, neither having to do with the other, but both comprising the context of human life. Use of Jesus' response as concession to government in all good conscience has served as variant of this view, perhaps its most celebrated illustration in the Howard Hawks' production of "Sergeant York," the conscientious objector from rural Tennessee, alone with his dog in the Appalachians, musing over "render to Caesar what is Caesar's, and to God what is God's," in the end enlisting in the army, and with his unit taking one hundred thirty Germans captive during WWI. Matched against the New Testament perspective, the interpretation and its variant are too facile.[30] In the New Testament those "two kingdoms" are not co-equal or coterminous. The one is on the point of being displaced, even overwhelmed by the other, as witness, for example, the hymn in Revelation 11:15: "The kingdom of the world has become the kingdom of our Lord and of his Messiah, and he will reign forever and ever." The view is decidedly apocalyptic, and whether or not Jesus himself was an apocalypticist, his Gospel witnesses certainly were, and from their point of view Jesus' response could only mean that giving to the emperor (Tiberias?) what was his, and from whatever motive, in good conscience or bad, and in whatever form, willingly or under restraint (!), spelled allegiance to bankruptcy, to a kingdom on the way to disappearing, while giving God what was his meant deliverance and life. But whatever his would-be assassins took Jesus' word to mean, their plot had

---

30. While, together with his theology of the cross, Luther's recovery of the eschatology of the New Testament in its apocalyptic form is regarded as constitutive of his theology, he does not deal at any length with the specific aspect of this aeon and whatever belongs to it as passing away. Cf. e.g., Luther, Martin. "Temporal Authority: To What Extent It Should Be Obeyed," Vol. 45: *Christian in Society II*, trans. Schindel, J.J., rev. Brandt, Walther I. (Philadelphia: Fortress Press, 1962); Cf. also Nestigen, James Arne, "The End of the End: The Role of Apocalyptic in the Lutheran Reform," *Word & World* 15, no. 2 (Spring 1995): 204, and the authors cited there.

been foiled. Mark writes: "They were utterly amazed at him" (Mark 12:17); Matthew: "they left him and went away" (Matthew 22:22), and Luke: "they became silent" (Luke 22:26). The plan to entrap will reach its climax in the passion narrative, with the chief priests' and the scribes' (Mark 14:1–2; Luke 22:1–2)), or the elders' (Matthew 26:1–3), or the chief priests and the Pharisees' (John 11:47–53) plot to kill Jesus.

In the Synoptics the next in line of Jesus' opponents and critics are the Sadducees, described as denying the resurrection, then as putting their question: in the resurrection, whose wife will the widow be who has lost one, two, three, up to seven husbands, and without issue? Here, not only old animosities, but Sadducaic boast in strict adherence to written Torah is transcended in giving the question a form calculated to render the old Deuteronomic law a joke.[31] As Matthew's use of the verb (*epigambreuo*) indicates, the widow had to have had seven brothers-in-law to fulfil the obligation—a Gulliver's leap for any family in that period. The query was nasty, and in reply Jesus asks "Is not this the reason you are wrong, that you know neither the scriptures nor the power of God?" (Mark 12:24). While the NRSV translates Jesus' response with a "you are wrong," the verb used suggests a being led astray, as in "you are deceived" (Mark 12:24) or "you are much deceived," (vs. 27). Jesus' reply to the question has two parts, the first of which is a statement regarding the state of existence in the resurrection: "When they rise from the dead" (Mark 12:19), "in the resurrection" (Matthew 22:30), "those who are considered worthy of a place in that age and in the resurrection from the dead" (Luke 20: 34–35). . . neither marry nor are given in marriage, but are like angels in heaven." In Luke Jesus goes on to contrast those "considered worthy" with "those who belong to this age," and further describes them as unable to die anymore, "because they are like angels and are children of God, being children of the resurrection" (Luke 20:34–35). The second part of Jesus' reply calls Moses to witness, in whose "book" with its "story about the bush" God identifies himself to the patriarch, says "I am the God of Abraham, Isaac, and Jacob."[32] Whether the pronoun lacks the copula as in Mark and the original Hebrew (*ego*, "I" = Hebrew, *anochi*), or is supplied as in Matthew (*ego eimi*, "I am"), the copula in the present tense is obviously assumed, as is clear from its use in the later revelation to Moses of the name by which God is to be remembered: "I AM

---

31. Deuteronomy 25:5–6: "When brothers reside together, and one of them dies. . .the wife of the deceased shall not be married outside the family to a stranger. Her husband's brother shall go in to her, taking her in marriage. . .and the first born whom she bears shall succeed to the name of the deceased brother. . .."

32. Exodus 3:6.

WHO I AM."[33] Thus, whoever is *of*, whoever belongs to that God, whether Abraham, Isaac, or Jacob, to that one the same tense applies as to the One to whom it belongs. The Sadduccee cannot affirm the one without the other; cannot deny the existence of the one without denying the existence of the other. God *is*, thus of whomever that God is it must be said that he is, whether Abraham, Isaac, or Jacob. For that God is "God not of the dead, but of the living." Mark puts the period there, while Matthew writes that "when the crowd heard it, they were astounded at his teaching" (Matthew 22:33), and Luke adds that "they (the Sadduccees) no longer dared to ask him another question" (Luke 20:40).

The succession of critics begun with Pharisees and Herodians, continues with Sadduccees, ends with a scribe (Mark) or a lawyer attached to the Sadducees (Matthew), who asks which commandment is first of all, or another lawyer who asks what he must do to inherit eternal life (Mark 12:28; Matthew 22:36; Luke 10:25). In Matthew's and Luke's version, the questioner's purpose is to put Jesus to the test, to lure him into compromising himself (Matthew 12:35; Luke 10:25)[34] In Mark and Matthew Jesus replies to the question, and in Luke it is the lawyer who replies with the *Shema Yisrael* ("Hear, O Israel") of Deuteronomy,[35] the most important part of the Jewish prayer service, adding the command in Leviticus to love the neighbour as oneself.[36]

Was the questioner serious, did he assume that a Jew born in Galilee would be ignorant of what was read weekly in the synagogue, and recited twice daily? Did he assume the parents of Jesus were ignorant of the command to teach their children to recite the *Shema* before getting under the covers?[37] Or, as Matthew and Luke report, was the interrogator's intent to entrap? In that case, the questioner was dissembling, hoping for an answer to upend what for every Jew comprised a *mitzvah*, a command. But if so, one would have expected Jesus to unmask the attempt, as occurs, for example, in the dialogue about taxes (Matthew 22:18) But he does not. Mark and Matthew record Jesus' acceding to the scribe's question without reprimand. In

---

33. Hebrew: eyeh hasher eyeh, Exodus 3:14.

34. The verb used with its object in the accusative (peirazon or ekpeirazon auton) means to tempt, to put to the test.

35. "Hear, O Israel: The Lord is our God, the Lord alone. You shall love the Lord your God with all your heart, and with all your soul, and with all your might" (Deuteronomy 6:4–5).

36 "You shall not take vengeance or bear a grudge against any of your people, but you shall love your neighbor as yourself: I am the Lord" (Leviticus 19:18).

37 "Recite (these words) to your children and talk about them when you are at home and when you are away, when you lie down and when you rise" (Deuteronomy 6:7).

fact, in Mark and Luke, the interrogator is complimented upon his recitation of the *Shema* in answer to Jesus' answer. Mark writes: "When Jesus saw that he answered wisely, he said to him, 'You are not far from the kingdom of God'" (Mark 12:34), and Luke: "You have given the right answer; do this, and you will live" (Luke 10:28). Whether, as with Matthew and Luke, the purpose was to ensnare, or as with Mark, simply to follow up a dispute with a question that needed answering among the elite, Jesus' response is unexpectedly mild, evidence that his reaction to challenge or attack could not be predicted. Mark ends his report of the dispute to read that "after that no one dared to ask him any question" (Mark 12:34), a comment which Luke attaches to the dispute over the resurrection (Luke 20:40). The authorities' plan to do away with Jesus reaches its climax at the outset of the passion narrative. In Mark and Luke the plot is instigated by the chief priests and scribes (Mark 14:1; Luke 22:2), in Matthew by the chief priests and elders (Matthew 26:3), and in John by the chief priests, Caiaphas at their head, along with the Pharisees (John 11:47, 49). Once more, whatever differences existed between the various parties was surmounted by a hatred shared in common.

In John's Gospel, the reports of opposition to Jesus have no counterparts in Mark, Matthew, or Luke. The first has to do with Jesus' healing of the man by the Pool of Bethesda (John 5:1–18). The narrative begins with Jesus' arrival in Jerusalem for "a feast of the Jews" (John 5:1).[38] At the pool with its five stoa or porches, a dialogue ensues between Jesus and a paralytic who for thirty eight years has lain unaided at the pool. Following Jesus' command to get up the man is immediately "made well" (in the Greek: *egeneto hygies*) takes up his mat and begins to walk. Some have suggested that the adjective "well," used five times in the narrative (John vss. 6, 9, 11, 14–15), carries allusions to Hygeia, the daughter of Asclepius, the Greek god of healing, and to the possible existence of an Asclepion in Jerusalem.. Excavations indicate that an asclepion once existed outside the city, was later brought within the city walls by Herod Agrippa and then expanded into a large temple by Emperor Hadrian. Is it legitimate to assume that these allusions suggest John's purpose was to "scupper" the Asclepius tradition? After all, the "sign" at Cana pointed in the same direction, that is, toward Jesus' power to leave the Olympian god Dionysus leagues behind. But to assume that John's intent to "scupper" Asclepion tradition reduces the narrative to a "yarn" hides from the principle of the excluded middle: the healing of the paralytic is true or it is not true. Now, since the healing occurs on the Sabbath, it rouses the ire of Jesus' adversaries. "It is the sabbath," they say, "it is not lawful for you to

---

38. If the reference in 5:1 is to Passover, in John the number of Jesus' visits to Jerusalem for Passover is increased to four (cf. 2:13; 6:4 and 12:1).

carry your mat." If the first century BC Zadokite Document is indicative of Jewish law obtaining in Jesus' day, activity on the Sabbath was seriously hampered. The document, presumably prepared by a sub-group of the Sadducees reads:

> No man shall carry anything from the house to the outside or from the outside into the house and if he be in the gate he shall not carry anything of it or bring in any thing into it. . . .And if any person falls into a gathering of water or into a place of. . .he shall not bring him up by a ladder or a cord or instrument.[39]

Ignorant of the one who healed him the man encounters Jesus in the temple who reproaches him ("See, you have been made well! Do not sin any more, so that nothing worse happens to you" (John 5:14). Later in John's narrative, Jesus sees a man born blind, and rejects the disciples' assumption that the infirmity resulted from the man's or his parents' sin (John 9:1–3). Does Jesus' word here, "do not sin any more," endorse the mathematics rejected later? Or, does it mark an exception, referring, perhaps, to some particular wrong doing that brought about the man's calamity? Or, is it the word spoken at the healing of the man born blind ("neither this man nor his parents sinned," John 9:3) that proves the exception? A word from one of the best known apologists of the twentieth century may help clear the air:

> I used to think it was a "cruel" doctrine to say that troubles and sorrows were "punishments." But I find in practice that when you are in trouble, the moment you regard it as a "punishment," it becomes easier to bear. If you think of this world as a place intended simply for our happiness, you find it quite intolerable: think of it as a place of training and correction and it's not so bad.[40]

In any case, the man's confession that it was Jesus who cured him led to an attack for his having breached the Sabbath. And when he iterated that "my Father is still working, and I also am working," his adversaries were all the more eager to kill him, since he not only broke the Sabbath but called God his Father.

John chapter seven contains a cluster of conflict narratuves, According to 7:1–9, Jesus is intent on remaining in Galilee to avoid assassination in

---

39. Schechter, Solomon. *Fragments Of A Zadokite Work*, edited from Hebrew Manuscripts in the Cairo Genizah Collection and provided with an English translation, introduction and notes (Cambridge: At the University Press, 1910), VIII, 7–9, 16–17. xlix.

40. Lewis, C.S. *God In The Dock, Essays on Theology and Ethics*, ed. Walter Hooper (Grand Rapids: William B. Eerdmans Publishing Company, 1970), 52.

Judea. His brothers urge him to reverse his decision and engage in public display at the Festival of Booths or Ingathering ("Leave here and go to Judea so that your disciples also may see the works you are doing; for no one who wants to be widely known acts in secret. If you do these things, show yourself to the world" (John 7:3-4). The Festival, *Sukkot*, literally "booths," one of the three at which the Jews were commanded to perform a pilgrimage, was celebrated on the fifteenth day of the seventh month (*Tishrei* from late September to late October).[41] To their urging the evangelist appends the remark that "not even his brothers believed in him" (John 7:5). We are not told whether that unbelief spelled an inability to see beyond the "works" he was doing to what those works were intended to signify, or whether they disbelieved those "works" out of hand, in which case their urging was a mockery. Then follows Jesus' contrast between his "time" as not yet come, and that of his siblings as "already here," between the world's hatred of him and its absence toward them, the implication being that they belong to that world whose hatred of him is roused by his testimony against its evil works. The report concludes with Jesus' dismissal ("Go to the festival yourselves," John 7:8a), and the repetition of his refusal to go to Jerusalem since his "time has not yet fully come" (John 7:8b). Once more the term translated "time" (*kairos*) is used in that peculiarly Johannine sense, the "hour" of his "going to the Father" the "hour" of his glorification- crucifixion (John 14:12; 17:1), has not yet come.

As object of inquiry ("where is he?"John 7:11), and of debate for and against ("some were saying, 'He is a good man,' others were saying, 'No, he is deceiving the crowd'"7:12), Jesus reverses his decision to avoid the festival, attends it incognito, and in the end proceeds to teach openly in the temple. Here he faces the opposition initially voiced during his absence. The Jews first register surprise at his teaching ("How does this man have such learning, when he has never been taught?" 7:16), a comment implying a lack of learning, or learning gleaned apart from an accredited teacher. As if to say his education far exceeds that of any on earth Jesus responds that his teaching does not originate with him but with God (7:16), that whoever resolves to do the will of God will know whether that is so or whether he speaks on his own (7:17). Adding that those who speak on their own seek their own glory, and that the one who seeks the glory of him who sent him is true (7:18), he asks "Did not Moses give you the law? Yet none of you keeps

---

41. Cf. Exodus 34:22: "You shall observe the festival of weeks, the first fruits of wheat harvest, and the festival of ingathering at the turn of the year." Cf. also Leviticus 23:42-43: "You shall live in booths for seven days; all that are citizens in Israel shall live in booths, so that your generations may know that I made the people of Israel live in booths when I brought them out of the land of Egypt; I am the Lord your God."

the law. Why are you looking for an opportunity to kill me?" (7:19). The crowd answers, "You have a demon! Who is trying to kill you?" (7:20). There is a certain spiraling ascent to the dialogue: the crowd begins with asking after Jesus' whereabouts, then divides over its opinion of him, then registers surprise at what he knows absent any formal training, then accuses him of demon possession. Jesus begins with asserting a learning gotten from God, then challenges the crowd to admit it by doing God's will, then attacks it as given the law but intent on killing him. And at the center of the spiral the axiom that whoever speaks on his own is after his own glory, whereas truth is in the one who speaks for another. The dialogue ends in a reprise of his attacker's inconsistency, allowing circumcising on the Sabbath, but accusing him of breaching it with healing. And at center another axiom: circumcision did not originate with Moses but with the patriarchs (7:21-24).

In John 7:25-31 some in Jerusalem find disingenuous the crowd's denial that it wants to do away with Jesus. They ask whether or not he is the one "they seek to kill," note that Jesus is speaking openly in the temple, and inquire after the reason for it: "Can it be that the authorities really know that this is the Messiah?" (John 7:26). They themselves do not, since they know where "this one" is from, whereas when Messiah comes no one will know where "he" is from (John 7:27). Talmud and Midrash echo references to the Messiah's unknown origin. According to the tractate *Sanhedrin,* a certain Rabbi Huna, commenting on Eve's word on giving birth to Seth after Abel's death, says: "It is written, For God hath appointed me another seed (Genesis 4:25) that is, seed from another place, referring to the Messiah,"[42] and a midrash reports that a Rabbi Zera, encountering scholars calculating the time of the Messiah's arrival, would say: "I beg of you, do not postpone it, for it has been taught: Three come unawares: Messiah, a found article and a scorpion."[43] There, in the temple, and in a loud voice, Jesus says: "You know me and you know where I am from" (7:28). Is the intent to counter the demurrer of the crowd, echoed in Talmud and Midrash, and by implication to call himself Messiah, or simply to state that his vital statistics are public property? If the latter, the crowd "knows" of Jesus' physical origins, but does not "know" the one who sent him, pitting knowledge of his "historicity" against the knowledge of the one whose agent he is, the one who is "true." But Jesus "knows" him because he is "from him," because he originates in him. That last "knowing" enrages the crowd. Whether or not that initial "you know me, and you know where I am from," is meant to counter the

---

42. *Babylonian Talmud: Tractate Sanhedrin,* Folio 97a.

43. Santala, Risto. *The Midrash Of The Messiah* (Finland: Tummavuoren Kirjapaino Oy, 2002), 83.

traditon of Messiah's appearance unawares, Jesus' declaration that he knows the one who sent him, because he is from him, is infinitely more than an affirmation of Messiahship. It is nothing if not a reprise of the opening words of the Prologue: "In the beginning was the Word, and the Word was with God, and the Word was God." (1:1). The crowd tries to arrest Jesus, but none lays a hand on him, because his "hour," the "hour" appointed him by God for his "glorification" has not yet come.

In 7:32-36, the Pharisees overhear the crowd's muttering, murmuring, grumbling about Jesus, and with the chief priests send temple police to arrest him. The temple police ("gatekeepers," *sho'arim*), headed by Levites, guarded the entrance to the Temple mount. They stood at twenty-one posts in the Temple court, at three of which priests kept watch during the night. A captain patrolled to see that the keepers were at their posts, and was given the right to beat anyone who fell asleep and set fire to his garments. In addition to opening and closing the gates to the temple, the gatekeepers kept watch over the chambers and treasures of the temple, its utensils and other articles used for service, and prepared bread for the sabbath. (Cf. I Chronicles 9:17, 24-27; 26:12-18). What happened with the temple police's attempt to arrest Jesus? The evangelist allows us to assume that it failed, as did the earlier attempt of the crowd. After this dual failure Jesus, presumably still in the temple, announces that he is going to the one who sent him. and ends with the word that "where I am you cannot come" (7:34). Tripping over what proves to be one more entendre, the adversaries construe the "going" geographically: "Where does this man intend to go that we will not find him?" suggesting Greece as destination (7:35-36). The scene borders on the comic. The crowd hasn't dared to arrest Jesus, so the police are called, ardently to no avail, Jesus persists in talking in the temple, says he is going to the one who sent him, and the crowd takes the "going" to mean a hiking off to Greece, and that at a distance of over a thousand kilometers, as the crow flies. Jesus' opponents at least deserve credit for allowing him Olympian prowess. In John 7:42-44, upon hearing Jesus' invitation to come to him and drink, and of those who believe in him says they are a source of living water—according to the evangelist the latter postponed till the coming of the Spirit—the crowd divides into three groups. The first acknowledges Jesus as "the prophet," the one whom the Lord would raise up like Moses.[44] This group could hardly have missed Jesus' invitation to drink as reminiscent

---

44. Deuteronomy 18:15, 18: " The Lord our God will raise up for you a prophet like me from among your own people; you shall had such a prophet. . . . . I will raise up for them a prophet like you from among your own people; I will put my words in the mouth of the prophet, who shall speak to them everything that I command."

of Moses' bringing water from the rock at Meribah.[45] The second group roundly declares Jesus as the Messiah,[46] while the third matches his Galilean origins with the scripture's prophecy of the Messiah as the Davidic descendant from Bethlehem, city of the great king.[47] Eagerness on the part of both Jews and Christians to establish the Messiah's birth in Bethlehem is not dispelled in Mark 12 and parallels where Jesus asks: "David himself calls him Lord; so how can he be his son?"[48] There, Jesus is not questioning the Messiah's paternity, but his status. The scene once more concludes with the evangelist's note that some of the crowd wanted to arrest Jesus, but no one laid hands on him. It is the third time the desire to do away wth him fails, a repetition that demands the inference that it will be quite another hand that takes the inivitative respecting his "hour."

In John 7:45–52, the evangelist describes priests and Pharisees as totally confounded over the temple police's excuse for not arresting Jesus ("Never has anyone spoken like this!" (7:45), proposing that the police were duped ("Surely you have not been deceived too, have you?" 7:47), registering a total lack of support on the part of the authorities, and laying the blame on the lower class (houtos *ho* ochlos = "this people," 7:49) ignorant of the law, and damning it to hell ("they are accursed," 7:49). It is no secret that the lay movement of Pharisaism, with its iron clad adherence to the oral and written law, in addition to its "fence" around the Torah, comprising three hundred sixteen rules and regulations, held "the people" in contempt, regarded them equal to the heathen, and themselves as the true Israel. Into the fray steps one of their own, Nicodemus, advocating for the 'madding crowd' ("Our law does not judge people without first a giving them a herring to find out what they are doing, does it?" 7:51), only to hear that his advocacy may be politically motivated ("Surely you are not also from Galilee, are you?" 7:52), and a rehearsal of the argument that no prophet comes from Galilee.

The evangelist's narratives of the rejection of Jesus does not end with chapter seven. In 8:43–47, he records an intense and extremely caustic exchange between Jesus and his opponents over their respective relation to Abraham and to God ("They answered him, 'Abraham is our father.' Jesus said to them, 'if you were Abraham's children, you would be doing what

---

45. Exodus 17:1–7; Numbers 20: 13.

46. In the New Testament, the Greek term *Christos* which translates the Hebrew *mashiah* or the Aramaic *meschiha, and* meaning "the anointed one," is the one used most of Jesus.

47. Cf. Micah 5:2: "But you, O Bethlehem of Ephrathah, who are one of the little clans of Judah, from you shall come forth for meone who is to rule Israel,whose origin is from old, from ancient days."

48. Mark 12:35–37; Matthew 22: 311–46; Luke 29:41–44.

Abraham did, but now you are trying to kill me'. . ..They said to him, 'we are not illegitimate children; we have one father, God himself.' Jesus said to them, 'If God were your Father, you would love me,'" (8:39–40; 41–42). Denying his opponents any vestige of religiosity, and tracing their paternity to the devil, a "murderer from the beginning and does not stand in the truth," who when speaking "speaks according to his own nature, for he is a liar and the father of lies" (8:44, his opponents accuse him of being a Samaritan and demon possessed, repeating the charge made at the festival of booths (7:20). The conflict ends with Jesus' opponents picking up stones to throw at him after hearing him declare not only that Abraham rejoiced "that he would see my day," but that "before Abraham was, I am.'" (8:56, 58).

In John 9:13–34, after hearing how the man born blind was healed the Pharisees insist the one who performed the deed cannot be "from God" since he is a Sabbath breaker. Restrictions regarding the Sabbath were severe, but calling a man who healed the blind on the Sabbath a sinner had to be extreme. Though others suggest such a person could not be a sinner, the man's interrogators approach him a second time, only to hear the man declare that his benefactor is a prophet. Disbelieving the man's story, they go to his parents, who admit the man involved is their son, but are ignorant of the entire affair, and, fearing expulsion from the synagogue add that their son is of age, thus able to put their questions to rest. Apparently, the parents have no qualms over placing their son in jeopardy. It would not be surprising if the memory of the later separation between the followers of Jesus and those who remained with the synagogue were somehow reflected here.[49] At any rate, the Pharisees approach the man healed, telling him to give glory to God, that they know his benefactor is a sinner, assuming that calling Jesus a sinner would give glory to God. The man replies that he does not know whether or not he is a sinner but whereas he was blind now he sees. When asked how the act was performed, the fellow, certainly by this time wearied with the interrogation, asks if they want to become Jesus' disciples. To this his questioners respond that they are disciples of Moses, but have no idea where Jesus comes from—reversing the opinion in 7:2[50], and, wittingly or unwittingly fitting Jesus out with a Messianic genealogy. In reply the man expresses his amazement over his interrogators' position states that if Jesus were not from God he could not do what he did, and is summarily thrown out of the synagogue.

49. Cf. the report in John 12:22 in which it is noted that many, even of the authorities, believed in Jesus, but feared to admit it for fear of being expelled from the synagogue. Cf. also Jesus' note in 16:2, that the same fate awaited those who were his.

50. John 7:27: "We know where this man is from; but when the Messiah comes, no one will know where he is from."

THE HARD SAYINGS 97

In John 10:18-21, the evangelist records that just as at the Festival of Booths there was division among the people (John 7:40-44) so also here after hearing Jesus seak of himself as "gate" and good shepherd" (John 19:7-18). Many say that Jesus has a demon, and is out of his mind, a repetition of the charge made at the Festival of Booths, and later (7:20; 8:49), while others insist that his words are not those of one who has a demon, and ask, "Can a demon open the eyes of the blind?" (10:18).

In John 10:22-39, Jesus is reported as walking in the temple, in the portico of Solomon, the colonnade on the eastern side of the outer court. It was winter, festival time, presumably Hanukkah or the Festival of lights, sometimes called the Festival of the Maccabees. The festival commemorated the purification of the temple following the pollutions of Antiochus IV, dubbed "Epiphanes," "Manifest God, "a Seleucid who in 168 BC or 169 marched on Jerusalem, dedicated the temple to Zeus, erected the image of the god in his own image on the altar, and there, according to some, sacrificed a pig. The temple's sacred treasures were robbed, copies of the Torah were destroyed, and the city rebuilt as a Seleucid fortress. According to legend a cruse of oil remained in the temple and was used to light a candle which, miraculously, burned for eight days, hence, the extension of the feast to last a week. It was this king's sack of Jerusalem and desecration of the temple that led to the Maccabean revolt. During this festival another dialogue ensues between Jesus and his adversaries. His opponents demand that he relieve the suspense and acknowledge he is the Messiah. Jesus responds that he has already done so, but his adversaries have not believed, nor have they believed that his works testify to him since they are not of his sheep. After adding that his sheep follow him and that none can snatch them from his hand, the Jews once more take up stones to kill him. Jesus then asks for which of his good works will they stone him, to which they reply it is not for any good work but for blasphemy, for making himself God. Jesus asks, "Is it not written in the law, 'I said, you are gods?' (10:34) , then how could it be said of one the Father has sent that he blasphemes because he says he is God's Son. If they do not believe him, they ought to believe the works he does, thus would know he is in the Father and the Father in him. At this, his opponents try to arrest him, but once again he escapes from their hands. The word Jesus quotes is not in the law, the Torah, but in the writings, the Kethubim, in the Psalms. And, the reference is not to those who enjoy "equality with God," but to those who "shall die like mortals, and fall like any prince" (Psalm 82: 6-7). We may assume that by referring to "the law" Jesus has in mind the Tanak as a whole (Torah, Nevim, prophets, and Kethubim). But in view of the distance between the mortality of the "gods" of the Psalm and what Jesus says of himself ("the Father is in me and I am in the Father"), his remark could be construed as disingenuous, unless, of course, the evangelist intends us to see a *wachomer* here, a move in the argument from the lesser to the greater. In other words, Jesus is saying that if his adversaries are gods, the same is truer of him, whose deeds testify to his oneness with the Father. In either case, the charge of blasphemy is denied.

In John 12:36, in the wake of his triumphal entry into Jerusalem Jesus, contrary to current expectation of the Messiah's" remaining forever" announces the death of the "Son of Man." To the question "who is this Son of Man" he gives the oblique answer: "The light is with you for a little longer. Walk while you have the light." At this point the evangelist writes that though Jesus had performed many signs among them, the people did not believe him, thus fulfilling the prophecy in Isaiah 6:9 that they could not. The conjunction used to render this sense (Greek = hina) is the same as in Mark 4:12, and makes the sentence read, "he has blinded their eyes and hardened their heart, *so that* they might not look with their eyes, and understand with their heart and turn—and I would heal them" (John 12:40). "In Matthew 13:13 the conjunction used in the operative clause (Greek = *hoti*) makes the sentence read, "*because* seeing they do not perceive, and hearing they do not listen" (not as in the NRSV "so that seeing they do not perceive . . ."). Thus, in John as in Mark, the blinding and lack of understanding are construed as an act of God, whereas in Matthew as a human activity. In John, however, the entire scene is wrested from its context in Mark and Matthew who use the Isaiah quote to indicate the purpose of the parables. The evangelist's purpose is to attach it to the series of events described in chapter seven and the chapters following to indicate that God is their author, for which reason all human attempts to make an end of Jesus are thwarted in face of the divine initiative. It is God who sets the time for the Son's glorification.

For years, anti-Semitism has been fueled with references to Jewish involvement in Jesus' death. For just as long the Jewish response has been to deny any complicity in it. Both positions reflect neglect of a fundamental biblical tenet. First, that tenet disallows assigning any group or groups more than mere human agency in that death. In his sermon recorded in Acts, Peter declares that "*this man. . .*[was] *handed over to you.*" Second, that tenet disallows assigning any particular group exclusive complicity in that death, whatever the agency. In the same sermon, Peter describes his Jewish audience as having crucified and killed Jesus "*by the hands of those outside the law,*" in other words, by the Romans. Third, and most important of all, Peter refers to that "handing over" as having occurred "*according to the definite plan and foreknowledge of God*" (Acts 2:23). This accent on the divine initiative in the event of Jesus' death comes from his own mouth in the Gethsemane narrative: "Father, for you all things are possible; remove this cup from me; yet, not what I want, but *what you want*" (Mark 14:36; Matthew 26:39). It appears elsewhere in the New Testament, certainly by implication in John 3:16: "God so loved the world that *he gave his only Son*," or in I Peter 1:18–19: "you were ransomed. . .with *the precious blood of Christ. . .destined before the foundation of the world*," but clearly and explicitly in Revelation with its reference to "the book of life of the Lamb, *slain since the foundation of the world*" (Revelation 13:8, *The Revised English Bible*), Finally, the tenet is reflected in the innumerable New Testament applications to Jesus of the *Eved Yahweh*, the Isaian Servant, of whom the prophet writes in his fourth and final Song: "Surely he has borne our infirmities and carried our diseases; yet *we accounted him stricken struck down by God, and afflicted*" (Isaiah 53:5). Finally, according to the biblical witness, wherever and to whatever extent that tenet is declared or proclaimed, there, and to that extent, whoever hears it is implicated in the deed, no matter the generation, tribe or nation.

On the Attack

The instances in which Jesus engages his adversaries are many and varied. Again, following the Markan outline, one of Jesus' earliest engagements follows the report of his family's opinion regarding his mental state, and his parable in reply to the scribes' charge that he expels the demons by the power of Beelzebul. In that engagement he gives warning to whomever "blasphemes against the Holy Spirit" (Mark 3:28–30; Matthew 12:31–32; Luke 12:10). Mark then adds, "for they said, 'He has an unclean spirit'" (Mark 3:30). Clearly, the addition assumes precisely the opposite. It identifies Jesus and his activity with the Spirit, thus hides the following syllogism: a) Major premise: blasphemy against the Holy Spirit is an eternal sin. b) Minor premise: "they said" Jesus had an "unclean spirit." c) Conclusion: therefore, they blasphemed against the Holy Spirit. Mark, who typically avoids thetical or dogmatic statements respecting Jesus' identity, preferring to leave it to the reader to draw the proper conclusion, has left the passage as a stunning identification of Jesus with Jahweh, implied in the parable of the bridegroom in 2:19–20. Matthew and Luke omit the addition.

In Mark 7:1–23 and its parallel in Matthew 15:1–20, Pharisees and scribes from Jerusalem gather around Jesus, notice that his disciples eat without washing their hands, and ask him to explain the omission. In Luke 11:37–41, Jesus is invited to dinner at the home of a Pharisee, and to the amazement of his host eats without washing his hands. After posting the query, Mark spends two verses (7:3–4) educating his readers in matters of Pharisaic scruple respecting ritual observance. The scrupulosity is well attested in Jewish teaching. For example, in the Babylonian Talmud the tractate "Berakoth" ("Blessings") records a *Baraitha* (a tradition in Jewish oral law not recorded in the Mishnah), according to which Leviticus 11:44 refers to handwashing before and after meals: "'Sanctify yourselves.' This refers to washing of the hands before the meal; 'And be ye holy:' this refers to washing of the hands after the meal."[51] The tractate "Shabbath" ("Sabbath") refers to three things which bring a man to poverty, one of which is to treat the washing of the hands with disrespect.[52] The tractate "Sotah" ("Suspected Adulteress") cites one rabbi who states that whoever eats bread without previously washing the hands is as though he had intercourse with a harlot. Another in the name of Eleazar, the great fourth century Mishnaic teacher, states that whoever makes light of washing the hands [before and after a meal] will be uprooted from the world. Still another is cited who states that with the first washing [before the meal] it is necessary to lift the hands up; with the latter washing [after the meal] it is necessary to lower them. Finally, according to a similar teaching, whoever washes his hands before the meal must lift them up lest the water pass beyond the joint, flow back and render them unclean.[53]

The extent to which Talmudic teaching reflects usage in the period of the Second Temple, that is, in Jesus' day, can only be surmised, but if Mark's "aside" in the two verses cited has less to do with contempt for Jewish tradition than with an intent to instruct, meticulousness in the matter of ritual purity was a hallmark of "orthodoxy." It was such that raised Jesus' ire, denouncing his critics in the words of the prophet respecting their captivity to human tradition matched against their disobedience toward God. "Isaiah prophesied rightly about you hypocrites...You abandon the commandment of God and hold to human tradition" (Mark 7:6-8; Matthew 15:7-9).[54] There was nothing general about the attack. Jesus was acutely specific: his critics' hypocrisy lay in their pious affirmation that whatever support might have been given their parents was given to God. "Moses said ("God said," Matthew 15:4), 'Honor your father and your mother . . . but you say that if anyone tells father or mother, 'Whatever support you might have had from me is *Corban*[55] (that is, an offering to God) then you no longer permit

---

51. Berakoth 53b, *Socino Babylonian Talmud*, trans. Rabbi Dr. I. Epstein (London: The Soncino Press, n.d.), chapter VIII.

52. Shabbat 62b, in *Ibid.*, Chapter V.

53. Sotah 49, in *Ibid.*, Chapter I.

54. Typically, Mark sets the prophetic word ahead of the event, a commitment to the word as constitutive of the event, whereas Matthew sets the word at the end of the event, a commitment to the event as fulfillment of the prophetic word.

55. The Greek transliteration of the Hebrew term meaning "offering."

doing anything for father or mother, thus making void the word of God through your tradition" (Mark 7:10–13; Matthew 15:4–6). In other words, what had been given to God, God neither needed nor wanted.

In Luke's altered scene, Jesus attacks his host and fellow religious reformers by way of metaphor:: "You Pharisees clean the outside of the cup and of the dish, but inside you are full of greed and wickedness. You fools!. . .Give for alms those things that are within, and see, everything will be clean for you" (Luke 11:39–40. Then follow woes in clusters of three: *Woe to you Pharisees!* For you tithe mint and rue and herbs of all kinds, and neglect justice and the love of God. . .*Woe to you Pharisees!* For you love to have the seat of honor in the synagogues and to be greeted with respect in the market places. *Woe to you!* For you are like unmarked graves" (Luke 11:42–44). Lawyers are attacked in a second cluster of three: "*Woe also to you lawyers!* For you load people with burdens hard to bear; and you yourselves do not lift a finger to ease them. *Woe to you!* For you build the tombs of the prophets whom your ancestors killed." The woe reaches an intensity never uttered over a Pharisee. As if in the face of all reason or sense Jesus charges his contemporaries responsible for the protection of human life with murdering, not merely John Q. Public, but all the God-sent prophets, and from the beginning of the world, "from the blood of Abel to the blood of Zechariah, who perished between the altar and the sanctuary" (Luke 11:50–51), in other words, from those whose stories appear in the first pages of the Jewish canon (Genesis 4:8) to those in the very last (II Chronicles 24:21). Finally, "*Woe to you lawyers!* For you have taken away the key of knowledge; you did not enter yourselves, and you hindered those who were entering" (Luke 11:46–52). It needs noting that Jesus does not attack the professions to which the objects of his rage belong, but their neglect to exercise what those very professions at bottom demand: justice and love of God, humility, the easing of burdens, overturning ancestral resistance to the prophetic word, and an open mind, thirsting to know.

In Mark 8:11–12; Matthew 12:38–42; and Luke 11:16, 29–32, Jesus' opponents demand for a sign is set in varied contexts. In Mark, Jesus has just fed the four thousand and left for Dalmanutha,"an unidentifiable district by the shores of Galilee. In Matthew he has exorcized a blind and mute demon, warned against blaspheming the Spirit, and addressed his attackers as a brood of vipers, destined to give account of every careless word. In Luke the demand for a sign is sandwiched in-between Jesus' exorcism of a dumb spirit and his response to the charge that he is in league with the devil. A "doublet" or second account of the scene appears in Matthew 16:1–2. Mark prefixes Jesus' reply with a look-see into his psychic states—a feature his fellow-evangelists in almost every instance are careful to avoid—writing that "he sighed deeply in his spirit" (Mark 8:12)[56] And while Mark simply reports Jesus' refusal to give "this generation" a sign, Matthew and Luke quote Jesus's reply that no sign will be given "an evil and adulterous generation" but "the sign of the prophet Jonah" (Matthew 12:39; Luke 11:29). In Matthew's account Jesus likens Jonah's three nights and days in the belly of the fish to the Son of Man's three days and night in the "heart of the earth," while Luke simply states that the Son of Man will be a sign to "this generation" as was Jonah to his. Finally, both evangelists conclude with Jesus' word concerning the judgment of Sheba ("queen of the south") and Nineveh waiting for those who resist "something here" that is greater than Solomon or Jonah. The demand for a sign addressed to Jesus alone, his linking the fate of the prophet with that of the Son of Man, finally his reference to that "something" greater than Solomon or Nineveh, allow the conclusion that despite the debate over whether Jesus used the Son of Man title as self-designation or whether it was later applied to him,[57] here, for Matthew and Luke, with that "Son of Man," and that "something," Jesus is referring to himself.

The scene is vastly different in the Fourth Gospel. There, following his feeding of the five thousand, Jesus is pursued by the crowd ready to make him king, and withdraws to "the mountain." He then appears to the terrified disciples walking on the water toward Capernaum, and is pursued again. He remonstrates with the crowd for not looking for him but for more to eat, announces that the Son of Man will give food that endures for eternal life, and in answer to the question regarding the work of God that needs doing summons to faith in the one on whom God the Father "has set his seal." Then, finally, comes the question: "What sign are you going to give us then, so that we may see it and believe you?" (John 6:15–30), and to the veiled suggestion that he match Moses' performance in the desert, replies that it

---

56. Cf. a similar reference following Jesus' encounter with the leper: "moved with pity, Jesus stretched out his hand and touched him" (Mark 1:41); following the criticism of his curing the man with the withered hand on the sabbath: "he looked around at them with anger; he was grieved at their hardness of heart (Mark 3:5); his reaction to the rejection at Nazareth: "he was amazed at their unbelief" (Mark 6:6); his compassion for the hungry crowd (Mark 6: 34; 82); his indignation at the disciples' treatment of children: "he was indignant and said to them, 'Let the little children come to me'" (Mark 10:14); his love for the rich man: "Jesus, looking at him, loved him" (Mark 10:21), and his state of mind at Gethsemane: "He began to be distressed and agitated" (Mark 14:33). In two instances, the Fourth Evangelist allows for a glimpse into Jesus' inner life. At the sight of Mary and others weeping over the death of Lazarus, Jesus "was greatly disturbed in spirit and deeply moved." Again, "greatly disturbed," he came to Lazarus' tomb (John 11:33, 38).

57 —which, according to one scholar of the last century, would have been inconceivable, had not Jesus been conscious of himself as Messiah. Cf. Bacon, Benjamin W. "The 'Son of Man' in the Usage of Jesus," *Journal of Biblical Literature*, XLI (1922): 181–2.

was not Moses but his Father who gave the manna, more, that the bread he gives is life for the world, and to the plea that he, Jesus, supply it, answers "I am the bread of life. Whoever comes to me will never be hungry, and whoever believes in me will never be thirsty" (John 6:35). Whatever the doubts respecting Jesus' self-identification, the Fourth Evangelist has none. The appellations, "Son of Man," "him on whom the Father has set his seal," "the bread of life," all come cascading down to their end at Jesus himself, object of the crowd's pursuit. As for Mark, he will later take his turn, principally in his accounts of the passion predictions.

In Mark 8:14–21 Jesus warns the disciples against "the yeast of the Pharisees and the yeast of Herod," in Matthew 16:5–12 against "the yeast of the Pharisees and Sadducees," and in Luke 12:1, simply, against "the yeast of the Pharisees." For the afore-mentioned Wellhausen, Matthew's coupling of the Pharisees with the Sadducees in this event is of "doubtful nature," since in ordinary life and outside the Sanhedrin the appearance of the two parties in common is "striking," for which reason he assigns historicity to the narrative in Mark.[58] Wellhauen's demurrer does not belong to the reasons for assigning priority to Mark. The appearance of Pharisees with Sadducees, however "striking," is not without parallel in human history. More than once bitter enemies have joined forces against a common foe, and for Matthew that is precisely what is occurring here. On the other hand, if we adhere to Mark's version of the event, once more Jesus' disciples display their obtuseness. Earlier, they had missed the point of the parables, had been aghast at the miracle at sea, and flummoxed at the summons to feed the five, then the four thousand in the desert.[59] And here they missed the metaphor in Jesus' warning against the yeast of the Pharisees and Herod, as if it were a matter of comestibles: "It is because we have no bread" (Mark 8:16). In Mark the obtuseness is unrelieved. It belongs to his "Messianic secret," his drawing the shadow of the cross over the entirety of Jesus' life and career, broken only by the demons' recognition of his identity, or the centurion's confession beneath the cross, but with all the rest, family, disciples, and adversaries, misunderstanding, misinterpretation, blind ignorance. Mathew could not leave the lack of understanding unrelieved. He writes that following Jesus' correction of the disciples' lack of perception "they understood that he had not told them to beware of the yeast of bread, but of the teaching of the Pharisees and Sadducees" (Matthew 16:12).

58. Wellhausen, *op. cit.*, p. 44, note 1.

59 Cf. e.g., 4:13: "Do you not understand this parable? Then how will understand all the parables?"; 4:41: "Who then is this, that even the wind and the sea obey him?"; 6:52: "Are we to go and buy two hundred denarii worth of bread, and give it to them to eat?" 8:4: "How can one feed these people with bread here in the desert!"

As for the "yeast of Herod," the reference is to that of the son of Herod the Great (ca. 20 BC–ca. AD 39), nicknamed "Antipas," tetrarch of Galilee and Perea, a client of Rome and protégé of Tiberius to whom he dedicated a capital on the Galilean western shore. Jesus' linking the yeast of the Pharisees with that of Herod scarcely implies material similarity between the two. Abandoning his wife, the daughter of a desert king, to wed the wife of his half-brother, Herod II, Antipas would have been condemned by any strait Pharisee. As it happened, the task fell to John the Baptist, who lost his head for his pains. The link between Herod Antipas and the Pharisees thus had to do with the "negative assist" which the one gave the other, since the decline of Jewish political authority with the advent of Roman rule and its fawning clients proved advantageous to the Pharisees who shunned the secular in favor of total devotion to the religious life. In other words, it was a case of "the enemy of my enemy is my friend." Later, hearing reports of Jesus, Antipas would declare that the Baptist had risen from the dead (Matthew 14:2), an instance, perhaps, of similarity between the two yeasts. Later yet, when Pilate sent Jesus to Herod for arraignment, since he belonged to the tetrarch's bailiwick, Herod urged him to produce a sign, lacking which he returned Jesus to Pilate, whereupon the two became fast friends. Still later, when accused of conspiracy against Caligula, Tiberius' adopted son, he was exiled to Gaul where he breathed his last.

As is obvious to any reader, Jesus' cleansing of the temple in the first three Gospels differs markedly from the report of it in the fourth. In Mark 11:15–19, Matthew 21:12–13 and Luke 19:45–46, the temple cleansing is part of the overture to the passion, an event that heightens his opponents' appetite for doing away with him. In John 2:13–17, the event is set at the outset of Jesus' ministry, initiating the conflict between him and his enemies threading throughout the Gospel, the raising of Lazarus thus taking on the function of the overture in the Synoptics (John 11:53). Unless two cleansings are assumed, opting for the synoptic over the Johannine dating of the event, while allowing that the fourth evangelist was aware of traditions that rendered him independent of the first three, appears the best course.

There is a surface and a depth to the narrative. As to the surface, first of all, the selling of oxen and sheep and doves in the temple does not mean they were all running wild in the sanctuary. "In the temple" (Mark 11:15) means somewhere in the temple precincts, outside, in the courtyard. Second, in order to act Jesus makes a whip of cords or rushes—-carrying clubs and weapons about in the temple was tabu. Third, in John, the word the disciples remember—"zeal for your house will consume me"—is from Psalm 69. Finally, John's reference to "the Jews" who ask for a sign reflects a time when Jewish Christians had left or been thrown out of the synagogue and called their non-Christian cousins "Jews."

In John's account, after turning the tables Jesus says, "do not make my father's house an emporium, a shop, a store, a marketplace!" "My Father's house" he says to those sitting there at their tables, changing Roman coins for temple shekels, at home in that place, as if it were their own, their own house, their own temple. And since God was believed to be there, only there, in that temple, in Jerusalem and nowhere else on earth, whatever else it might have meant, "*my Father's* house" meant that encounter with God was Jesus' affair.

In their narrative, the three evangelists write that after turning the tables and chasing out those selling doves—the cheapest offering for sacrifice—Jesus said, "my house shall be called," or as in Luke, "shall be a house of prayer!" To which, according to John (2:18) his adversaries reply, "What sign can you show us for doing this?" Jesus' answer is a weave. It braids two ideas, two themes, so tightly woven that the one cannot be pulled without pulling the other. "Destroy this temple, and in three days I will raise it up." Those who heard him thought he meant: "Demolish this thing made of stone with its inner and outer court and its Holy of Holies," which is what the prophets predicted the Messiah would do. Now, nothing is left of that place but a wailing wall, and men with their sidelocks (*peyot*) and yarmulkes bobbing back and forth, pushing little slips of prayer between the cracks, and a huge Muslim mosque with verses from the Koran around it where their temple used to be. Later, in John four he will say to the woman at the well, "Woman, believe me, the hour is coming when you will worship the Father neither on this mountain nor in Jerusalem" (John 4:21).

Or, did "Destroy this temple" mean "put me to death and I will come to life again over the week-end"? When they asked, "this temple has been under construction for forty-six years, and will you raise it up in three days?" it is clear they had no idea he was speaking of himself, that *he* was the temple to displace what Herod had built, to put an end to the entire cult of sacrifice surrounding it. John writes that after he was raised the disciples remembered he had spoken of the temple of his body (John 2:22), but his co-evangelists might not have added the words from Isaiah ending with God's coming to save Zion and rebuild the cities of Judah if they had not thought it meant the end of Israelite worship as well.[60] That was *his* word, *his* command.

---

60. Isaiah 56: 7b-8: "My house shall be called a house of prayer for all peoples. Thus says the Lord God, who gathers the outcasts of Israel . . ."

At the middle of his narrative John writes that the entire affair reminded the disciples of the Psalmist's word: "zeal for your house will consume me."[61] "It will eat me up!" may be a better translation. The disciples remembered the contingent event, recalled the details, presumably, whatever would satisfy an officer of the law eager for the facts. That was only the first strand, the first thread in that weave. At the end of his story John writes that they believed the writing and the word he spoke (John 2:22). That had to mean they believed that what was eating him whole would lead to a death of such a kind that nothing ever said, done, or thought would not somehow be touched by it, be impinged upon by it, that the death of Jesus of Nazareth was the one thing to stick in time and history from which they'd never get free. That believing was the second strand, the second thread in that weave. According to John, it was when Jesus was raised from the dead that the disciples remembered and believed. The mere remembering would not need a tomb's opening and a dead man's throwing off his shroud. Remembering is one thing, believing another. The disciples needed a resurrection to bring them to faith.

In the first three Gospels Jesus questions a favorite dogma of his time: "How can the scribes say that the Messiah is the son of David?" (Mark 12:35), or as in Matthew he asks the Pharisees: "What do you think of the Messiah? Whose son is he?" Then, following the citation of Psalm 110:1, in which David calls him Lord, incidentally, a reference appearing more than any other from the Old Testament, Jesus asks, "so how can he be his son?" This, in face of The Old Testament reference to the Messiah (the "righteous Branch," or the "one shepherd") as from the lineage of David, to say nothing of his *physical descent* from the great king.[62] The Davidic ancestry of the Messiah has had long history in the literature of Judaism, as witness the apocryphal *Testament of Judah*,[63] the *Babylonian Talmud, Tractate Sanhedrin*,[64] and the *Shemoneh Esre* ("Eighteen Benedictions"), prayed by

---

61 Psalm 69:9: "It is zeal for your house that has consumed me; the insults of those who insult you have fallen on me."

62. As to lineage, cf. Jer. 23:5; Ezek. 34:23, etc. As to physical descent from David, cf. II Sam. 7:12; Ps. 132:11; Isaiah 11:1–9, etc.

63 "And after these things shall a star arise to you from Jacob in peace, And a man shall arise [from my seed], like the sun of righteousness, Walking with the sons of men in meekness and righteousness; And no sin shall be found in him. . . ..Then shall the scepter of my kingdom shine forth; And from your root shall arise a stem; And from it shall grow a rod of righteousness to the Gentiles, To judge and to save all that call upon the Lord," Charles, R.H. *The Apocrypha and Pseudepigrapha of the Old Testament.* Oxford: Clarendon Press, vol. 2 (1913): 323–324.

64. Cf. *Babylonian Talmud: Tractate Sanhedrin*, Chapter XI, folio 98a, p. 98: R. Hanina said: "The Son of David will not come until even the pettiest kingdom ceases

the Orthodox three times a day.[65] The New Testament itself is at great pains to accent Jesus' Davidic Messiahship.[66] Why then the question? Why pit the Psalm quotation against the remainder of the Old Testament reference? Or, as many suppose, does the question hide the rejection of a political Messiah? With the collapse of the Maccabean kingdom, and under the rule of Rome and Herod the Great, Jews did in fact begin to yearn for a deliverer who would throw off the yoke of the usurper and establish a kingdom of justice and peace. But if Jesus' question hides rejection of that notion, why ride into Jerusalem like a monarch suing for peace? Further, it would be a singular instance in which Jesus did not directly attack a notion or practice held by his critics, and without horns and teeth. Mark ends the narrative with the note that the crowd was listening to him with delight, and Matthew with the comment that no one was able to answer him, and from that day did not dare ask him any more questions (Mark 12: 27; Matthew 22:46). Do these remarks somehow furnish a clue, that Jesus' intent is not to engage in dialogue but to leave things hanging in the air, deliberately to puzzle, befuddle, throw off balance? After all, he dealt in *mesalim*, in everything from narrative to similitude, from proverb to riddle. And if, after this, his critics ever bothered to wrestle with the question, they would have had to wrestle over the identity of the one who put it. So there may have been a kind of maieutics functioning here, a kind of "Socratic" putting of the question to make one's hearers think—to think about him.

In Mark 12:38-40, and Luke 20: 45-47, Jesus' denunciation of the scribes is reduced to a simple warning against those who go about in long robes, love to be greeted in public, enjoy choice seats in synagogues and at banquets, devour widows' houses, and pray long prayers. In Matthew 23:1-36, the lengthiest denunciation of scribes and Pharisees in the New Testament is prefaced by a description of their taste in dress and behavior, as per that of Mark and Luke, framed by the summons to do what they teach, not what they do, and by the summons to refuse their titles, whether of rabbi, father, or instructor, since all who exalt themselves will be humbled, and vice versa. Then follow what must be Jesus' bitterest attacks in a series

---

[to have power] over Israel, as it is written, He shall both cut off the sprigs with pruning hooks, and take away and cut down the branches. . . in that time shall the present be brought unto the Lord of hosts of a people that is scattered and peeled."

65. "May the Seed of David Thy servant flourish speedily and may You exalt in Your salvation. For in Your salvation do we hope all the day. Blessed are You, Lord, Who brings forth the Horn of our salvation. " *Hebrew for Christians*, copyright John J. Parsons. https://www.hebrew4christians.com/About_HFC/about_hfc.html

66 Cf. Matthew 1:1; 12:23; Luke 1:32; John 7:42; Acts 2:30; 13:23; Rom. 1:3; 15:12; Rev. 22:16.

of seven "woes," each with its appositive, "hypocrite," and punctuated with epithets ("blind guides," "blind fools," "snakes, brood of vipers"). Each of the woes gives the reason for the attack in adversative style: they lock out those who would enter the kingdom *but* do not go in themselves; they cross land and sea to make converts *but* turn them into types more vile than themselves; they distinguish between oaths *but* ignore the binding nature of each; they tithe trivia *but* neglect weightier matters of the law; they fuss over externals *but* are full of greed and self-indulgence; they appear righteous *but* are full of lawlessness, finally, they build the prophets' tombs *but* murder the prophets as did their fathers. Despite the brevity of their reports, Mark and Luke contain what must have been Jesus' bitterest indictment of the scribes: "They devour widows' houses," a patent violation of Jewish law.[67] Then Jesus adds, "and for the sake of appearance say long prayers" (Mark 12:40; Luke 20:47). The indictment thus adds hypocrisy to their avarice. They pray fervently for the most vulnerable in Jewish society (in their homes?), and in this way hide their rapacity.

Matthew has been indicted for casting Jesus in a legalistic role, his "five books"[68] reflecting the Pentateuch, with Jesus as the new Moses, and the Beatitudes as the new Torah. It is true, nowhere else in the New Testament does Jesus enjoin the crowds or disciples to do what those who "sit on Moses' seat" teach them to do. Nowhere else are they described as failing to practice what they preach, as if practice were the be-all and end-all, and nowhere else are they excoriated for omitting what can only be described as obedience to Torah. The indictment needs correcting in the face of Matthew's portrait of Jesus, for whom giving his life as a ransom for many (Matthew 10:45) forms the substance of his life and career; who demands that the righteousness of those who follow him exceed that of scribes and Pharisees (5:20), a righteousness given shape in curing the sick, raising the dead, cleansing the leper, and casting out demons (10;8); who at his appearing will grant inheritance in his kingdom to those who gave food, drink, welcome, clothing, and care for "one of the least of these " (25:34–40). As an old friend insisted, "we know of no one else who in the name of God did not want to make the godless pious and the pious more pious, but rather went to publicans and sinners and said to them: God is there for you."[69]

---

67 Cf. Exodus 22:22–23: "You shall not abuse any widow or orphan. If you do abuse them, when they cry out to me, I will surely heed their cry; my wrath will burn, and I will kill you with the sword, and your wives shall become widows and your children orphans."

68. Each concluding with the formula, "when Jesus had finished speaking," in 7:28; 11:1; 13:53; 19:1, and 26:1.

69 Käsemann, Ernst. „Die Gegenwart des Gekreuzigten," *Kirchliche Konflikte*

Matthew and Luke alone report Jesus' woes over the Galilean cities of Chorazin, Bethsaida, and Capernaum (Matthew 11:20-24; Luke 10:12-15). Chorazin (= "a secret. Here is a mystery"?) lay in northern Galilee, a few miles from Capernaum on a hill above the northern shore of the Sea of Galilee. The name of the city appears only in the woe pronounced against it, though it may have been prominent during Jesus' lifetime. It was already deserted in the time of Eusebius, who places it two miles from Capernaum. Identified today as *Khirbet Kerazeh*, it is a desolate ruin, with a few carved stones among the heaps, and traces of a Roman road connecting the city with a highway between north and south. Bethsaida (= "house of fishing") was perhaps located on the shore of the Sea of Galilee about two miles / three kilometers east of Capernaum. In Mark it is the scene of the healing of the blind man (Mark 8:22-25); in Luke site of the feeding of the five thousand (Luke 9:10-17), and in John listed as the home town of Peter, Andrew and Philip (cf. John 1:43-45; 12:21). Capernaum, a small village in the Bronze age, its population reduced during the Babylonian conquest in the sixth, and restored in the fifth century when the exiles returned, then rebuilt during the Roman period, is now identified as *Kefar Nachum* (="village of Nahum"?), located at the north corner of the Sea of Galilee, on the highway toward Syria. The city with its fifteen hundred inhabitants was Jesus' home (cf. Mark 2:1; 6:1; Matthew 4:13; 9:1). There, in the synagogue, he healed the man with the unclean spirit (Mark 1:21, 27; Luke 4:31, 36-38), and at sundown cured many and cast out demons (Mark 1:32-34). At Capernaum he healed the paralytic (Mark 2:1-12); healed the man with the withered hand in the synagogue (Mark 3:1), healed the servant of the Centurion (Matthew 8:5-13, 22; Luke 7:1-10), called Matthew (Matthew 9:18), and walked toward the city on the water (John 6:16-21).

The reason for Jesus' attacks on these cities or villages is that none of his miracles had led their inhabitants to repentance, to a radical transformation of the self in favor of God and the other. Their obduracy was of such a sort that it exceeded that of Tyre and Sidon: "For if the deeds of power done in you had been done in Tyre and Sidon, they would have repented long ago in sackcloth and ashes." And, if those deeds had been done in Sodom, it would have avoided its fate: "For if the deeds of power done in you had been done in Sodom, it would have remained until this day."

There was scarcely anything Simon pure about the island of Tyre or of Sidon. For the island's wreaking havoc on the mainland, Ezekiel prophesied that the Lord would destroy its walls, break down its towers, scrape its soil from it, make it a bare rock, and at its ruin the coastlands would tremble

---

(Göttingen: Vandenhoeck & Ruprecht, 1982), 81.

(Ezekiel 26:4). For Sidon, having with Tyre treated Israel with contempt, God promised pestilence, blood in her streets and death by the sword (Ezekiel 28:23). As for Sodom, for its shameless sinning, from Deuteronomy to Isaiah to Jeremiah to Ezekiel to Amos to Zephaniah, nothing awaited it but a "burning waste of salt and sulfur."[70] The only event comparable to its fate would be the revelation of the Son of man.[71] And in midst of these two woes the bitterest left for Capernaum, scene of the heart of Jesus' activity: "And you, Capernaum, will you be exalted to heaven? No, you will be brought down to Hades. For if the deeds of power done in you had been done in Sodom, it would have remained until this day."

How could the conflict of Chorazin and Bethsaida trump the havoc of Tyre, or the contempt of Sidon? And, how could Capernaum, Jesus' home, outdo the shameless sinning of Sodom? Is there irony here, or hyperbole in the extreme, precedent for it or no?[72] What of the obduracy of Chorazin, Bethsaida and Capernaum did Tyre, Sidon, and Sodom lack, to the point where they would have turned around? The answer must be those deeds of power by the one who did them. He and what he did created the inequality between Chorazin and Tyre, Bethsaida and Sidon, Capernaum and Sodom. He and what he did made those cities of his day and time all the worse, since those ancient towns would have bent to his will had he done in them what he had done in those cities of his day. These woes and the naked wrath they reflect exceed by a Gulliver's leap all other attacks on the religious sects and political parties of Jesus' time.

---

70 Deuteronomy 29:23; Isaiah 1:9–10; 3:9; 13:19–22; Jeremiah 23:14; 49:17–18; 50:39–40; Lamentations 4:6; Ezekial 16:48–50; Amos 4:1–11; Zephaniah 2:9.

71 Luke 17:28–30: "Likewise, just as it was in the days of Lot: they were eating and drinking, buying and selling, planting and building. But on the day that Lot left Sodom, it rained fire and sulfur from heaven and destroyed all of them—it will be like that on the day that the Son of Man is revealed."

72. In Ezekiel 16:48, God says to Jerusalem: "As I live . . . Your sister Sodom and her daughters have not done as you and your daughters have done."

PART THREE

Schooling the Disciples

The Sermon on the Mount

In the four Gospels, with the exception of the passion narrative, the number of speeches or instructions addressed by Jesus to his disciples and followers far outweighs the rest of the New Testament record. The best known is the cluster known as the Sermon on the Mount, recorded in Matthew, or the Sermon on the Plain in Luke. In Matthew the cluster is restricted to chapters five through seven, but in Luke appears in chapter six, as well as in segments elsewhere in his Gospel. Following the sequence in Matthew, the Sermon opens with the eight Beatitudes in 5:3–12, four of which are repeated in Luke 6:20b–23. In seven of the eight the adjective "blessed" is followed by its subject in the nominative plural ("Blessed are those who, etc."), and in the eighth ends in direct address, in the first person plural ("Blessed are you, etc."). The list begins with the "poor in spirit," continues with," "those who mourn," "the meek," "those who hunger and thirst for righteousness," "the merciful," "the pure in heart," "the peacemakers," those "persecuted for righteousness' sake," and ends with those reviled and persecuted "on my account." There is no move from the lesser to the greater, though the first and seventh beatitudes serve as frame for the remainder with the refrain: "for theirs is the kingdom of heaven. " The eighth beatitude and its direct address ("Blessed are you when people revile you and persecute you and utter all kinds of evil against you falsely on my account") gives the clue to interpreting all eight beatitudes as applying to each disciple. Though the term "reward" (*misthos*) for the attitude or action described is used explicitly only in the eighth beatitude ("Blessed are you when people revile you and persecute you . . . Rejoice and be glad, for your reward is great in heaven") the idea is obviously implied in the others. Any standard dictionary would define the term as recompense or requital for services rendered, that is, for something earned, merited, deserved. If these beatitudes are intended to portray Jesus as dealing in *quid pro quo*, then the description of Matthew's

Gospel as a neo-legalistic document characterized by an emphasis on deeds that demand payment, is apt, on the mark. If, on the other hand, these beatitudes involve a denial of self that rules out the thought of gain, and if the evangelist elsewhere records Jesus as condemning desire for reward,[1] then "reward" must take its definition from the beatitude ("Blessed are you"), thus as the favor of God apart from desert or merit.

After the beatitudes follow Jesus' description of the disciples in metaphor: "You are the salt of the earth...You are the light of the world" (Matthew 5:13–14), then the announcement that he did not come to abolish but rather to fulfill the law and the prophets, adding that not one letter or stroke of it would pass away till all is fulfilled. The terms translated "letter" or "stroke of a letter" are *iota*, corresponding to the Hebrew *yod*, tenth letter of the alphabet, and *keraia*, a transliteration of the Hebrew term for "horn," one of those tiny strokes by which similar Hebrew letters are distinguished from each other. Jesus is saying that not even the smallest letter or diacritical mark attaching to the law will disappear till all is fulfilled. And here again it appears as if Jesus has sat for the portrait of Moses. But before labeling Matthew an Ebionite, advocate of a law-oriented Christianity, one needs to read to the end of this speech, with its demand that the righteousness of the disciples exceed that of the scribes and Pharisees (Matthew 5:20). What might such righteousness be if not the denial of self and action on behalf of the other as reflected in the beatitudes? For the appearance of this righteousness, the law and the prophets would wait. This righteousness, this self-denial and action on behalf of the other, would be their fulfillment.

Next, in Matthew 5:21–43 follow six antitheses dealing with murder, adultery, divorce, oaths, taking revenge, and love for enemies, each opening with "you have heard that it was said," or "it was also said," and in each instance countered by Jesus with a "but I say to you," followed by Jesus' radicalizing of the Mosaic command. The command respecting murder is radicalized to a prohibition against anger or insult; the command respecting adultery to a prohibition against lust; the allowance of divorce except for unchastity is radicalized to countenancing adultery; the command against swearing falsely radicalized to a prohibition against oaths of any kind; the command against taking revenge abolished, and the distinction between

---

1. Matthew 6:1: "Beware of practicing your piety before others in order to be seen by them;" 6:2: "So whenever you give alms, do not sound a trumpet before you, as the hypocrites do in the synagogues and in the streets;" 6:5: And whenever you pray, do not be like the hypocrites; for they love to stand and pray in the synagogues and at the street corners, so that they may be seen by others; 6:7u: "When you are praying, do not heap up empty phrases as the Gentiles do; for they think that they will be heard because of their many words."

love for friend and hatred for the enemy radicalized to a command to love without distinction. Only once do Mark and Luke repeat Jesus' sayings respecting the commandments in antithetical form, in Mark in an editorial "but Jesus said to them" concerning divorce, and without citing the exception (Mark 10:2-9), and in Luke regarding love for enemies (Luke 6:27-29). In form and content the antitheses are breath-taking. With the radicalizing or abolishing of these commands Jesus sets his word against that of Moses, laying claim to a status greater than that of Judaism's primary legislator, at the least implying that Moses missed what God had in mind when he gave the commandments. According to one well known Medieval and Renaissance scholar and apologist,

> A man who said the sort of things Jesus said would not be a great moral teacher. He would either be a lunatic —on a level with the man who says he is a poached egg —or else he would be the Devil of Hell. You must make your choice. Either this man was, and is, the Son of God: or else a madman or something worse. You can shut Him up for a fool, you can spit at Him and kill Him as a demon; or you can fall at His feet and call Him Lord and God. But let us not come with any patronizing nonsense about His being a great human teacher. He has not left that open to us. He did not intend to.[2]

The words of the Sermon that immediately follow appear among the two hundred to two hundred-fifty verses which Matthew and Luke have in common and are absent in Mark.[3] Following the sequence in Matthew, they include the treasures in heaven that need storing up; the health of the eye as lamp of the body; the impossibility of serving two masters; casting off worry over food, drink, and clothing in favor of seeking first the kingdom; the response to prayer; the Golden Rule; the two ways; knowledge of false prophets by way of the analogy of the tree and its fruits, the vanity of appealing to God apart from doing his will, and the hearer and doer likened to the one who builds his house on the rock (Matthew 6:19-34; 7:7-27). Just as the beatitudes and the antitheses in Luke do not follow the sequence of Matthew, and reflect a peculiarly Lucan cast,[4] so also with the remainder of the Sermon. To his account of the Sermon Matthew adds

---

2. Lewis, C.S. *Mere Christianity* (New York: Harper Collins, 1952).

3. With the exception of the word about Judging, and the Lord's Prayer the Sermon does not appear in Mark (Mark 4:24-25; 11:25),

4. For example, the first beatitude in Luke is unmodified, and reads: "Blessed are you who are poor, for yours is the kingdom of God" (Luke 6:20b).

four admonitions regarding alms and prayer (Matthew 6:1–6); fasting and profanation (Matthew 6:16–18; 7:6).

The speeches that remain make up a veritable cascade of instructions, and can be grouped according to Jesus' call to discipleship, the conditions of discipleship, its rewards and fate, the responses to be anticipated, and the commitment and character of discipleship.

The Call to Discipleship.

As to the call, Matthew writes of a scribe, Luke of an anonymous person, who informs Jesus that he will follow him wherever he goes, and is told that "foxes have holes, and birds of the air have nests; but the Son of Man has nowhere to lay his head" (Matthew 8:18–20; Luke 9:57–58).[1] Another "of his disciples"[2] asks permission first to bury his father, only to hear Jesus' reply to "let the dead bury the dead" (Matthew 8:22), to which Luke adds, "but as for you, go and proclaim the kingdom of God" (Luke 9:60). However peripheral mourning and burial of the dead may have been in Israel, prompt burial of the dead to avoid defilement and as a matter of respect was paramount. Jesus' response to the man's petition to observe the normal obsequies before following him seems harsh and uncompromising, if not coarse and rude. And, who are "the dead" that should "bury the dead"? Members of the man's family or household, members of his community whom custom dictated should share the task? In this instance, at least one thing is certain: Jesus' call to follow urged a priority that spelled collapse of the basic social structures, a radical breach of the norms by which his contemporaries lived. That Jesus' relation to his own family involved such collapse is implied in the complaint registered in the first passage ("the Son of Man has nowhere to lay his head").[3] Luke, not content with the single incident reported in Matthew, heightens the priority of the call to follow over familial obligation by adding the petition of "another" who bids permission to say goodbye to his family, then hears the response that none who puts his hand to the plow and turns back is fit for the kingdom of God (Luke 9:62). Later, Matthew describes

---

1 Here, Jesus' identification of himself with "the Son of Man" represents the first, if not the earliest type of reference to that heavenly figure.

2. At this point the designation has not been narrowed down to the twelve.

3 Cf. Mark's report of Jesus' reply to his mother's and brothers' remonstrance: "Who are my mother and my brothers!" (Mark 3:33).

Jesus as engaged in a whirlwind of activity throughout Israel, "proclaiming the good news of the kingdom, curing every disease and every sickness" (Matthew 9:35), and, by implication, ending in exhaustion over the impossibility of any further extension of his mission, summoning the disciples to ask the Lord of the harvest to add more laborers (Matthew 9:37-38). Again, not content with the single incident Luke embroiders, setting the summons within the context of the commissioning of the seventy,[4] the list of instructions to be followed: "Carry no purse, no bag, no sandals; greet no one on the road. Whatever house you enter, first say, 'Peace to this house!' Remain in the same house, eating and drinking whatever they provide . . . Do not move about from house to house. Whenever you enter a town and its people welcome you, eat what is set before you, cure the sick . . . say to them, 'The kingdom of God has come near to you'"—and what will result from a welcome refused (". . . it will be more tolerable for Sodom . . ." Luke 10:4-12). Much later, following Peter's confession at Caesarea Philippi, Jesus announces that to follow him spells denial of self and taking up one's cross (Matthew 16:24-25; Luke 9:23-27). That call to denial of self is more than a call to emulate Jesus as the highest ethical goal. Like his call to repentance it involves a radical transformation by which the self is no longer at the center of thought and action, but shoved to the periphery in favor of God and the other. The acuity, the "bite" of Jesus' word cannot be missed: life and death are at issue. Radical transformation of the self spells life, while allowing it to remain at center spells death: "For those who want to save their life will lose it, and those who lose their life for my sake will find it" (Luke 16:25). Thus, metaphor aside ("let the dead bury the dead. . .lord of the harvest. . .take up their cross. . .."), priority of the call over whatever the norms by which life is arranged, a petitioning to add to the number of those called, and a radical transformation involved in the answer to it.

Perhaps one of the most massive and suggestive portraits of Jesus in the Gospel is Mark's description of Jesus' call in 3:13: "And he went up the mountain and called to him those whom he wanted, and they came to him." Reference to "the mountain" is less for a geographical than for a theological purpose. Just as the mount of transfiguration (9:2), or of Olivet, site of Jesus' prediction of Jerusalem's ruin and end of the world (13:3), "the mountain" here is a site of revelation and command. From this height Jesus does not merely "appoint," as the NRSV translates, but "creates" the twelve. Similarity to the Greek of Genesis One ("In the beginning God created. . ..") is deliberate.

At the conclusion of his Gospel, Matthew records the disciples' "Great Commission." The scene is that of "the mountain" (Matthew 28:15), which,

---

4. Again, the list is not limited to the twelve.

like that of the Beatitudes (Matthew 5:1) and the Transfiguration (17:1), is for Matthew as much a site of revelation as for Mark, though his mountains are not identical to those in Mark (Mark 3:13; 9:2; 13:3). From this height Jesus calls "the eleven" (Judas excluded) who on seeing him "worshipped him, but some doubted." The verb translated "doubted" appears only twice in the New Testament, both times in Matthew, here, and in the narrative of Jesus' walking on the water in Matthew 14. Matthew may have intended that the worship of some and the doubt of others at Jesus' appearing reflected the faith of the one group and the lack of it of the other. This appears to be the burden of his narrative of Peter's attempt to walk toward Jesus on the water, and at his fear of drowning hears the word, "You of little faith, why did you doubt?" (Matthew 14:31). But Matthew may have intended simply to record the disciples' reaction to a phenomenon they had never experienced, and to the effect that some could not believe their eyes. Such was their reaction when seeing Jesus walking on the water and in terror said "it is a ghost!" (Matthew 14:26), the very same reported by Luke in his narrative of Jesus' resurrection appearance to the disciples ("they were startled and terrified, and thought that they were seeing a ghost," Luke 24:37). At any rate, to all, whether believing or doubting, whether able or not to acknowledge the phenomenon occurring before them, Jesus asserts his authority over heaven and earth, summons the eleven to call "all nations" to discipleship, baptizing and teaching them to obey all he has commanded, and promising to be with them to the end of the age. Could it be that Jesus' commission together with his summons to baptize in the name of the Trinity reflects the influence of earliest (hellenistic Jewish) Christianity's rite of initiation on the Gospel narrative, and thus consists of a "cultic legend," trajected back into the mouth of Jesus?[5] However intriguing the interpretation, it reflects commitment to the idea that no two similar events (in this case, the Great Commission and earliest Christianity's rite of initiation) can have occurred within relatively the same time frame without the one being dependent on the other.[6] And even if it could be proved that the Great Commission reflected such influence, a Gulliver's leap would be needed to deny the historicity of the event, to say nothing of adding Matthew into the bargain.

---

5 Bultmann, Rudolf. *Geschichte der synoptischen Tradition* (Gottingen: Vandenhoeck & Ruprecht, 1961), 169, 310, 313.

6 I have forgotten the author of the phrase: "similarite n'est pas identite." English: "similarity is not identity."

The Marks of Discipleship

In Mark 9:33-39 and parallels in Matthew 18:1-5, and Luke 9:46-48, on arrival in Capernaum, Jesus asks what the disciples were arguing about on their way to the city, Mark adding that the subject dealt with who was greatest. In response Jesus urges humility ("Whoever wants to be first must be last of all"), then takes a child into his arms and declares that whoever welcomes such "in my name" welcomes him, and whoever welcomes him welcomes the one who sent him. There is nothing unusual about the argument over rank. Political contests are continual reminder that modernity has not erased such carryings on. Nor is Jesus simply "trying to make clear" what he means by the example of the child."[1] He is establishing an equivalency between welcoming a child "in [his] name" and welcoming him, and an equivalency between welcoming him and giving welcome to God. His response to the conflict over rank is deliberately opaque, reaches beyond illustrating the need for humility to a summoning to give status to a child "in my name," an act equal to giving honor to God, calculated to put to death contest over rank and with it whatever else belongs to self-interest.

If that child in Mark 9:39 is still in the scene, then the theme just struck has its variation in Mark 9:42 and parallels in Matthew 18:6-7, and Luke 17:1-3a. There Jesus declares that being hanged by a millstone, large enough, perhaps, to be turned by an ass, and being drowned in the sea, would be preferable to causing "one of these little ones who believe in me" to stumble. The scene concludes with stern warnings against yielding to temptation. Variation on the theme is crystal clear in Mark 10:13-16 and parallels in Matthew 19:13-15, and Luke 18:15-17. Rhetorical criticism would describe this pericope as an "expanded" action *chreia*." First, there is the *description of the situation*: in Judea beyond Jordan Jesus is accosted by

---

1. Cf. *Das Jesus Handbuch*, 287.

people who bring little children to him to touch them, a procession which irritates the disciples. Then follows the *response*, expanded by an *introduction with emotion*, Jesus' ire (a feature omitted by Matthew and Luke who characteristically avoid all such glimpses into his inner life) followed by an *exhortation:*:"Let the children come to me," then by an *explanation:* "for it is to such as these that the kingdom of God belongs" (a translation in need of some correction, so as to read that the kingdom of God "is of these," that is, "consists of, is made up of, is composed of, these.") Then, in a *restatement in the negative* Jesus says: "truly I tell you" (the translation of a term—*Amen*—calculated to assert an authority given him directly by God) "whoever does not receive the kingdom as a little child will never enter it." The scene ends with a threefold *actione*: Jesus takes the children into his arms, blesses them and lays his hands on them. That little adverb "as" in "as a little child," allows entry to anyone, but only "as a little child." Nowhere outside the New Testament is such status given the child, on condition that it be "in my name."

Apparently the lesson did not sink in, since later, in Mark 10:41–45, and parallels in Matthew 20:24–28, and Luke 22:24–30, the disciples are once more described as squabbling over rank. According to Mark, the ten disciples are angry with James and John who have just petitioned Jesus for the chief seats in his glory, one on his right, the other on his left hand. Jesus rebukes the quarrelers with citing Gentile taste for power and authority, declaring that such has no place among them, reiterating, that whoever wishes to be great or to be first must be their servant or their slave, ending with the word that the Son of Man came not to be served but to serve and give his life a ransom for many.

The Conditions of Discipleship

In Mark 8:31–9:1, following Peter's confession of Jesus as the Christ and preceding the Transfiguration, Jesus gathers the crowd together and calls to discipleship.[1] The definition given following is stark, severe: If any want to become my followers, let them deny themselves and take up their cross and follow me." Taking up the cross is further defined by "losing life for my sake, and for the sake of the gospel." The alternative is more severe: "Those who want to save their life will lose it," even if saving life means gaining the whole world—a paltry, miserable exchange for taking up the cross. Unwilling to end the argument there, Jesus continues with citing the consequences of being ashamed of him in "this adulterous and sinful generation," a generation for which taking up the cross and following would be a matter of which to be ashamed. Of such, he says, "the Son of Man will be ashamed when he comes in the glory of the Father with the holy angels." Once more, Jesus uses that self-designation so irritating to interpreters, but for Mark of a piece with his portrait of Jesus as hidden Messiah.

The majority of passages involving the conditions of discipleship appear in Matthew and Luke, presumably from the stereotyped oral or written source dubbed "Q" (for *Quelle* = "source") by the scholars, used by Matthew and Luke along with Mark to construct their Gospels, and comprising two hundred to two hundred and fifty verses. In Matthew 10:1–6, Jesus authorizes "the twelve disciples" to exorcise unclean spirits, and cure every disease and malady, following which their names are listed, the number limited to the twelve. In Matthew 10:17–25 and Luke 12:11–12, Jesus predicts the disciples' fate, remanded before councils, flogged in the synagogues, dragged before governors and kings, with brother betraying brother, father the child, children their

---

1. In Matthew 16:24, Jesus speaks only to the disciples, whereas. In Luke 9:24, he speaks "to them all," presumably to the five thousand, though the reference is interrupted by Peter's confession.

parents, hated by all "because of my name." In Matthew 10:26–33 and Luke 12:2–9, Jesus' words of comfort to the threatened disciples (Matthew 10: 26: "have no fear of them," vs. 31: "do not be afraid") furnish the frame for a promise (vs. 26b-"nothing is covered up that will not be uncovered, and nothing secret that will not become known"), in light of which they are to act ("what I say to you in the dark, tell in the light; and what you hear whispered, proclaim from the housetops"), all followed by a warning (vs. 28: ". . .rather fear him who can destroy both soul and body in hell"), made explicit in vss. 32–33 ("who acknowledges me before others, I also will acknowledge before my Father in heaven; But whoever denies me before others, I also will deny before my Father in heaven"). The effect of the promise and warning is to render surrendering allegiance to Jesus equivalent to incurring the judgment of God. In Matthew 10:37–39 and Luke 14:25–33, discipleship requires giving first place to following over obligation to family ("Whoever loves father or mother more than me is not worthy of me; and whoever loves son or daughter more than me is not worthy of me," (Matthew 10:37)). To this Luke adds an extended caveat respecting the need for reflecting on the price such discipleship exacts ("Which of you, intending to build a tower, does not first sit down and estimate the cost. . .what king, going out to wage war against another king, will not sit down first and consider whether he is able with ten thousand to oppose the one who comes against him. . ..? (Luke 14:28–32). In Matthew 10:40–42 and Luke 10:16, Jesus declares that whoever welcomes a disciple welcomes him, and the "one who sent [him]"—an obvious reference to God—and throwing a wide arc adds the promise of reward to whomever welcomes a prophet "in the name of a prophet," a righteous person "in the name of a righteous person," or gives "to one of these little ones" a cup of cold water "in the name of a disciple." The accent is not on similarity, as if welcoming a disciple were *like* welcoming Jesus, or the one who sent him, or as if welcoming someone in the name of a prophet, or a righteous person were similar to welcoming a prophet or righteous person, or again, as if giving a cup of cold water to one of these little ones in the name of a disciple were like slaking a disciple's thirst. "*In the name of*" *means the deed done to the one named.* Jews and Christians alike agree to the equivalency.[2] The equivalency is given further accent

---

2. "A man's agent is like to himself," Berakoth 5.5, Danby, *The Mishnah*, p. 6; "Let not a brother who has entered your house depart without a prayer *(You have seen a brother,* it says, *you have seen your Lord),* Tertullian, *De Oratione,* (Tertullian's tract on The Prayer), Edited and translated by Ernest Evans, 1953, para. 26 (S.P.C. K. 1953, Reproduced by permission.); "Let him grown up in my service be as the one who serves," Agraphon 296 in Resch, Alfred. *Agrapha,* Ausserkanonische Schriftfragmente (Leipzig: J.C. Hinrichs'sche Buchhandlung, 1906): 50; "The Master's servant must be received as the master, the bishop as Christ," Ignatius to the Ephesians 6.1, *The Apostolic Fathers,* Part II, by Lightfoot, J.B. (London: Macmillan and Co., 1889), 46.

in Mark's and Luke's addition of the narrative of the strange exorcist, in which the disciples encounter an anonymity casting out demons, order him to stop, and are rebuffed by Jesus who declares that whoever does a deed of power "in my name" will be unable to speak evil of him. The Markan addition then answers the question earlier left hanging respecting the identity of "one of these little ones." The disciple, the one who "bears the name of Christ," belongs to "these little ones" (Mark 9:41). Later, Matthew will expand and Luke will abbreviate Jesus' warning against causing offense to "one of these little ones who believe in me" (Mark 9:42; Matthew 18:6; Luke 17:1-2). After inserting a general threat against anyone who causes stumbling, despite its inevitability, Matthew repeats Mark's record of Jesus' summons to the disciple to cut off his hand, foot, or tear out his eye should the one or other member cause offense, "for," he adds, "it is better for you to enter life maimed . . . lame . . . with one eye" than to go with two hands, feet, or eyes into hell (Mark 9: 43-48; Matthew 18:8-9). In Matthew 18:15-16 and Luke 17:3, Jesus addresses the problem of the erring member of the community. If the erring member will not heed the remonstrance of the injured party alone or when accompanied with two others, or, all else failing, will not listen to the church, such a member is to be treated as a heathen or tax collector. In Luke Jesus' word seems softened by his summons to an "unlimited readiness to forgive,"[3] even if sinned against seven times, but the difference is only apparent, since forgiveness is on condition of repentance (Luke 17:3-4: ". . .if there is repentance, you must forgive. . .if the same person sins against you seven times a day, and turns back to you seven times and says, 'I repent,' you must forgive"). It is in Matthew, and not in Luke, that Jesus summons to a forgiveness without conditions when Peter asks how often he should forgive (Matthew 18:21-22). In Matthew 18:19-20, following instructions for disciplining an erring member, the disciple is promised that whomever he binds or looses on earth, that is, whomever he indicts or absolves here below is indicted or absolved by "my Father in heaven." Yet again the equivalence, this time between the disciple and "my Father." In the "Little Apocalypse" of Mark and its parallels in Matthew 24:9-14 and Luke 12:12-19, a section in the earliest Gospel which may more than any other reflect the situation of the evangelist's hearer/reader, Jesus predicts the fate of the disciples. They will be handed over to councils, beaten in synagogues, stood before governors and kings, and hated "because of my name"— once more, the equivalency of the one named with the deed or action done. The predictions are repeated earlier in Matthew 10:17-25 and Luke 12:11-12, probably from that elusive second Synoptic source. Matthew 19:23-30 and

---

3 *Jesus Handbuch*, ed. Jens Schroter & Christine Jacobi (Tubingen: Mohr Siebeck, 2017), 352.

Luke 18:24–30 reprise Jesus' words about the conditions of discipleship, but not before prefacing them with Mark's narrative of the rich young man (Mark 10:17–22). The young man kneels before Jesus, addresses him as "Good Master," and asks what he must do to inherit eternal life. Jesus replies: "Why do you call me good? No one is good but God alone" (Mark 10:19), a response omitted by his co-evangelists, presumably to avoid what appears to be a denial of deity, but which belongs to his occasional habit of turning his listener on his ear, as, for example, occurs later in his question concerning the Messiah as David's son ("David himself calls him Lord; so how can he be his son?" (Mark 12:37), in this instance a remark not avoided by Matthew and Luke Jesus continues, "you know the commandments," proceeds to list those belonging to the second table of the law but one (the command to love father and mother), to which the young man responds that he has kept them all. Mark then gives his readers one more glimpse into Jesus' inner life ("Jesus, looking at him, loved him," vs. 21), a window never opened in Matthew or Luke, as if it somehow spelled trespassing. Then Jesus calls him to sell what he has, to give the money to the poor, and follow him, at which the young man is shocked and disappears grieving from the scene. First adverting to the difficulty of a rich man's entering the kingdom ("How hard it will be for those who have wealth to enter the kingdom of God"), with his metaphor of the camel and needle's eye, Jesus describes it as well nigh impossible. However tempting to take the needle's eye as a (till now undiscovered, unexcavated) gate into Jerusalem through which a camel would have to kneel, will not suit the accent on the impossibility. Nor can it explain the disciple's astonishment at such upping of the ante, clearly indicating they had applied the maxim to themselves: "Who then can be saved?" they asked, and, they were not people of wealth. As Peter later put it, they had left all to follow. But if that maxim applied to them, if entry into the kingdom was as impossible for them as for the rich young man, then Jesus' word, "for mortals it is impossible, but not for God" had also to apply to them. Then Jesus' promise that having left house, family, and field for his sake and for the sake of the good news meant riches "in this age," and eternal life "in the age to come," had to come under that possibility that belonged to God.

There is an instance in which Luke alone and once with Mark records sayings regarding the conditions for discipleship. The first trails the parable of the unjust steward and framed by two maxims urges the necessity of faithfulness. After the first maxim ("Whoever is faithful in a very little is faithful also in much, and whoever is dishonest in a very little is dishonest also in much" (Luke 16:10)) Jesus addresses the disciples: "If then you have not been faithful with the dishonest wealth, who will entrust to you the true riches? And if you have not been faithful with what belongs to another, who will give you what is your own?" (Luke 16:11–12). Then, following the second maxim ("No slave can serve two masters; for a slave will either hate the one and love the other, or be devoted to the one and despise the other," Luke 16: 13a), Jesus once more addresses the disciples: "You cannot serve God and wealth" (Luke 16:13b). First of all, the reference to wealth (Greek: *mammon*) as "dishonest" (Greek *adike*) suggests that for the Jesus of Luke wealth spelled "filthy lucre," or even ill-gotten gains, whereas poverty bridged the way to the kingdom, as per Luke's recitation of the first beatitude ("Blessed are you who are poor," Luke 6:20), absent the qualification in Matthew 5:3 ("Blessed are the poor *in spirit*"). Second, in these passages faithfulness appears in ascending fashion, from faithfulness in what is "a very little," defined as faithfulness with "dishonest wealth" (the "if then" following the "whoever is faithful in a very little, etc." urges the definition), to faithfulness with what belongs to another, to faithfulness as an undivided heart ("no slave can serve two masters"), and reaching its height in a faithfulness to God that allows no parity ("You cannot serve God and wealth"). Third, if it should appear that Jesus' words make little sense in light of the disciples' having left all to follow (cf. Mark 10:28; Luke 18:28), he is addressing a characteristic that adheres to every human being, rich or poor, disciple or unbeliever, that is, the *amor sui*, the tendency to set the self at the center of one's universe, and of which greed, avarice or the desire to acquire may be the most telling symptom.

Immediately following an indictment of the scribes, Mark and Luke include the narrative of the widow's "mite" (Mark 12:41–44; Luke 21:1–4). When Jesus came to Jerusalem, the Temple had just been rebuilt by Herod the Great who enlarged its size to about thirty-five acres. Of the eight gates leading into the temple, fourteen steps led through the "Beautiful Gate" to the Court of the Women, once without buildings, and later surrounded with a gallery, so that the women would see from above, and the men from below. According to the *Mishnah*, in that Court was located the treasury with its thirteen "Shofar" (trumpet-shaped) chests, designated "New Shekel dues," "Old Shekel dues," "Bird-offerings," "Young birds for the Whole-offering," "Wood," "Frankincense," "Gold for the Mercy-seat," and on six of them, "Freewill-offering." The main source of income was the half-shekel (Exodus 30:13ff.), paid by every Israelite "twenty years and upward," before the first of Nisan each year. Seated opposite the treasury, where he may often have taught (cf. John 8:20), Jesus watches the crowds throw coins into the treasury, sees a widow cast two *lepta* into a chest, calls his disciples together, remarks on the difference between those who give from out of their superfluity, and the widow who gives all she has. Since Jesus calls his disciples to note the event, he clearly intends to draw a lesson from it. Again the question is whether or not the lesson makes sense if directly applied to the disciples, who, again allowing for some attention to chronology in Mark's Gospel, had earlier reported through Peter that they had left all. Still, it would not have been out of character for Jesus to use the event, this time in oblique manner, to accent once more the conditions of their discipleship: Doing for him what the widow had done—giving all they had.

The famed Rudolf Bultmann (1884-1976) described this narrative as a "biographical apothegm," of the type ending with a decisive word of Jesus, seldom on his own initiative, rather evoked by the action of another. Interpreting the narrative as an idealistic scene created by the Palestinian community for instruction regarding the proper criteria for evaluating offerings, Bultmann asks, "how could Jesus observe what the single donor put in, and how could he know that the widow gave all she had?" Bultmann concluded that such biographical apothegms are not historical reports, "no less for Jesus than for any other historical personality."

More than once Mark and his co-evangelists credit Jesus with a knowledge independent of sense perception. For example, in Mark and Luke, following the hemorrhaging woman's touching his cloak, he is immediately aware that power has gone out of him (Mark 5:30; Luke 8:45-46). In the three Synoptics, approaching his triumphal entry into Jerusalem, Jesus tells two of the disciples to go into a village, untie a colt no one has ridden, and bring it to him (Mark 11:2; Matthew 21: 2; Luke 19:30). Or again, in Mark and Luke, at the feast of unleavened bread, he sends two into the city to follow a man carrying a water jar who would show them where they would eat Passover (Mark 14:13-16; Luke 22:10-12). According to whatever rabbinical or classical pattern the evangelists may have shaped their portrait of Jesus, if, indeed they did so shape it, they clearly regarded Jesus as having a knowledge not given the average human being. That conviction deserves attention before attempt is made at interpretation. Next, the attempt to get at the life which a saying or doing of Jesus enjoyed before being written down, more, to get at the context of the community (in the case of this narrative, the Palestinian), in which that saying or doing had a life, was nursed, and transmitted, thus to determine its historicity or lack of it, may have been one of the most ingenious projects undertaken in the last generation, but is totally without analogy in the study of texts outside the New Testament. The part of prudence is simply to give this narrative a name, whether "biographical apothegm" or no, to admit to whatever parallels may exist in the literature and religion of other communities, but to avoid the attempt to get behind the text to some original, pristine state, so as to document its genuineness. Let the text be as it is, with the interpreter challenged to be open to the claim of transcendence it makes.

The Specifics of Disciplesip

The Gospels yield a virtual catalogue of Jesus' specific instructions of the disciples. They may occur in Jesus' response to a report. In Mark 9:38–41 the disciples report the activity of an anonymous exorcist whom they ordered to stop because he did not follow them. Jesus says, "Do not stop him; for no one who does a deed of power in my name will be able soon afterward to speak evil of me. Whoever is not against us is for us." To this Jesus adds the promise of reward to whomever gives them a cup of water because they bear the name of Christ.

In Mark 10:17–31, the task is framed by Jesus' encounter with the young man unable to follow him due his great riches. Jesus comments that it is easier for a camel to go through the eye of a needle than for a person of wealth to enter the kingdom. The disciples in amazement construe the word as denoting the impossible, obviating all subsequent attempts at removing the edge of Jesus' remark by inventing the fiction of needle's eye gate in the Jerusalem wall through which a camel might kneel and go. Then Jesus says, 'for mortals it is impossible, but not for God . . . " Then, as if to point out the contrast, Peter states that he and the rest have left all to follow Jesus, and to which he replies that no one who has left house, siblings, parents for his and the gospel's sake will not receive a hundredfold in this age and the age to come.

In the same chapter Jesus instruction is a response to the petition of James and John that they sit at his right and left in his glory. Jesus descries their ignorance, not other impudence, asks if theory are able to drink this cup, and to their reply in the affirmative states they will indeed drink the cup, will be baptized with his baptism, meaning they will imitate him in suffering and death, but awarding the place of honor is a prerogative reserved to God (Mark 10:35–43).

In Mark 11:20–25 the narrative of the withered fig tree furnishes the frame for Jesus' instruction. Peter, amazed at the withering of the tree Jesus has cursed, along with the rest hers that if they were to say to to "this mountain, 'Be taken up and thrown into the sea,'" it would take place on condition of a believing heart; that whatever they ask for in prayer will, on condition of faith, come to pass. These words are hard to reconcile with actual experience. The removal of a mountain on condition of faith begs to raise that condition to a level beyond human possibility. And, given that unlikely possibility, would not the promise that one will get whatever one asks for guarantee disappointment? One solution, perhaps, lies in reserving these words for the disciples, later recorded as performing mighty works. Or, is it possible Jesus is indulging in hyperbole? One thing is certain, over the years these words have taken on a heuristic cast, moving generations to persist everlastingly in prayer on condition of faith. Jesus then adds that "standing" in prayer and forgiving anyone against whom they may have a complaint will end in the forgiveness of their trespass by the Father in heaven. Could all this have been prompted by that irritatingly odd event of the curing of a a fig tree ? (Mark 11:13: " . . . for it was not the season for figs").

In Mark 12:28–34 Jesus' instruction is not intended for a disciple but for a scribe who asks "which commandment is the first of all." After hearing Jesus recite the *Shema Yisroel*[1] and its the second in the command to love the neighbor[2] the scribe affirms Jesus' response (" you are right, Teacher . . . "), repeats Jesus' response, adding that "this is much more important than all whole burnt offerings and sacrifices." Jesus replies that the scribe is not far from the kingdom of God. Not the mere repetition of Jesus' word put the scribe within reach of the kingdom, but the fact that the repetition carried an affirmation of the one who uttered it. Following the exchange between Jesus and the scribe, Mark adds, after that no one dared to ask him any questions." (Mark 12:34). The sentence cannot mean that Jesus' adversaries feared to face him, this left off putting questions to him. It may be that the sentence belongs to the secret of Jesus' Messiahship threading throughout this Gospel, except that in this instance it is not Jesus who enjoins to silence, but his adversaries who assume the initiative for it. In Luke's parallel version, a layer puts the question, affirms Jesus' response, but receives no approbation, but attempting to justify himself asks "and who is my neighbor?" (Luke 10:29), evoking Jesus' reply in the parable of the Good Samaritan.

The entire tenth chapter of Matthew is devoted to Jesus' instruction of the disciples. In Matthew 10:5–15 Jesus sends the twelve out on their

---

1. Deuteronomy 6:4–5: "Hear, O Israel: The Lord is your God the Lord alone. You shall love the Lord your God with all your heart, and with all your soul, and with all our might."

2. Leviticus 19:18: "You shall not take vengeance or bear a grudge against any of your people, but you shall love your neighbor as yourself: I am the Lord."

mission, ordering them to announce exclusively to the "lost sheep of the house of Israel" that the kingdom of heaven has come near. They are to cure the sick, raise the dead, cleanse the lepers, and cast out demons without receiving payment. They were to take nothing with them but the shirt on their backs, totally dependent on their hosts. In whatever town they entered they were to determine who was "worthy," and remain there. On entering the house they were to greet it. If the house was "worthy" they were to let their peace come upon it. If not, they were to let their peace return to them. If none would welcome or hear them they were to remove the dust from their feet on leaving the town, on which a judgment would fall far greater than on Sodom and Gomorah. The term "worthy" denotes what befits or corresponds to what is at issue; here too welcoming and hearing the proclamation of the kingdom's having come near. Jesus' word concerning the disciples' peace ("if the house is worthy, let your peace come upon it; but if it is not worthy, let your peace return to you," vs. 13) cannot refer to what is owned by the disciples but is rather a peace given them to share. Just as the ability to cure the sick, raise the dead, cleanse the leper, and cast out demons was an "authority" given them by Jesus (vs. 1), so also was the peace they were to share or receive back.

The section in Matthew 10:16–23, further developed in 24:3–44 parallels the "Little Apocalypse" of Mark 13. Prefacing his instruction with the statement that he is sending the disciples out like sheep in the midst of wolves, so that they are to be "wise as serpents and innocent as doves," vs. 17), Jesus predicts a dark future. Because of him the disciples will be hauled off to councils and flogged, dragged before governors and kings, and this as a "testimony to them and the Gentiles" (vs. 18). When handed over, they are not to worry about how or what to speak, since the Spirit will be speaking though them. Then Jesus continues, families will be split apart, even to death. They will be hated by all, but the one who endures to the end will be saved. Finally, Jesus says, "when they persecute you in one town, flee to the next; for I tell you, you will not have gone through all the towns of Israel before the Son of Man comes" (vs. 23). First of all, if it should be imagined that following Jesus requires abandoning cranial activity, the summons to be "wise as serpents" should dispel it. Specifically, the disciples are to beware of their persecutors' ability to force them to recant, to revoke their witness, and are thus to rely on the Spirit. Jesus continues, in this period families will be split apart, ending in fratricide and patricide "because of my name," but whoever endures to the end will be saved. Then he adds that when persecuted in one town they should flee to another; that they will not have gone through all the towns of Israel before the Son of Man comes. Clearly, the sayings Matthew has assigned to Jesus deal with the "tribulation" or "woes" preceding the advent of the Messiah for judgment and deliverance. The reference to the Son of Man's coming before the disciples have gone through all the towns of Israel needs the correction of Jesus' statement in Mark 13: "But of that day or hour no one knows, neither the angels in heaven, nor the Son, but only the Father" (Mark 13:32). As will be discussed below, in apocalyptic discourse, two contradictories are held in tension, the one respecting the Son of Man's imminent arrival, the other ignorance respecting the time of its occurrence. Here, Matthew has recorded only one of those two contradictories.

Appended to Jesus' prediction of the disciples' persecution is the "moral" of the story. For the disciple, as for the slave, it is enough to be like the teacher or master. If the one, the master, is reviled, called "Beelzebub"(the devil's nickname, derived from "Baal" of the Canaanites, meaning "lord of the flies"), his household can expect worse treatment (Matthew 10:24–25). Later, the insult will be directly applied. When hearing of Jesus' exorcism of the demon inhabiting a deaf mute, the Pharisees will say, "it is only by Beelzebub, the ruler of the demons, that this fellow casts out the demons" (Matthew 12:24).

"Therefore," or "these things being so," what follows in 10:26–33 is a loosely connected cluster of instructions. First, framed by sayings telling the disciples to have no fear of "them" but of him who can destroy both soul and body in hell.[3] Jesus states that what he says to them in the dark they are to proclaim from the housetops (Matthew 10:26–28). The statement is reminiscent of Jesus' word in Mark 4:32" there is nothing hidden, except to be disclosed; nor is anything secret, except to come to light." Then follows further admonition not to have no fear; if a sparrow worth only a penny does not fall to earth without the Father, those whose hairs on their heads are numbered, are worth more than many sparrows. To this Jesus adds that anyone who acknowledges him before others he will acknowledge before his Father in heaven. And that anyone who denies him before others he will deny (Matthew 10:29–33).

In this cascade of instructions Jesus says he has not come to bring peace but a sword, and in a reprise of Micah 7:6[4] describes the effect of that "sword"

---

3 The term used by Jesus is *Gehenna,*. In Matthew's Gospel he uses it seven times to denote a place of torment. In the Old Testament and in later Judism *Gehinnom* or *Gehenna* was used of such a place. In early Judaism *Sheol* denoted the place of the dead beyond God's reach., but toward which he could engage in pursuit. Here, the implication is that God can work his will directly within the place of torment.

4 ". . .the son treats the father with contempt, the daughter rises up against her mother, the daughter-in-law against her mother-in-law;your enemies are members of our own household."

as division within one's own kith and kin.[5] And that "sword" will create division between those closest and Jesus: "Whoever loves father or mother more than me is not worthy of me; and whoever loves son or daughter more than me is not worthy of me" (Matthew 10:37). And as if to sum up what was just said, he adds, "whoever does not take up the cross and follow me is not worthy of me." And again, as if to hammer the point home concludes, "those who find their life will lose it, and those who lose their life for my sake will find it" (Matthew 10:38–39). Thus, to "find life" spells suffering division within the innermost circle; spells love for Jesus beyond love for those tied closest by blood, here defined as "carrying one's cross" and following. Discipleship of Jesus involves a more radical attachment than any humanly conceived.

At the end of Matthew 10 Jesus says that whoever welcomes the disciples welcomes him and whoever welcomes him welcomes the one who sent him; that whoever welcomes a prophet or righteous person in the name of a prophet or righteous person. or gives a cup of cold water to "one of these little ones" in the name of a disciple, will not lack a reward (Matthew 10:40–42). Those welcomed are listed in an ascending and descending order respecting status; first, in an ascent from a disciple to Jesus, then to "the one who sent me," then in a descent from a prophet to a righteous person to "one of these little ones." Then, as if to fracture all regard for status, Jesus promises a reward to whomever gives a drink to those last in the order of descent, to "one of these little ones." And this since it is given "in the name of a disciple," of one welcomed two rungs away from "me" and "the one who sent me."

In Matthew 11:2–19 Jesus' instruction takes the form of a response to messengers sent by the Bapist, now in prison and asks whether or not Jesus is "the one who is to come," or are they to await another. Jesus orders the messengers to return to the Baptist, relating to him what they have heard and seen of his miraculous deeds, ending with the blessing on anyone who takes no offense at him. Then follows a long encomium in praise of the Baptist, identifying him with the Elijah-forerunner of Malachi 3:1 ("See, I am sending my messenger ahead of you, who will prepare our way before you."). Having thus assigned John a status unequalled by any born of women, he relegates him to a level beneath the "least in the kingdom." Then follows the word of the kingdom's suffering violence, and of the violent takng it away. Situated within Jesus' "biography" of the Baptist, the sentence relates to the effect of the Baptist's activity, that the urge to acknowledge him and his message resembles the warriors' siege of a city.[6] But once more Jesus

5. Ibid.

6. Thus the NIV translates: "12 From the days of John the Baptist until now, the kingdom of heaven has been subjected to violence,[a] and violent people have been raiding it."

cites that division in the history of the divine activity, stating that all of law and prophecy reach their crest in the Baptist ("for all the prophets and the law prophesied until John came," Matthew 11:13), again assigning him the status of the Elijah-messenger to come. The inference to be drawn is clear: it is the kingdom Jesus brings that has created the caesura in the history of the divine activity. The work of the Baptist, great as it is, only leads up to it, not away from it.

In chapters nine through twenty of his Gospel, Luke contains responses of Jesus for the purpose of schooling the disciples and others. In 9:51–56, to the question of James and John whether he wanted them to bring down fire on the village of the Samaritans who would not receive him, the evangelist tersely states that "he turned and rebuked them."

In 12:13–14 someone in the crowd asks Jesus to intervene in a dispute over an inheritance, to which he reples in the parable of the rich fool taxed to the limit with the yield of his acreage he resolves to replace the old with bigger barns, and in soliloquy says, "Soul, you have ample goods laid up for many years; relax, eat, drink, be merry." "You fool," says God, "this very night our life is being demanded of you. And the things you have prepared, whose shall they be?" "So it is" Jesus concludes, "with those who store up treasures for themselves but are not rich toward God" (12:21).

In Luke 13:1–5, when told by some present about the Galileans whose blood Pilate had mixed with their sacriices, Jesus replied in question form: "Do you think that because these Galileans suffered in this way they were worse sinners than all other Galileans?" Then he adds, "No, I tell you; but unless you repent, you will all perish as they did." Then, referring to the eighteen persons crushed by the tower of Siloam, he asks: "Do you think that they were worse offenders than all the others living in Jerusalem?" And again he adds, "No, I tell you; but unless you repent you will all perish just as they did."

In 14:1–6, about to eat at the home of a leader of the Pharisees on the Sabbath, and being closely watched, a leper approaches Jesus who asks his audience whether it is lawful to perform a cure on the Sabbath. Then he heals the leper, dismisses him, and giving point to the earlier question asks if on the Sabbath it would be lawful to rescue a child or an ox that had fallen in a well. In other words, would the three hundred sixteen regulations with which the most observant had surrounded the *Torah* as its "fence," with its prohibition against, for example, setting a broken bone or taking an artificial emetic, disallow doing on the Sabbath what simple humanity demanded? Luke writes that the company "could not reply to this" (14:6). Jesus' reduction of their alleged Sabbath observance to the absurd left them mute, unable to answer.

Luke 17 contains several episodes of Jesus' intention of the disciples. In 17:1–4 he says that causes for stumbling are bound to occur, but it would be better for whomever caused "one of these little ones" to stumble that a millstone were hanged about his neck and he were thrown into the sea. He adds that if any disciple sins, he must be received back; if repentant he must be forgiven, and if a disciple[7] sins against another seven times a day and seven times says "I repent," he is to be forgiven. Here Jesus establishes the form of existence that should obtain among the members of his community. It is radical. The number "seven" denotes times without number. No matter how often one is sinned against, the offender is to be forgiven. What would tear apart any other society, to to say nothing of reducing such practice within it to an absurdity, must prevail among those who belong to Jesus. No interruption, no breach, nothing however heinous, must put this fellowship at risk. Every other community or persuasion, ethical, moral or political, may be severed, and for what anyone with a bit of moral sense would call good reason, but not this company, this society, this persuasion. All, everything is to be borne.

In Luke 17:5–10 the apostles say to the Lord,[8] "increase our faith!" Jesus replies that if they had faith the size of a mustard seed, they could say to this mulberry tree, "Be removed and planted in the sea, and it would obey you." The scene is roughly parallel to Mark 11:20–25, but unlike Mark who sets the disciples' surprise at the withered fig tree as the occasion, Luke omits the occasion. Further, what Jesus says according to Mark will occur ("if you do not doubt in your heart, but believe that what you say will come to pass, "Mark 11:23) in Luke is on condition of a faith no larger than a mustard seed. In Luke the mountain in Mark's account as been reduced to a mulberry bush. No matter whether Mark or Luke have tailored the size of faith to its outcome, with the one the promoting of a mulberry bush by a faith no larger than a mustard seed, with the other a mountain removed by faith free of doubt and confident in the outcome, the situation remains the same: what is assumed is an existence beyond human capability. The clause is conditional: "If you had faith . . . " No one had, and no one in the world has such faith; no one but he.

Again, without citing the occasion in 17:20–23 Luke writes that Jesus "once" was asked by the Pharisees when the kingdom of God was coming. He answered, not with things that can be observed, but "in fact, the

---

7 In the Greek "the brother" in verse 3 is subject of the verb in verse 4. The NRSV translates "the same person."

8 Reference in like to title "apostles" and "Lord" rather than "they," the disciples, or "Peter's addressing Jesus as Rabbi" in Mark's account, reflects attention to a period this side of the passion.

kingdom of God is among you." It has been the habit of some to take the last two Greek terms in that sentence (*entos hymin*) to mean "within you," thus to interiorize the kingdom or rule of God. But the kingdom is something apart, something brought, from the outside, not, say, a disposition that can be summoned up from within; it can only draw near, come nigh, as something alien and unbidden, at no one's call, and for that reason hidden, "not coming with things to be observed."

In the Fourth Gospel the conditions, task, and rewards of discipleship are clustered in chapters thirteen through sixteen. In chapter thirteen, following reference to Jesus' awareness that his "hour" had come, the evangelist describes him as washing the disciple's feet while they are at table. The contrast involved cannot be missed. Removing outer clothing, wrapping a towel about oneself, pouring water into a basin, washing others' feet are obviously all acts of a servant or house-slave, but here performed by one whom ordinary reckoning would distance by miles from such service, who knew that "the Father had given all things into his hands, and that he had come from God and was going to God" (John 13:3). Peter, in left-handed fashion marks the contrast by refusing the service, to which Jesus responds, "unless I wash you, you have no share with me." Then, as if to make clear the point that had escaped them, Jesus instructs the disciples to act toward one another as he has acted toward them, leaving them no room for elbowing to the top. The action is preceded and followed by reference to Judas' plot to betray, in essence excluding him from the reward given such service ("If you know these things, you are blessed if you do them," John 13:17), an exclusion chosen by Jesus ("I know whom I have chosen," John 13:18), in order to fulfill the scripture: Psalm 41:9 ("The one who ate my bread has lifted his heel against me," John 13:18). Following his summons to Judas to "do quickly" what he is about to do, and the betrayer's exit from the company, Jesus gives the disciples "a new commandment, that they love one another" (John 13:34). Commentators have been at pains to describe the newness of the commandment in light of its having been uttered in the past.[9] Historical continuity between the new and the old commandment cannot be denied. The term "new" as used in the New Testament demands recognition of the historical, temporal. At the same time, the term demands recognition of the contrast between the new and the old. And in this case what is new is the fact that it is Jesus who gives the commandment: "I give you a new commandment, that you love one another. Just as I have loved you, you also should love one another" (13:34). It is precisely because he reveals the new

---

9. Cf. e.g., Lev. 19:17-18: "You shall not take vengeance or bear a grudge against any of your people, but you shall love your neighbor as yourself: I am the Lord."

within this temporal, historical framework and on an historical occasion that the occasion itself takes on the character of the new. And it is obedience to the commandment that gives evidence of discipleship.

In John 14:15–31 Jesus discourses on his farewell and the giving of the Spirit. The discourse is laced with repetition, contrasts, and seeming paradox. First, Jesus declares that love for him means keeping his commandments, or his word, that they who do so will be the object of his and the Father's love (vss. 15, 21, 23). For this reason he will ask the Father to give them an Advocate, the "Spirit of truth" who will teach them everything and remind them of what he had said (vs. 26). By contrast, "the world" neither sees nor hears him (vs. 17), nor does whoever does not love him keep his word (vs. 24). In midst of these remarks there is the seeming paradox of Jesus' "going" and "coming." In verse 19 he says, "in a little while the world will no longer see me," and in vs. 28 says, "I am going away. . .I am going to the Father." But in vs. 18 he says, "I am coming to you," and in vs. 21 of those who love him says "I will love them and reveal myself to them.," and in the verse following declares that he and the Father will make their home with them. Jesus' word regarding the giving of the Spirit and the word of his "coming" to the disciples when they will see him, live, and "on that day" will know he is in the Father and they in him (vss. 18–20), are clue to the paradox. The two occurrences are identical. The Advocate, the Spirit of truth and the presence of Christ with those who are his are one and the same, and both occur "on that day." It will be left for the future to construe that presence as an essence equal to the Father and the Son. Could there be a hint here of the "procession" of that essence from the Father and the Son? In vs. 15, Jesus says, "I will ask the Father, and he will give you another Advocate," but in verse 23, "those who love me will keep my word, and my Father will love them, and we will come to them and make our home with them." Following his promise of the Spirit, Jesus extends his peace to the disciples, tells them neither to be troubled in heart nor to fear, rather, if they love him, to rejoice that he is going to the Father, "who is greater than I" (vs. 28). Given what some might term the Fourth Gospel's exalted Christology, the Jesus of John is functionally, if not essentially, subordinate to the Father. In verse 29 Jesus says that when "it occurs," i.e., the gift of the Spirit, the disciples may believe, he is not grouping them, say, with Thomas (20:26–29), who needed to see before he believed, for the "seeing" that will lead to believing will be inward, "in them." The discourse ends with reiterating that the events about to occur have God for their initiator: "I go as the Father has commanded me" (vs. 31)

In John 15:1–6. Jesus said, "I am the true vine, and my Father is the vine grower." Earlier he had said, "I am the bread of life," "I am the light," "I am the door," "I am the good shepherd,' "I am the resurrection , and the life," "I am the way, the truth, and the life. " Those seven utterances were calculated to conjure up the scene with Moses and the burning bush in Exodus. Moses had said,

> "if I come to the Israelites and say to them, 'The God of your ancestors has sent me to you,' and they ask me, 'What is his name?' what shall I say to them? God said to Moses, "I am who I am."[10]

Here, in John 15:1–8, and for the last time, struggling to explain who he is and what this little group of hangers-on means to him, and what is the connection is between them, Jesus says, "I am the vine." Before deciding these utterances are mere figures of speech, it should be noted that they all have to do with life, more, with Jesus as source of life. And when he says, "I am the *true* vine," that suggests contrast, exclusion, distance between him and others who promise life. Discipleship of Jesus of Nazareth spells allegiance to him alone. Then he adds, "and my Father is the vine grower." He is the "true vine" because what he is his Father has made it so. As if he were to say, I am because he is who he is; we two are one, and any who comes within range of me is liable to everything that will happen to me." Then he says, "he removes every branch in me that bears no fruit. Every branch that bears fruit he prunes, to make it bear more fruit." (vs.2). Whatever type of Christianity Freud thought he was describing when he wrote that it celebrates peace above all things, the disciple's relation to God would not be a matter of perpetual peace and quiet, but disturbance.[11] Tradition has it that John was boiled in oil, and Peter crucified upside down.

Now Jesus turns to the disciples and says, "You have already been cleansed by the word that I have spoken to you" (vs.3), giving sense to what follows. Something has happened to the disciples; a word had been spoken to them. Earlier Jesus had said that it was not his but the Father's word he was sent to speak. The entire operation was out of their hands, evidently the translators decided not to pursue the pruning metaphor, though the verb earlier translated "prune" deserves its original force: "You've been pruned, trimmed by a word, the word of the spontaneous, unmerited, and uncaused favor of God. by his word, and his word alone."

Then follows the word "Abide!" And it introduces what reads like a condition: "Just as the branch cannot bear fruit by itself unless it abides in the vine, neither can you unless you abide in me" (vs. 4). And later. "if you abide in me, and my words abide in you ask for whatever you wish" (vs.

---

10. Exodus 2:13–14
11. Cf. Edmunson, Mark. *The Death of Sigmund Freud* (NY: Bloombury, 2010).

7), or "If you keep my commandments. you will abide in my love" (vs. 10). "Unless," "if:" Is this abiding something apart from what was done to them, something to be added to the cleansing, the pruning, as though the pruning were somehow left behind when the abiding needed doing?

When Jesus says, "you have already been cleansed by the word that I have spoken to you," or when he says, "abide in me as I abide in you," he allows no separation between the one action and the other. When he says, "apart from me you can do nothing" (vs. 5), he admits of no activity without him. The two are one. The command is embraced, rolled up in the promise. Christ is both subject and agent. And because this is so, he says, "ask for whatever you wish, and it will be done for you" (vs.7) One scholar asks, "what else could you] pray for than for the abiding of the Revealer in you and your abiding in him?" I am not sure that scholar has covered all the territory making up that "whatever." Whatever else it may cover will need an entire lifetime to see.

And the end of it all is that his Father is glorified, and they are his disciples. We have come round once more to the first and greatest commandment. For if he is the vine grower's vine, and the disciples are his branches; if they take all their life from the vine grower's vine, this must mean that they are one constant, incessant, everlasting evidence of the glory of God.

In John 16:12-15, and in the context of his farewell, Jesus says to the disciples that the future is the Spirit's affair. He says "when the Spirit of truth comes. . . he will guide. . .he will speak. . .he will declare (vs. 13). . ..he will glorify" (vs. 14). In those verses the future tense of the verb is used eight times. Thus, discipleship of Jesus means to be aimed, poised toward the future. The French Jesuit, paleontologist, biologist and philosopher, Pierre Teilhard de Chardin, wrote that everything in the universe and everything and everyone in it was evolving toward a final unity he called the "Omega Point." It was all a process converging toward last things, toward God, toward Christ. When Paul wrote to his Corinthians, "thanks be to God, who in Christ always leads us in triumphal procession,"[12] he expressed the same idea, Jesus is telling the disciples that because of this Spirit not yesterday nor today but tomorrow gives them their identity. What they had been and were now derived its meaning from what they were to be. Again, when Paul wrote to the Romans that the entire creation was groaning in labor, that they themselves were groaning while waiting for the redemption of their bodies,[13] he was repeating himself. Not that the future was something the

---

12. II Corinthians 2:14.
13. Romans 8: 22–23.

disciples possessed. The future was *something that possessed them* because of the Spirit sent to them.

Further, everything this Spirit is and does has to do exclusively with Jesus, without remainder. "All the truth" into which he will guide the disciples is the truth concerning him. What the Spirit speaks is not his own; what he hears is what he speaks and speaks concerning Jesus; whatever things to come he declares are things to come with Jesus. There is nothing to suggest that the coming of the Spirit means anything else but that what Jesus said and did would still come into their own. There is an exclusivity laid claim to here to leave one breathless; an exclusivity not even religious people have been able to concede.

In John 16:24 Jesus expands on the motif elaborated on in 14:18–31. The discourse begins with reference to that "little while" in which, according to chapter 14, the world would no longer see him; here, in which the disciples would not see him. In either instance Jesus provokes a question, in chapter 14 from Judas (not Iscariot) regarding Jesus' word that he would reveal himself to those who love him, while here a group of the disciples asks: "What does he mean by saying to us, A little while and you will no longer see me, and again a little while, and you will see me," and "Because I am going to the Father'"? We do not know what he is talking about" (vss. 17–18). In chapter 14 Jesus opens this portion of the larger discourse stating he will not leave the disciples orphaned, thus only implying a separation, while here the separation is made explicit in the declaration that they would weep and mourn while the world would rejoice. The separation is spelled out as a "going to the Father." The phrase appears in 14:12, 28, in 14:12, and later in 16:28 to end the Johannine circuit of the Word, beginning with his coming from God, his coming into the world, and his leaving the world, the event embracinghis glorification-crucifixion and ascension. In either instance the separation comes to an end, in chapter 14 with the coming of Jesus and the Father to the disciples and making their home with them (14:23), and here with the disciples' seeing him again. To illustrate the end to their separation Jesus, suggestive of a Jewish wisdom teacher, cites the pain of a woman and her resultant joy at having birthed a child. Finally, the disciples' joy over their reunion with Jesus will be made complete when "anything" they ask of the Father in his name (and this for the first time), it will be given them (16:23)—again, that "anything" needing a lifetime to give it content. The utterances in chapters 14 and 16, involve a reversal. Evidently the evangelist intended that the giving of the Spirit on which Jesus discourses in chapter 14 should anticipate the "go to the Father" in John 15:21.

The Last Things

Jesus' longest discourse in the Synoptic Gospels appears in Mark 13, and parallels in Matthew 24, and Luke 21. The discourse opens with Jesus' predicting the destruction of the temple (Mark 13:1-2; (Matthew 24:1-2; Luke 21:5-6). Judaism had hoped for a renewal of the temple in the end-time, but according to Jesus that time would only bring its destruction. Then, to the disciples' question respecting the time of its occurrence, the sign of Christ's coming, and the end of the age, Jesus again counters Jewish expectation with the prediction of woes (Mark 14:3-8; (cf. Matthew 24:3-8; Luke 21:7-11), the first sign of which will be the appearance of those who come "in my name" (Mark 13:6), that is, with the name and titles of Messiah, characterized by the mysterious "I AM." Wars are a further sign of the woes of the end-time, a concept occurring often in Jeremiah. And all of it happening according to divine necessity: "This must take place" (Mark 13:6), and in the words of Daniel 2:28, the first apocalypse, "But," Jesus' longest discourse in the Synoptic Gospels appease in Mark 13, and parallels in Matthew 24, and Luke 21. The discourse opens with Jesus' predicting the destruction of the temple (Mark 13:1-2; (Matthew 24:1-2; Luke 21:5-6). Judaism had hoped for a renewal of the temple in the end-time, but according to Jesus that time will only bring its destruction. Then, to the disciples' question expecting its occurrence, the sign of Christ's coming, and the end of the age, Jesus again counters Jewish expectation with the prediction of woes (Mark 14:3-8; (cf. Matthew 24:3-8; Luke 21:7-11), the first sign of which will be the appearance of those who come "in my name" (Mark 13:6), that is, with the name and titles of Messiah, characterized by the mysterious "I am he." Wars are a further sign of the woes of the end-time, a concept occurring often in Jeremiah. And all of it happening according to divine necessity: This must take place" (Mark 13:7), and in the words of Daniel 2:28, the first apocalypse." This," Jesus adds, "is but the beginning of the happenings" (Mark 13:8). In other words, the Christ does not come with war, again, in contrast to Jewish tradition. Then follow the persecutions (Mark 13:9-13;(cf. Matthew 24:9-14; 10:17-21, 34-36; Luke 21: 12-19; 12:51-53), in Judaism an essential part of the Messianic "woes." In this period the Christian will be hated "because of my name (Mark 13:9); there will be betrayals, increase in lawlessness, but also the good news of the kingdom will be proclaimed throughout the world (13:10-12). Then, Jesus says, follows the last tribulation (Luke 13:14-23;(Matthew 24:15-25; Luke 21:20-24), a final distress before the Son of Man's coming. There are two basic motifs here: expectation of the Antichrist in vss. 14, 21f., and foretelling the flight in vss. 14-18. The term "abomination" in vs. 14—reference to the Antichrist—is from Daniel 9, 11, and 12. Whether of Antiochus or of Caligula who attempted to set up his statue in the temple in AD 37-41, or of many others who sat for his portrait, the reference is deliberately veiled: "let the reader understand" (Luke 13: 15). After all this, Jesus states, the Son of Man will appear (13:24-27; Matthew 24:29-31; Luke 21:25-28). This portion of the discourse is ripe with Old Testament language. At midpoint, 13: 26, is a word from Daniel 2:13. "When the new heaven and earth appear, the old world must pass away (13: 24-25)." Then they will see him. Now, the Son of Man is veiled in humiliation and weakness, in "mystery," then exalted in glory. There is nothing here that could not appear in Jewish apocalyptic. What is important is that what was awaited in the Old Testament faith and what was fulfilled in the earliest Christian community has its point of intersection in Jesus. Finally, Jesus declares, comes the end (Mark 13:28-37;(Matthew 24:32-36; Luke 21: 29-36). This part of the discourse contains a tiny parable in Matthew ("wherever the carcass is, there the vultures will gather," Matthew 24:28), more or less isolated words regarding the earth's mourning at the coming of the Son of Man who will gather his elect from the four winds (Mark 13:30-31), and the summons to watch (Mark 13: 33-37), all grouped about the parable of the fig tree (13:28), and which has its parallel elsewhere in gospel tradition. Jesus then summons the disciples to keep awake, since the day or hour of the coming of the Son of Man is known neither to him, nor to the angels, abut only to the Father. Contrary to average interpretation, just as Jesus does here, so apocalyptic expectation embraces the two contradictories: expectation of imminent crisis, and ignorance of the time of its advent.

From this discourse it is clear that Jesus shared the general expectation of his time. What the specific events or conditions were that moved him to share them is another matter. It would hardly be an exaggeration to state that the Israel of his day was a land torn by civil unrest. The revolt of Judas of Galilee (4 BC) may have made an impression on him. His own appearance urged comparison with Judas (cf. Acts 5:37).[1] Earlier, Julius Caesar's anti-Semitic measures may have provoked apocalyptic sentiment. Later occurred, the revolt of AD 66–70, based on Daniel, chapter 9. And the revolt of Bar Kochba in AD 132–135 may have resulted from apocalyptic reckonings. At any rate, the idea that it was living at the end of days was common to Christians and Jews. As for the argument that Jesus was not interested in fixing the date of the end-time, it need only be noted that neither was apocalyptic. The two ideas could live together: "He is coming soon," and "no one knows the day or the hour."

Specifically, Jesus awaited his exaltation as Son of Man. At the heart of Son of Man usage is the expectation that God would choose someone to exalt him to heavenly status. In Jesus' preaching and teaching the Son of Man is none other than himself. If we follow the probabilities it is probable that before Easter the disciples waited for another, then after Easter directed their attention to Jesus. At Easter the original, apocalyptic expectation divided into the certainty he had been exalted, and that he would come again at the end-time.

But if Jesus was conscious of himself as Son of Man, did he reckon on his death? Humiliation, to be sure, but death? In Luke's record of the Last Supper Jesus' expectation is heightened to the extreme (Luke 22:15), as though he awaited the visible manifestation of God, and all the more his death came into view. Mark's and Matthew's description of Jesus' agitation in the garden, the contest of wills ensuing in the "yet not what I want, but what you want" (Mark 14:36; Matthew 25:39), is not merely for the purpose of adjusting Jesus' story to the plight of his readers. And, although, there is merit to the suggestion that Jesus' passion predictions in Mark 8:30; 9:30; 10:32, and parallels are a trajection from the actual events of his crucifixion and death, it is surely one thing to predict one's death and quite another actually to suffer it.

---

1. Judas of Galilee. https://en.wikipedia.org/wiki/Judas_of_Galilee

The Inner Life of Jesus

There are instances in the New Testament which give glimpses into Jesus' inner life or psychic states. These glimpses almost exclusively appear in Mark's Gospel. In Mark 3:5, Jesus' adversaries wait see if he will heal a man with a watered hand on the Sabbath, and in the synagogue. After bidding the man to come forward, he asks whether it is lawful to do good or evil on the sabbath, to give life or to kill. Then, at their silence, Jesus looks around at them "with anger...grieved at their hardness of heart." The word translated "with anger" denotes wrath, temper, and the word rendered "grieved" is a compound denoting sympathy. The report suggests a mood compounded of passion on the one hand and fellow-feeling on the other. Thus, Jesus is torn in his attitude toward his critics, a mood to which any human could attest. The refence does not appear in Matthew's or Luke's record of the scene (Matthew 12:12–13; Luke 6:10).

In Mark 6, Jesus' teaching in the Nazareth synagogue elicits a host of questions on the part of his listeners who take offense at him.[1] In response Jesus cites a maxim: "Prophets are not without honor, except in their hometown, and among their own kin, and in their own house" (Mark 6:4). Mark then reports that Jesus could do no deed of power there,[2] except for laying hands on a few sick and healing them. Mark concludes "And he was amazed at their unbelief" (6:6). Had Jesus expected another reaction to his teaching,

---

1. Mark 6:2–3: "Where did this man get all this? What is this wisdom that has been given to him? What deeds of power are being done by his hands! Is not this the carpenter, the son of Mary and brother of James and Moses and Judas and Simon, and are not his sisters here with us?"

2. Incidentally, Matthew emits the verb translated "could not," leaving the impression that because of Nazareth's unbelief, Jesus refused to do a mighty work there. And it would not be the fist time Mark indicated Jesus' inability. He writes in 1:45 that Jesus is unable openly to enter a town; in 7:24 that he is unable to be hid.

acceptance, affirmation, perhaps, or, at least, the courtesy of a hearing? And is it possible that the reason for Matthew' and Luke's omission of his reaction stems from a hesitation at assigning such a human quality to him (cf. Matthew 15:38; Luke 4:24)? The verb used and translated "amazed" means to wonder at, to marvel. There may be a touch of irony here. Jesus' critics have just exclaimed at the deeds of power being done by his hands, then Mark adds his laying laid hands on a few sick and healing them, and this compounded with reference to his inability to do any mighty work. What could trump what Nazareth had seen, could witness to at first hand? If there is no irony here, then we are left either with the author's disappointment, an obvious impossibility, or with his intent one way or another to warp the scene into the weave of the "Messianic secret," that theme of Jesus' incognito threading throughout Mark's work.

In connection with Mark's description of the feeding of the five thousand (Mark 6:30–44) and of the four thousand (8:1–10) Jesus is described as having compassion on those who follow him, "for they are like sheep without a shepherd"(6:34), or Jesus himself says, "I have compassion for the crowd, because they have been with me now for these days and have nothing to eat" (8:2). In Matthew's and Luke's parallel versions (Matthew14:13–21, Luke 9:10–17), reference to Jesus' compassion is omitted. Uncharacteristically, Matthew's account of the feeding of the four thousand (Matthew 15:32–39, repeats Jesus' statement recorded in Mark 8:2 (Matthew 15:32). Whereas Luke omits the event altogether evidently Mathew has decided to follow his Markan exemplar.

When, following the feeding of then four thousand the Pharisees come to Jesus to argue with him, asking him for a sign from heaven to test him, Mark writes that "he sighed deeply in his spirit" (8:12). The verb used denotes a sigh drawn from the bottom of the breast, or, as Mark writes,"in his spirit," that is, within that power by which the body is animated, thinks, feels, and decides. Again, in Matthew's account of the scribes and Pharisees who demand a sign (Matthew 15:38–52) Mark's look-see into Jesus' inner state is omitted. In his account in 11:29–32, Luke omits the reference.

In 10:13–16 Mark records that people were bringing children to Jesus for a blessing, that when the disciples "spoke sternly" to them (10:23), Jesus was "indignant" and invited the children to come. The verb used and translated "indignant" denotes irritation, vexation, displeasure. In the Matthaean and Lukan reports (Matthew 19:13–15; Luke 18:15–17) there is no mention of Jesus' indignation.

In this same chapter (Mark 10:7–22), Mark records Jesus' encounter with the rich young man who addresses him as "Good Master," and asks what he must do to inherit eternal life. Jesus replies, "why do you call me good? No one is good but God alone" (Mark 10:18). He then recites the commandments, which, the young man responds, he has kept from his youth. Following this exchange Mark adds that "Jesus, looking at him, loved him" (Mark 10:21). In this parallel version Matthew (19:16–22) has undertaken two major revisions. First, apparently sensing Jesus' initial response as liable to misinterpretation, he alters it to read "Why do you ask me about what is good?" (Matthew 19:17). Second, he omits Mark's reference to Jesus' love for the young man. By this time, the reader would expect his co-evangelist Luke to do the same (Luke 18:18–25), as indeed he does (25).

Finally, in his description of Jesus' arrival with Peter, James, and John at Gethsemane, Mark writes that Jesus "began to be distressed and agitated (14:33), then said to them, "I am deeply moved, even to death" (14:34). The passage contains a cluster of three verb forms, the first of which, translated "distressed," may denote amazement, but also extreme terror, the second translated "agitated," denotes anguish or depression, and the third, translated "deeply moved," such sorrow as to cause one's death. In this version Matthew substitutes the word translated "grieved, for the word translated "distressed" "perhaps to soften any intimations of terror, then repeats Jesus' statement in Mark to the effect he is sorrowful even unto death. In his version (Luke 22:39–46) Luke collapses the references simply to read that "in his anguish he prayed earnestly, and his sweat became like great drops of blood" (Luke 22:44). In the Fourth Gospel, there is no hint of the Gethsemane scene such as appears in Matthew or Luke, to say nothing of Mark's doubling the motif of Jesus' agitation and grief. There is simply the notice that he crossed the Kidron with his disciples toward the garden where Judas would betray him (John 18:1–11).

It is remarkable that Mark's Gospel, whose initial portrait of Jesus strikes the reader as massive, colossal, should in these scenes place such stress on his humanity as his co-evangelist are reluctant, or, in John's case, totally unable to share, since such reference may have seemed to them inappropriate, perhaps to detract from his divinity. At any rate, the scenes portray an altogether human figure, leaving it to later generations to wrestle with the "communication" between the divine and the human. There is something of a refraction of Mark's Gethsemane scene in the Epistle to the Hebrews, whose author writes that "in the days of his flesh, Jesus offered up prayers and supplications, with loud cries and tears, to the one who was able to save him from death" (Hebrews 5:7).

If Mark should have the lion's share of references to Jesus' inner life, they are not absent from the other Gospels. In Matthew and Luke, Jesus delivers a series of woes over the Galilean triangle of cities where he performed most of his miracles "Woe to you Chorazin! Woe to you Bethsaida!

For if the deeds of power done in you had been done in Tyre and Sidon, they would have repented long ago, in sackcloth and ashes. . .And you, Capernaum, will you be exalted to heaven? No, you will be brought down to Hades" (Matthew 11:20–24; Luke 10:13–15).

If these woes do not allow inferring anything regarding Jesus' inner life, what he says to the crowds and disciples in Matthew, and to the scribes and Pharisees in Luke, certainly does so. In Matthew Jesus excoriates the scribes and Pharisees, initially in the third person plural: "They tie up heavy burdens, hard to bear. . .they do all their deeds to be seen by others. . .they love to have the place of honor at banquets. . .to be greeted with respect in the market places." In Luke's account the attack begins in the first-person plural: "You Pharisees clean the outside of the cup and of the dish, but inside you are full of greed and wickedness. You fools! Did not the one who made the outside make the inside also? . . . . . woe to you Pharisees! For you tithe mint and rue and herbs of all kinds, and neglect justice and the love of God. . .Woe to you Pharisees! For you love to have the seat of honor in the synagogues and to be greeted with respect in the marketplaces. Woe to you! For you are like unmarked graves, and people walk over them without realizing it" (Luke 11:39–44). Matthew's longer account contains a seven-step cascade of woes: "Woe to you, scribes and Pharisees, hypocrites! For you lock people out of the kingdom of heaven. . ..Woe to you, scribes and Pharisees, hypocrites! For you cross sea and land to make a single convert, and you make the new convert twice as much a child of hell as ourselves. Woe to you, blind guides, who say, "Whoever swears by the sanctuary is bound by nothing. . ..Woe to you, scribes and Pharisees, hypocrites! For you tithe mint, dill, and cumin, and have neglected the weightier matters of the law. . ..Woe to you, scribes and Pharisees, hypocrites! For you clean the outside of the cup and of the plate, but inside they are full of greed and self-indulgence. . ..Woe to you, scribes and Pharisees, hypocrites! For you are like whitewashed tombs . . . Woe to you, scribes and Pharisees, hypocrites! For you build the tombs of the prophets (Matthew 23:1–7, 13–28).

If these events do not allow a glimpse into Jesus' psychic states his response to the return of the seventy, sandwiched between the woes, certainly does. When informed that even the demons submitted to them, Jesus says: "I watched Satan fall from heaven like a flash of lightning, " and following his caveat ("do not rejoice at this. . .but that our names are written in heaven") Luke writes that "at that same hour Jesus rejoiced in the Holy Spirit and said, "I thank you, Father, Lord of heaven and earth, because you have hidden these things from the wise and the intelligent and have revealed them to infants" (Mark 10:17–22; Matthew 11:25; 28:18).

In his record of the Last Supper, Luke writes that Jesus said, "I have eagerly desired to eat this Passover with you before I suffer" (Luke 22:15). The noun and verb translated "eagerly desired" stem from the same root, denoting desire, craving, often translated "lust." More, the repetition of the stem in noun and verb to allow for the old King James translation "with desire I have desired," indicating a state or condition heightened to the extreme, scarcely denoted by the NRSV adverb "eagerly." The reference does not occur in Matthew.

Initially, Like omits explicit reference to Jesus' agony in the garden, but allows the inference, reporting that an angel appeared which "gave him strength," then arrives at an explicit reference to the agony in the garden, stating that "in his anguish he prayed more earnestly, and his sweat became like drops of blood falling down on the ground" (Luke 22:43-44). This reference also does not appear in Matthew.

If the Fourth Evangelist was wary of referring to Jesus' inner life, there were certainly occasions when he could have made an exception. The evangelist records that following Jesus' discourse opening with the word, "unless you eat the flesh of the Son of Man and drink his blood, you have no life in you," and ending with the statement, "no one can come to me unless it is granted by the Father," many of his disciples "turned back and no longer went about with him" (John 6:53, 65). At this He turns to the twelve and asks, "do you also wish to go away?" (John 6:67). Here would have been an instance where the evangelist could have given a glimpse into Jesus' interior. But if not here, certainly in his reference to the scene in the garden. But there is nothing, not one word until his betrayal; not one word of the agony reported by Mark, Matthew, and Luke, merely the statement that Jesus entered the garden with the disciples and there was betrayed by Judas and arrested. With the Fourth Evangelist the inducement to avoid referring to Jesus' emotional states had to have been excessive. Could awe toward his subject have led him to believe that engaging in it spelled a kind of blasphemy? As noted, to a degree, Matthew and Luke share the same attitude, but with them Gethsemane had to be an exception. Curiously, there is an instance in which John offends against his rule and makes repeated reference to Jesus' inner states. It occurs within the narrative of the raising of Lazarus. The evangelist records that when Lazarus' sister Martha left their home in Bethany to meet Jesus on the way , she said to him, "Lord, if you had been here, my brother would not have died," and seeing her and those with her weeping Jesus was "greatly disturbed in spirit and deeply moved" (John 11:33). Then, after inquiring where the body of Lazarus lay, and urged to "come and see," the evangelist writes that "Jesus began to weep" (John 11:36), an action not hidden from the audience which remarks, "See how he loved him!" With that remark the Fourth Evangelist has gone his co-evangelists one better, since they make no reference to a public reaction to Jesus' emotional response. Again, when Jesus approaches Lazarus' tomb, the evangelist writes that he was "again greatly disturbed" (John 11:38). The question is why these refences to Jesus' inner life are reserved for this particular occasion, and why exposed to public gaze. If our author is pursuing a specific goal with his work not haphazardly adding data concerning the sayings and doings of Jesus, then the Lazarus episode can be seen as a kind of water-shed toward which the Gospel narrative moves, and drives it toward its conclusion. In that case, the story of Lazarus and the data connected with it is a kind of prelude to the passion, an anticipation of Jesus' behavior and action yet to come. Clues to the possibility mount up, first in Jesus' reaction to the news of Lazarus' illness ("this illness does not lead to death; rather it is God's glory, so that the Son of God may be glorified through it" (John 11:4); the two-day delay in arriving at Bethany (John 11:6), and Jesus' joy at being absent at Lazarus' death ("so that you may believe" John 11:15). Glorification of the Son through death; a two-day delay, presumably ending in encounter (with Martha) on the third, and the call to the disciples to believe absent the evidence of the eyes, are all suggestive of an omen of the Passion. In the chapter that follows the Lazarus narrative retains the impetus. In midst of recoding the triumphal entry, the evangelist writes that the crowd that had been with Jesus when he raised Lazarus went out to meet him, after which he declared that his "hour" had come: "Now," Jesus adds, "my soul is troubled. And what should I say—'Father, save me from this hour'? No, it is for this reason that I have come to this hour. Father, glorify your name" (John 12:27–28). Again, the evangelist has outdone himself with a look-see into Jesus' psychic state.

PART FOUR

The Passion

The passion narratives of the Four Gospels are quite similar. Keeping to the sequence off Mark, the earliest account of the Passion, used by his co-evangelists as model or template, reference is made to important differences or additions as occur.

The Passover

The scene begins with the disciples' question regarding the site. In response Jesus tells two of them to go into the city, to encounter a man carrying a jar of water, and wherever he enters say to the owner, "The Teacher asks, 'Where is a guest room where I may eat the Passover with my disciples?'" The disciples are then to follow the owner to a large upper room, where they are to prepare the Passover (Mark 14:12–16). In Matthew the disciples are instructed to follow a "certain man," telling him that "the Teacher" will eat Passover at his house (Matthew 26:17–20). Did Matthew omit the matter of the jar because there was enough of the miraculous in Jesus' foreknowledge of the one the disciples were to follow? Luke repeats the narrative in Mark (Luke 22:7–13), whereas John merely mentions that before the festival of Passover Jesus, knowing the time of his departure was near, proceeded to wash his disciples' feet (John 13:1–11).

At least two features should be noted here. First, this will not be the only time Mark refers to that so-called "telepathic "sense or "second sight" exhibited by Jesus. In 2:8 he writes that Jesus knows the questions of his critics before they ask; in 12:15 he divines their hypocrisy; in 15:30–32 amid the press of the crowd he perceives power has gone from him, and asks, "Who touched my garments"? In 11:26 he has foreknowledge of the beast on which he will ride into Jerusalem. Later, Mark will record that the identity of his betrayer, the disciples' dereliction at the crucifixion, and Peter's denial are all known to him beforehand (14:17–18, 42; 14:27, 30). More than any "telepathic" sense or logical inference, Mark is pointing to an omniscience signaled in the amazement of onlookers or followers, or as here, to Jesus' disciples having "found everything as he had told them" (Mark 14:16).

The second feature is that Mark sets the date on which the disciples ere to inquire after the site of the Passover as the first day of unleavened bread (Mark 14:12): On Mark's own admission it is the day on which the Passover lamb was sacrificed (i.e., Thursday, the 14th of Nisan). Reckoning backward two days from this point the death-plot was originally hatched on Tuesday, the 12th of Nisan. Jesus then held the last supper with his disciples on Wednesday, the 13th and was crucified on the Thursday following. The passage in Mark 14:1-2 ("it was now two days before the Passover and the Feast of unleavened Bread. And the chief priests and the scribes were seeking how to arrest him by stealth, and kill him; for they said, "'Not during the Feast, lest there be a tumult of the people'") clearly contradicts the actual course of Mark's narrative. Most interpreters give looser interpretation to the time reference in 14:1-2, or contend that Judas' offer to betray Jesus stimulated his enemies to act in contrast to their original intent, that is, publicly and precipitously—an explanation which has no support in the text. Mark's co-evangelists set the day of Jesus' crucifixion on the day the Passover lamb was eaten, not slaughtered, thus on the 15th of Nisan, the date subsequently chosen by the early church, which, incidentally, hereticized the so-called "quartodecimaners" or "fourteeners" who celebrated Jesus' crucifixion on the 14th of Nisan in conjunction with the Jewish Passover.

Here, as elsewhere throughout the Gospel accounts the figure of Jesus as dispenser of bread has as its purpose the portrait of the Messiah at whose banquet many from east and west will come to sit (cf. Matthew 8:11; Luke 13:29), a figure which Judaism never furnished with the attributers of divinity. The three Synoptics record that while at table Jesus took bread, blessed it and gave it to the disciples and said, "This is my body." He then took the cup, and after giving thanks gave it to them and said, "This is my blood of the new covenant, which is poured out for many" (Mark 14:22-24). Matthew adds Jesus' summons to the disciples to eat, and drink, and appends to the word "this is my blood of the covenant" the phrase "which is poured for may for the forgiveness of sins, "(Matthew 26:29). In Luke Jesus' anticipation of what is to happen to him is heightened in the words "I have eagerly desired to eat this Passover with you before I suffer" 22:15-16). How it is that Mark and his co-evangelists could quote Jesus as saying "this is my body," or "this is my blood of the new covenant," while sitting whole and "in the flesh" at table with his disciples, assumes an existence in time and space but unchecked, uninhibited by it, and here at the Supper a prolepsis, an existence assumed beforehand only later to be actuated in full, signaled in the word that he'll not drink of the vine again till he drinks it new with them in his Father's kingdom (Mark 14:25; Matthew 36:29), or will never "eat" of it till it is fulfilled in the kingdom of God (Luke 22:16). When, in the Fourth Gospel, Jesus identifies himself as "the living bread that came down from heaven" (John 6:51), and his critics ask "How can this man give us his flesh to eat" (John 8:52), it is the same unimpeded existence to which the author refers.

Earlier, having miraculously arranged for his Passover, and at Bethany foretold that the ointment the anonymous woman had poured on his head was for his burial (Mark 14:3–9), followed by his prediction of the treachery of Judas (Mark 14:18, 42), now, leaving the upper room for the Mount of Olives Jesus predicts Peter's denial. Predicting the defection of all the disciples as fulfillment of a bitter passage in Zechariah in which God prepares to destroy the southern kingdom for its idolatry and false prophesy ("Awake, O sword . . . Strike the sheperd, that the sheep may be scattered," Zechariah 13:7), Peter responds that though all desert him, he will not. To this Jesus answers that "This very night before the cock crows twice, you will deny me three times. Peter denies the denial: "Though I must die with you, I will not deny you," to which all say Amen (Mark 14: 29–31). In all of this, whether it be the incident of the woman with the jar, Judas' treachery, the disciple's defection, or Peter's denial, Jesus makes no attempt to forestall what he knows, as if allowing himself to be borne aloft on the stream of events. According to Mark, however, he is not caught by stealth. Aware of what is ahead for him he retains a certain sovereignty over what takes place.

Gethsemane

While Luke interposes a dialogue between Jesus and the disciples over whether he lacked anything, and is summoned to procure a sword so as to fulfill the prophetic word ("And he was counted among the lawless," Isaiah 53:23), Mark and Matthew move directly from the prediction of Peter's denial at Passover to the scene in Gethsemane. There he gathers the disciples, and about to pray, takes with him only Peter, James and John. The remainder are abandoned. Just as at the Transfiguration only these three are let in on the solitary event (cf. Mark 9:2). Then Jesus reflects a humanity in stark contrast to the initial portrait of him as God-like: "I am deeply grieved, even to death" (Mark 14:3). The words are a quotation from the Psalter (42:6, 12, 43). But while the Psalmist uttered them in prayer to God, Jesus addresses them to the three and adds "unto death." Is death the friend which can free him from this agony? For the three, at least, the enigma of the agony is not solved. They merely receive the recurring summons to "remain here, and keep awake" (cf. Mark 14:34, 37, 38). Jesus goes deeper into the garden, ascending the holy of Holies alone. His companions remain before the curtain. This is the "hour" and this the place of that service required of him. He falls to the earth, forehead and knee touching the ground. He prays. Mark first records the substance of the prayer ("He threw himself on the ground and prayed that, if it were possible, the hour might pass from him, (v. 35), then cites the direct quote, as though the hearer-reader had first to be prepared before the sacred winds themselves could be recorded. Jesus' prayer opens with a bilingual address common to the later Gentile community—"Abba, Father" (v. 36; cf. Romans 8:16). The prayer continues with an affirmation of the power of God—"all things are possible to thee" (v. 36). This power is able to avert not only what is humanly inescapable, but what is inescapable from the point of view of God. Then Jesus pleads, "remove this cup from me" whose cup? As the "hour" is God's, so is the cup." So it is not dark fate that hangs over him. The "cup" is the inescapable burden that God lays on him and him alone. Silence all around. Then come the words, "Yet not what I will, but what thou wilt." Nowhere else in the Gospels is the will of God set over against another's so directly and immediately. Jesus more than any other can claim a peculiar right to speak of his own will, bows to one higher. At this point some witnesses to Luke's Gospel record that following his prayer an angel appeared to Jesus, giving him strength, that in his anguish he prayed more earnestly, and that his sweat became like drops of blood, falling on he ground. Luke 22:43-44. Evidence of the secondary nature of these verses is the fact that they also appear after Matthew 26:39.[1] The earliest witnesses to these verses are early church fathers involved in the dispute over Jesus' humanity.

The Fourth Gospel does not reproduce the Gethsemane scene as appears in Mark, Mathew, and Luke. Following the washing of the disciples' feet at Passover, there is a lengthy discourse in which Jesus predicts the person of his betrayer, discourses on the new commandment, foretells Peter's denial; promises the coming of the Holy Spirit, speaks of him self as the "true vine," then of the world's hatred, of peace for the disciples and prays for them. There are reminescences of the Gethsemane scene in the extended discourse where Jesus says "Now my soul is troubled, and what should I say—Father, save me from this hour'? No, it is for this reason that I have come to this hour. Father, glorify your name," followed by a voice from heaven: "I have glorified it, and I will glorify it again" (John 12: 26-28). Again, toward the end of the discourse Jesus looks up to heaven and says, "Father, the hour has come; glorify your Son so that the Son may glorify you (John 17:1). And again, in the garden, where Peter attacks the high priest's servant, Jesus says to him, "Put your sword back into its sheath. Am I not to drink the cup that the Father has given me?" (John 18:10). Clearly, John has avoided painting the scene, altering the plea-name (Mount of Olives) in such dark colors as his co-evangelists. He reduces the aspect of Jesus' agony to a rhetorical question and answer ("what should I say, 'Father save me . . . ?' No, it is for this reason that I have come . . . "). Why this variation? Did John refuse to use the Old Testament to give shape to Jesus in this scene because it contradicted his portrait of Jesus as in control, not swept on the wave of events as in Mark, Matthew, and Luke? Mark might have warmed to that feature, but not without accenting the other facet of the prism—Jesus' humanity.

---

1. Cf. Metzger, Bruce M. *The Text of the New Testament: Its Transmission, Corruption, and Restoration* (Oxford University Press: 2005), 28.

Three times Jesus returns from prayer to find the three asleep. After the first, he summons them to "keep awake and pray that you may not come into the time of trial." (Mark 14:38). The summons is one more addition to those threading throughout Mark 13–15 (cf. 13:34, 33, 35, 37; 14:34, 37, 38; cf. also the admonitions to take heed in 13:5, 8, 23, 33). Earlier, in his apocalyptic discourse, Jesus had promised the Spirit "at that time" (Mark 13:11), had warned against misinterpreting the signs (Mark 13:3 vs. 5–8; 21–23,) and promised that the tribulations of the elect would end in his appearing and their victory (vs. 13–20, 35–38). Could that summons to keep awake against "that time" before he appears spring from a hope that in the end that the "cup" might pass from him, a hope that fired him to match this will against the Father's? And, that he reads off from those sleeping disciples the answer to his prayer, the summons to surrender his hope? According to Albert Schweitzer, Jesus, after initially unsuccessful attempts, ultimately resolves upon his death to bring in the Kingdom of God. The event never occurs, hence his cry of dereliction: "My God, my God, why have you forsaken me?" (Mark 14:34).[2] But if it is legitimate to see a connection between the disciples' sleeping and Jesus' prayer—three times he turns back to the three, after praying three times (Mark 14:37, 40, 41). At the first encounter he says to Peter, "Simon, are you asleep? Could you not keep awake one hour?" (Mark 14:37). The second time, Mark writes, the disciples' eyes were heavy; and they did not know what to say to him" (Mark 14:40). Finally, the third time he finds them still sleeping, and says, "Enough! The hour has come" (Mark 14:41). What if in those sleeping disciples Jesus has already gotten the answer to his prayer? Then that cry of dereliction is to be explained in a vastly different way. Then there is nothing of defeat in that cry. It rather results from what Jesus resolved to do, that is, to empty the cup at the Father's will. And, with that Father hidden. It is in obedience to that hidden God and his will that spells the erasure of what he had once hoped for and elicits the cry. It is the Father and what he wills that brings him agony. What lends support to this view is that it is immediately after encountering the three a third time that he says, "Enough. The hour has come; the Son of Man is

---

2. "The Baptist appears and cries: "Repent, for the Kingdom of Heaven is at hand." Soon after that comes Jesus, and in the knowledge that He is the coming Son of Man lays hold of the wheel of the world to set it moving on that last revolution which is to bring all ordinary history to a close. It refuses to turn, and He throws Himself upon it. Then it does turn; and crushes Him. Instead of bringing in the eschatological conditions, He has destroyed them. The wheel rolls onward, and the mangled body of the one immeasurably great Man, who was strong enough to think of Himself as the spiritual ruler of mankind and to bend history to His purpose, is hanging upon it still. That is his victory and this is his reign." Schweitzer, Albert. *The Quest of the Historical Jesus:*, Translated by W. Montgomery (A.&C. Black, 1910), 370-371.

betrayed into the hands of sinners. Get up, let us be going. My betrayer is at hand" (Mark 14:41–42). In the Greek, Mark will refer seven times to Judas' betrayal (Mark 14: 10, 11, 18, 21, 41, 42, 44), and fourteen times of Jesus' being "delivered up" (Mark 8:31; 9:31; 10:33; 14:10, 11, 18, 21, 41, 42, 44). There is no dialogue between Father and Son over glorification, as in John 12; no angel visitant as in Luke 22. Between Jesus' prayer and his summons, "Let us be going," only the snoring disciples. While Jesus is talking, Judas: "one of the twelve," arrives with a curiously armed crowd from the chief priests, scribes, and elders. Evidently the synoptics believed their readers needed to be reminded that Judas, despite having already been liberally identified, belonged to the inner circle, rendering his act the more heinous.

> With each mouth—he used it like a grinder—With gnashing teeth, he tore to bits a sinner, So that he brought much pain to three at once. The forward sinner found that biting nothing. When matched against the clawing, for at times. His back was stripped completely of hide. "That soul up there who has to suffer most," My master said: "Judas Iscariot—His head inside, he jerks his legs without."[3]

Judas had arranged with the authorities that they were to apprehend the one he should kiss. Mark simply states that the betrayer came up to Jesus, said "Rabbi," kissed him, and the crowd laid hands on him and arrested him (Mark 14:45–46). In Matthew's account, Judas encounters Jesus and says, "greetings, Rabbi!" to which Jesus replies, "Friend, do what you have here to do" Matthew 26:49–50). In Luke, the suggestion of predetermination in Matthew's account ("do what you have to do") is eliminated, and Jesus merely says, "Judas, Is it with a kiss that you are betraying the Son of Man?" (Luke 22:48). In John's account the dialogue between Jesus and Judas is entirely eliminated. Judas brings a detachment of soldiers with police from the chief priests and Pharisees, equipped with lanterns, torches and weapons. When Jesus asks whom they are after, they answer "Jesus of Nazareth," and at Jesus' reply, "I am he," step back and fall to the ground. Again Jesus asks "Who are you looking for?" and at their answer, "Jesus of Nazareth," he identifies himself once more, and orders his captors to let the disciples go, in fulfillment of his own word ("And this is the will of him who sent me, that I should lose nothing of all that he has given me . . . John 6:39). In the Fourth Gospel, whatever cold possibly detract from Jesus' control of the situation is eliminated or substitution made to enhance that aspect.

3. The Divine Comedy of Dante Alighieri, InfernoA Verse Translation with an Introduction by Allen Mndelbaum (The Quality Paperback Book Club Edition, Reprinted by Perrmission of Bantam Books, 1980), Canto XXXIV, p.296.

Did Jesus need betraying? Hadn't he taught openly in the Temple at Jerusalem, and within earshot of his opponents and adversaries? In view of that ease of identification, what need was there of Judas? Even if some of the soldiers and police could not recognize Jesus, certainly those who led them knew him. The question remains. But what if, according to the biblical writers, there is no "need" of Judas to fulfill the word of his betrayal, that he is rather the creature of that word. Then it is because of the word that there had to be a Judas to betray. The word in Matthew ("do what you have to do") and in John ("I did not lose a single one of those whom you gave me") give the clue to a reversal of the usual move from the event that fulfills the word, to the word that gives birth to the event. Then no "need" of Judas to fulfill a word, but rather need of a word to beget a Judas. And if this move should underlie all said and done in the context of the passion, then the entire drama deserves to be titled: "The lamb slain from the foundation of the world" (Revelation 13:8).

In the melee, according to the Synoptics, an unnamed figure draws his sword and stakes off the ear of the high priests' slave (Mark 14:47; Matthew 26:51; Luke 22:50). Luke prefaces his report of the act with the disciples' query whether they should strike with the sword, and both Luke and John record that it was the slaves' right ear, John, additionally naming both the assailant and his victim, Peter and Malchus. In Matthew's account, Jesus tells the unnamed actor to put his sword back into its place, that all who take the sword will perish by it, and that if he willed it he cold summon twelve legions to his aid (Matthew 26:52–53). In Luke Jesus says, "No more of this! Touches the slaves' ear and heals him (Luke 22:51). In John Jesus to Peter, "Put your sword back into its sheath. Am I not to drink the cup that the Father has given me?" (John 18:11). As far as Luke is concerned, the disciples or Peter had construed Jesus' earlier order to procure swords as a summons to engage in battle rather than to fulfill the prophetic word with merely being weaponed ("For I tell you, this scripture must be fulfilled in me, 'And he was counted among the lawless,'" Luke 22:37, the "scripture Isaiah" 53:12). It is one more instance of the move from event to its corroboration by the word, to the word as parent of the event.

At this point Mark interposes that curious reference to a young man who was following Jesus, wearing nothing but a linen cloth, escaping his captors and leaving the cloth behind (Mark 14:51–52). The reference has led to a congeries of interpretations, some taking it to be the author's autobiographical sketch. There may be nothing unusual about the reference to the escapee's age—he was a young man—but the reference to his being naked minus the linen cloth suggest a fellow improperly attired, at least by the standards of the day. The reference to his clothing—linen, smooth, non-elastic, easily come apart when repeatedly folded it the same place—suggests membership in a lower economic class. Young, a "follower," with barely the shirt on his back, fleeing for his life—can be said of the disciples, to sum up what occurred with the disciples following the encounter at Gethsemane. Mark may have resorted to metaphor. His co-evangelists are entirely silent on the matter.

Jesus before the High Priest

In the next scene, Jesus is taken to the high priest, Joseph Caiaphas, appointed in AD 18 by Valerius Grattus, the Roman prefect who preceded Pontius Pilate. Caiaphas was the son-in-law of Annas (also called Ananus). Deposed along with Pilate by Vitellius, governor of Syria, he was, amazingly, succeeded in office by five sons. While Mark writes simply of Jesus being taken where the high priest, chief priests, elders, and scribes were assembled, Matthew and Luke write that the gathering took place in the high priest's house (Mark 14:53; Matthew 26:53; Luke 22:54). According to John, it was first to Anna then to his son-in-law Caiaphas that the mob led Jesus (John 18:13–14). Nothing is said of a meeting in the temple where the seventy-one members of the Sanhedrin sat in a half circle, only an assembly likely to swamp the high priest's residence. Was it a rump session before which Jesus as arraigned, and in the dead of night?

Peter's Denial

While Mark and Matthew are content to relate Jesus' prediction of Peter's denial at the Supper, Luke and John interrupt the flow of events to give a detailed account of it. Following at a distance to witness the courtyard, Peter is accosted by a servant girl who announces that "This man also was with him." But he denied it and said, "Woman, I do not know him." A bit later, another came up to him and said, "You also are one of them." And again Peter denied: "Man, I am not!" An hour later insisted that "Surely this man also was with him; for he is a Galilean." Once again Peter said, "Man, I do not know what you are talking about!" And at that moment the cock crowed (Luke 22:60). In John's account an unidentified "they" first ask if Peter is one of "his" disciples. The next questioner is identified as the slave of the high priest, a relative of the man Peter attacked. The fourth evangelist makes no mention of a third query, only that the cock crowed (John 18:25–27). With a direct quote, Luke reminds his readers of Jesus' prediction: "Before the cock crows today, you will deny me three times," following which Peter "went out and wept bitterly" (Luke 22:61–62). Whether it is Jesus' word or that of the scripture needing fulfillment, the aura of inevitability is unabated. In this instance, Peter is caught in a web of circumstance, so he weeps. For himself, for Jesus, for the circumstance?

Jesus before the Council

In Mark and Matthew a dialogue follows between the high priest, Jesus, and the witnesses. The witnesses accuse Jesus of boasting he would destroy the temple and build another in three days. At this point Mark writes that their testimony did not agree. How did that happen? Did one witness say "in two days" and the other "in three"? (Mark 14:59). The high priest, likewise unable to negotiate the metaphor ("But he was speaking of the temple of his body," John 2:22), says "Have you no answer?" Here, before stating that the high priest asks Jesus if he is the Messiah, Son of God—Mark curiously, but in typical Jewish fashion, avoids referring to "God" outright and translates "Son of the Blessed" (Mark 14:61—Matthew affixes to the high priest's question the command: "I put you under oath before the living God, tell us. . .." (Matthew 26:63).[1] Jesus replies: "You have said so," adding that he will see the Son of Man coming on the clouds of heaven, at which the high priest tears his clothes over the alleged blasphemy, asks for a verdict, to which the crowd answers that he is worthy of death, while spitting in Jesus' face, striking and slapping him, and yelling "prophesy!" (Mark 14:53-65). It is clear that here Jesus is not speaking of two persons. His reply, that he is the Messiah, Son of God tethered to the declaration that "you will see the Son of Man seated at the right hand of Power. . ." (Mark 14:62), demands identifying "Son of Man" with "Messiah" and "Son of God" in the same breath. Whether nor not we are to supply the title "Son of God" with the content later centuries of faith and confession furnished it—equality with God in essence— or must rather view it synonymous with "Messiah"—Jesus lays claim to both before the high priest and his

---

1. The KJV translation: "I adjure you by the living God" gives the high priest's summons a heftier aspect.

court charging that Jesus has committed blasphemy, an affront to God (Numbers 15:30), in Jewish law carrying the death penalty (Leviticus 24:16), the high priest has reinforced the synonymity. At this point Mark and Matthew record the event of Peter's denial.

Jesus before Pilate and Judas' Death

Mark writes that as soon as it was morning the chief priests, scribes and elders, having held council, led Jesus away to the Roman procreator, Pontius Pilate. To conquered countries that posed a special threat to the empire a praocurator was assigned who was directly responsible to the emperor. Such was the situation in Israel, constantly in turmoil. Pilate served as procurator for about ten years, from AD 26/27 to 36/37, was ultimately discharged, sent to Rome, and according to one reading exiled to North Africa where he committed sicide.

After noting Jesus' appearance before Pirate, in chapter 27:3–10, Matthew digresses to record the suicide of Judas. Seeing that Jesus was condemned—an action yet to occur—Judas "repented," brought back the thirty pieces of silver earned for his betrayal, said "I have sinned by betraying innocent blood."[1] At this members of the council with a mendacity to take the breath away deny any responsibility in the affair, say "What is that to us? See to it yourself." Then Judas, throwing down the silver pieces in the temple, went out and hanged himself. The chief priests, noting that "blood money" could not be put into the treasury, bought a parcel of land designed for foreigners, "to this day," adds Matthew, "called the Field of Blood." Thus, according to this author, fulfilling the prophecy of Jeremiah, at which point Matthew resumes the hearing before Pilate. The Acts of the Apostles contains an alternate version of Judas' end. Gathered with the disciples in the upper room at Jerusalem, Peter indicates the need for a replacement of Judas, stating that the betrayer had "acquired a field with the reward of his wickedness; and falling headlong burst open in the middle and all his bowls gushed out" (Acts 1:18). Interpreters have been preoccupied with

---

[1] Whereas Mathew writes that Judas betrayed Jesus for thirty pieces of silver, Luke and John write that he was possessed by Satan (Luke 22–23 and John 13:27).

discovering the motive for Judas' betrayal. Obviously, the Gospel writers were not. What preoccupied them was its relation to the prophetic word. Judas, just as the other actors in this drama, would not act independently of the word that hung over him. That word could be the word of a prophet:

> they took the thirty pieces of silver, the price of the one whom a price had been set, on whom some of the people of Israel had set a price, and they gave them for the potter's field, as the Lord commanded me.

or of a word of Jesus himself. It would be left to future generations to wrangle over whether this perspective reduces the actors involved to persons devoid of will and responsibility.

The procurator asks Jesus, "Are you the King of the Jews?" Jesus answers, "You say so." Accused of multiple crimes, Pilate asks again "Have you no answer? See how many charges they bring against you." To Pilate's amazement, Jesus makes no answer (Mark 15:1–5).

Jesus or Barbabas

Now Mark, Matthew, and John introduce a scene unable to be verified in Roman or Jewish practice. They write of a custom attached to Passover of the Roman governor's commuting the sentence of a prisoner by public acclamation (Mark 15:6; Matthew 27:15; John 18:49). In this scene the crowd gathers to ask Pilate to act according to the custom. The prefect or governor gives the crowd a choice between Jesus and Barabbas (in the Aramaic "son of the 'father"), described by Matthew as "a notorious prisoner, by Mark and Luke as involved in a riot and murder. John refers to Barabbas as a bandit, a term used to indicate a revolutionary. The governor asks: "Do you want me to release for you the King of the Jews?" The chief priests stir up the crowd to demand the release of Barabbas. Pilate asks again: What do you wish me to do with the man you call the King of the Jews?" The crowd shouts back: "Crucify him!" Pilate asks yet again: "Why, what evil has he done?" The crowd shouts all the more: "Crucify him!" The scene concludes with the release of Barabbas, the flogging Jesus, and handing him over to be crucified (Mark 15:6–15; cf. Matthew 27:15–23; John 23:1–5).

According to Matthew, Pilate first asks "Whom do you want me to release for you, Jesus Barabbas or Jesus who is called the Messiah?" and with Mark records that it was out of jealousy that they had handed him over. Finally, flowing Pilate's hand-washing ceremony, he declares he is innocent of Jesus' blood, says, "See to it yourselves," to which the people respond, his blood be upon us and on our children!" (Matthew 27:6–26).

In the Fourth Gospel the exchanges between Pilate and the crowd, and between Pilot and Jesus, are more extensive. John writes that those who took Jesus from Caiaphas to Pilate did not enter the prefect's headquarters for fear of defilement, thus unable to eat the Passover. Pilate must go out to them. When he inquires about the charge against Jesús, the leaders respond that if "this man" were not a criminal, they would not have handed him over. To Pilate's word, "Take him yourselves, and judge him according to your law," Jesus' accusers reply that they are not permitted to levy the death sentence, thus, according to John, indicating what kind of death Jesus was to die. Pilate, returning to his headquarters summons Jesus and asks if he were King of the Jews, to which Jesus replies, "Do you ask this on your own, or did others tell you about me?" Pilate counters that he is not a Jew, that Jesus' own nation and the chief priests handed him over. Jesus, then, in a nonsequitur declares that his kingdom is not of this world, that if it were his followers would fight to rescue him. Pilate then asks, "So you are a king?" Jesus answers that Pilate agrees, that for this he was born, and came into the world, to satisfy the truth, that everyone who belongs to the truth hears his voice. To this Pilate replies: "What is truth?" The response is cynical, light years from someone celebrated in the Upanishads. Pilate then leaves his headquarters, goes out to the Jews, states that he finds no case against Jesus, rears to the Passover custom of prisoner release, asks whom the crowd wants released, the bandit Barabbas or Jesus, to which they answer, "Not this man, but Barabbas!" (John 18:28–40).

Commentators are quick to describe the scene as the invention of Mark with whom the others fell in step. Could it be that he has constructed a parable in order to set the true Messiah off in bold relief? And is it credible that Pontius Pilate, backed by Rome's might, could have been cowed by an unarmed crowd into releasing a prisoner condemned to death? The secretion that Yeshua bar Abbas and Yeshua the Messiah are one and the same, and the urging to choose between them a fiction, requires a Gulliver's leap, as does the notion that Jesus may have been the leader of a non-violent resistance to Pilate's setting up Roman eagles on the temple mount.[1] Lack of documentation for an event need not be read as the event's never having occurred. While it is true that Pilate's prefecture was notorious for roiling the Jews, this may have been an instance in which the bureaucrat turned feckless, decided to placate his subjects, or, being a superstitious fellow, on the advice of his wife—"Have nothing to do to do with that innocent man, for today I have suffered a great deal because of a dream about him" (Matthew 27:19)—avoided implication in the affair with histrionics, washing his hands. When Jesus was crucified Pilate had run out almost half his time in office, longer than most, and, like many of his ilk, could on occasion, counter a criminal incompetence leading to murder,[2] and finally ending in deposition, with a show of what he thought to be mercy.

1. Cf. the options offered in the Wikipedia article on Barabbas titled "Modern Views." https://en.wikipedia.org/wikindex.php?title=Barabbas&oldid=889726837#Modern_views.

2. Cf. Luke 13:1 which reports that some who were hearing Jesus formed him of

In midst of his detailing Jesus' trial before Pilate, Luke introduces a scene omitted by or unknown to his co-evangelists. After responding to the priests' and crowd's charges that he finds no basis of an accusation against Jesus, the crowd replies that "He stirs up the people by teaching thro throughout all Judea, from where he began even to this place" (Luke 23:4-5). Hearing that Jesus was under the jurisdiction of Herod Antipas, Pilate sends Jesus off to the tetrarch. In Jerusalem at the time, Herod is excited to see Jesus and ask him to perform a sign questioning Jesus at length but without getting an answer. Herod and his soldiers together with the priests and scribes proceed to mock Jesus, dress him up in finery and send him back to Pilate. From that day, writes Luke, the hostility of the two turned to mutual admiration. The scene gives further evidence of an occasional interruption of the Roman prefect's usual behavior.

Pilate's massacre of Galilean pilgrims in Jerusalem. The reference yields no data, though the action coheres with Pilate's character.

Jesus Flogged

All four Gospel writers continue their narrative with Pilate's release of Barabbas and handing Jesus over to be crucified, but not before having him flogged (Mark 15:15; Matthew 27:26; Luke 22:17; John 19:1). The verb used is *phragello*, from which the same-sounding English term derives. In the Roman empire, the practice of flogging had been in use since the second century BC and administered to non-citizens. Often used with strips of metal or bone, it easily caused trauma, in many cases severe pain and shock from loss of blood. The victim was stripped naked and bound to a low or upright pillar. Two, four or six lictors (officers attending the magistrates, bearing the *fasces* and executing offenders) aimed blows at the shoulders down to the soles of the feet, the number of blows left to those administering the punishment, and who were normally expected to leave the victim alive. Ancient authors refer to the one scourging as "half death." In Luke's version Pilate intends to release Jesus after having him flogged, but because the voices of those who demanded that Jesus be crucified prevailed, gave verdict that the crowd's demand should be granted (Luke 22:22–24). Apparently, according to Luke, Pilate believed the sight of the scourged Jesus would move the mob to pity and end in his release. It did not; Pilate let judgment be carried out. With all the handwashing, the interrogating of Jesus leading to the conviction of his innocence, with his refusal actively to participate in the execution, the flogging excepted, the Roman prefect ended with a crowd-pleaser.

The Soldiers Mock

Following the flogging, the soldiers lead Jesus to Pilate's headquarters, clothed him in purple, plait a crown of thorns and put it on his head. Matthew adds to the royal mockery that the soldiers put a reed in his right hand, as though it were scepter, signifying imperial power (Matthew 27:29) Then the prefect's troop begin to salute him, chorusing "Hail, King of the Jews!" striking him on the head, sitting on him and kneeling in homage to him. The similarity between Mark's description of the soldiers' mockery in 15:16–20 and the Isaiah Servant's giving his back to the smites, his cheeks to those who pulled out the beard, his face to shame and spitting (Isaiah 50: 6f.; cf. Isaiah 53:5) can hardly be coincidence. The charade ends with their stripping him of the robe, putting his own clothes on him and leading him away (Mark 15:16–20; Matthew 27:24–26). All three Synoptists contain the narrative of Simon of Cyrene come in from the country and forced to carry Jesus' cross (Mark 15:21; Matthew 27:32; Luke 23:26), Mark adding the reference to Simon's sons, Alexander and Rufus, conceivably members of his community. Did the evangelist by this reference intend to symbolize the requirement of faith? Again, Luke adds to the narrative the episode of the women along the way who beat their breasts and wail for Jesus, only to hear him warn of the imminent end: "Then they will begin to say to the mountains, 'Fall on us,' and to the hills, 'Cover us,'" prefaced with a blessing on those without child in those days—a mini-reprise of the extended apocalyptic discourse in Mark 23 (Luke 22:29–31). There is nothing of this narrative in fourth Gospel, according to which Jesus carries his own cross (John 19:17).

The Crucifixion of Jesus

According to Mark and Mathew, Jesus is led to his crucifixion by a Roman cohort. Luke is less precise, leaving it to the reader to infer the subject from the verb (Pilate handed Jesus over "as they wished. . ...As they led him away" (Luke 22:25, 26). All four evangelists identify the site of execution as "the skull," or as in the Hebrew, Golgotha. There he is nailed between two thieves or bandits, one on either side. At this point, occurs the passage in Luke recounting Jesus' first word from the cross: "Father, forgive them; for they do not know what they are doing" (Luke 23:34). It is not certain that his passage belongs to the original text. It is thus left to the student by way of the Greek critical apparatus to decide whether or not to include it. The NRSV translators have bracketed it in the text, and to that extent included it. Mark and Matthew write that on the cross Jesus was offered wine mixed with myrrh or gall (Luke and John simply writes wine), but that he refused to drink it. John writes that "when Jesus knew that all was now finished, he said (in order to fulfill the scripture), 'I am thirsty.'"[1] At which point the soldiers, presumably, put a sponge full of sour wine on a branch of hyssop and had it to his mouth. Then, John continues, when he had received the wine, he said, "It is finished," and gave up his spirit (John 18:28–30). Once more, and here in John, scripture is cited as destiny, as the efficient cause of the action described. Immediately prior to this event, John cites another word of Jesus from the cross, this time to his mother, standing near the cross with her sister, the wife of Cleopas, with Mary Magdalene and the "beloved disciple," that unnamed figure referred to six times in the Fourth Gospel and there alone.[2] Candidates for that title range from John

---

1. Cf. Psalm 69:21: "They gave me poison for food, and for my thirst they gave me vinegar to drink."

2. John 13:232, 25; 19:26, 27 20:2, and 21:20

the apostle to Lazarus to James the brother of Jesus, to Mary Magdalene, cited in the Gnostic *Gospel of Mary* as most beloved by Jesus, as well as in the Gnostic *Gospel of Philip*. To his mother Jesus says, "Woman, here is your son," then to the disciple, "Here is your mother," following which, John adds, the disciple took her to his own home (John 19:25b-27).

According to Mark, it was nine in the morning when Jesus was crucified.[3] Over his head read the charge against him: "The king of the Jews," or, as Matthew has it, "This is Jesus, The King of the Jews" (Matthew 27:38), or as Luke: This is the King of the Jews" (Luke 23:38). According to John the inscription in Hebrew, Latin, and Greek read: "Jesus of Nazareth, the King of the Jews." To the chief priests' objection to the simple declarative and their insistence that the inscription should read "This man said, I am King of the Jews," Pilate, in one more attempt at a show independence, said "What I have written I have written" (John 19:22).

---

3. As note above, on Thursday, the 14th of Nisan, while John and the remainder of the Gospel writers fix the date at Friday, the "Day of Preparation," on when the Passover lamb was slaughtered. Cf. John 19:31.Throughout his passion narrative, Mark takes special note of the da or hour of the day (cf. 14:1, 1, 12, 17, 30; 15: 1, 25, 33, 34, 42; 16:1, 2).

Jesus between Two Thieves

Of Isaiah's Servant it is written that he was "numbered with the transgressors" (Isaiah 53:12), and Mark records that with Jesus "they crucified two robbers, one on his right and the other on his left" (15:27). The Greek translations of Lamentations 2:15 ("they hiss and wag their heads") and Psalm 2:7 ("they make mouths at me, they wag their heads"); of Psalm 22:6 ("scorned by men, and despised by the people"); Psalm 69:9 ("the insults of those who insult thee have fallen on me"), and of Psalm 19:25 ("I am an object of scorn to my accusers,") contain the same barbs as appear in Mark 15:29: "Those who passed by derided him, wagging their heads," and in 15:32: "Those who were crucified with him also reviled him."

In Luke's account one of the bandits kept deriding Jesus, saying, "Are you not the Messiah? Save yourself and us!" The other criminal rebuked him and said "Do you not fear God, since you are under the same sentence of condemnation?" Acknowledging that he and the other thief had been condemned justly, and that "this man has done nothing wrong," he turns to Jesus and says, "Jesus, remember me when you come into your kingdom," to which Jesus replies, "Truly I tell you, today you will be with me in Paradise" (Luke 23:39–43). Used by Jesus alone, the prefix paraphrase ("Truly I tell you") frequently appears to accent the importance of what is to follow. As appears above, modern translators insert a comma after the prefix and before the rest of the sentence. Though grammatically allowable, connecting the adverb ("today") with the preceeding verb, so as to make the sentence read, "Truly I tell you today, etc.," assumes a delay in the penitent thief's arrival in paradise. The Fourth Evangelist merely notes that with Jesus two others were crucified, one on either side, with Jesus inbetween (John 19:18).

The Death of Jesus

Mark writes that when it was noon darkness covered the whole land, and at at three o'clock Jesus cried out with a loud voice, "Eloi, Eloi, lama sabachthani?' only to hear his prayer misunderstood ("Behold, he is calling Elijah" Mark 15: 34–35). In Mark, Jesus' cry is a mixture of Aramaic and Hebrew, and in Matthew is corrected according to the language of the temple, in the Hebrew. Jesus' cry repeats the lament of the Psalmist in Psalm 22. Perhaps Mark even intends his audience to hear behind Jesus' last and final shout (Mark 15:37) such a word as Psalm 31:22 "You heard my supplications when I cried out to you for help"). Little wonder his early readers described Mark's Gospel as accenting the spirit of prophecy, symbolized by the eagle, the fourth living creature in Revelation (4:7).

These may be only peripheral matters. Some might say that Jesus was in hell, since to be forsaken by God is to be in hell. Luther wrote that Christians have a similar experience, that to affirm God's will and be free of self may mean to endure hell. But what is happening to Jesus here is far from whatever may happen to a Psalmist or a Christian. For one thing, the Bible is clear as crystal that whatever hell is, or wherever it is, it is not out of God's reach. In the parable of the rich man and Lazarus, not even Abraham is beyond the cry of that man in torment. What is happening to Jesus, and leagues beyond understanding, is a separation from God beyond God's reach. He is in a state in which there is no Father, no God, no place where God will penetrate. Hence it makes little sense to say that Jesus is taking humankind's place here, for it is a place where humankind will never be. There is a rupture occurring in the Godhead; Father and Son are being torn apart in this event. Mark writes that those standing by the cross thought Jesus was calling Elijah, evidently thrown off by that mix of Aramaic and Hebrew. But whatever they may have thought, none was more "in on" the event than they. And as for that centurion who, after seeing how Jesus died said, "Truly this man was God's Son," witnessing to what he saw, does not mean he understood what was occurring. Nor have the theologians understood it any better. One by one they write that all this was happening to Jesus' human nature. But if Jesus is true God and true Man, attempting to split those two natures and leave to the one what does not belong to the other makes little sense. What is behind this cry of Jesus to the Father is unfathomable. And for what reason this fissure in God? Paul writes that Jesus was handed over to death for our trespasses. Can humanity's sin have been so profound that it caused this rupture in God? Some object to the idea of Jesus' death as an atonement for sin, arguing that it belongs to an outmoded theology, a theology shaped in commercial terms, terms of debt and payment, of a *quid pro quo*. But how will abandoning that idea help? One would still be left with an event that did not happen because God wanted to prove something to himself, to see if putting his hand to the stove would hurt. The event took place out of love for the human race. What religion or faith an equal such a thought, that the very God himself endured in himself such division, and for love of the world he created? Mark and Matthew write that at the moment Jesus breathed his last the veil of the temple was torn in two, from top to bottom. Then, Mark writes, when the centurion facing the cross saw that Jesus expired "in this way" (English translation of the Greek *houtoos*) he said: "Truly, this man was God's Son" (Mark 15:39), a cry that complements the confession of Peter in 8:29. But perhaps even with Mark that title "God's Son" does not carry the payload usually given it in the Nicene Creed: "Very God of very God, begotten, not made, being of one substance with the Father, by whom all things were made." Nonetheless, with an artistry that renders each successive title loftier and grander than the one preceding. The scoffers had said, "Let the Christ, the King of Israel, come down now from the cross" (Mark 15:32), and here he climaxes his passion story with the confession of the centurion who saw him "breathe his last" (Mark 15:39). In Matthew's account, along with the rending of the temple veil the earth shook, rocks were split, tombs were opened, and bodies of the "saints" were raised. Following the resurrection, they emerged from their tombs, entered the Holy City, and appeared to many (Matthew 27:51–53). At least two things are clear from this account, first, that by these incidents Matthew intended to accent the central importance of Jesus' death, and second, by reporting the appearance of the dead following Jesus' resurrection, it did not allow that event to anticipate it. Matthew writes that the centurion and those who were with him, keeping watch, saw the earthquake and what took place they were terrified and said "Truly this man was God's Son" (Matthew 27:54). In Luke's version , following the tearing of the temple veil Jesus cried with a loud voice, "Father, into your hands I commend my spirit," and breathed his last.

Luke then adds that when the centurion saw what had occurred he praised God and said, "Certainly this man was innocent" (Luke 22:36–37). There is nothing of this feature in the Fourth Gospel which reports that to prevent the hanging of bodies during the Sabbath, the Jews asked that the legs of the crucified be broken. Accordingly, the legs of the two criminals were broken, but on seeing that Jesus had already died, his side was pierced, out of which flowed blood and water. The evangelist adds that "he who sw this has testified so that you also may believe. His testimony is true, and he knows that he tells the truth," adding that these things occurred that the scriptural word might be fulfilled, that "none of his bones shall be broken," and again, that "they will look on the one whom they have pierced (John 19:31–37).[1] And once again the scriptural word is elevated to the status of efficient cause: the events do not corroborate the word but are created by it.

---

1. The scripture references are to Exodus 12:46 Numbers 9:12; Psalm 34:20, and Psalm 22:16; Zechariah 12:10.

The Burial of Jesus

Following his reference to the women who had supported Jesus while he was in Galilee, and now were standing at a distance, Mark writes that the evening on the Day of Preparation, Joseph of Arimathea went to Pilate and asked for the body of Jesus.[1] Amazed to hear Jesus was already dead, Pilate summoned a centurion to determine if it were so (a feature appearing neither in Matthew nor Luke), and on learning Jesus was dead released his body to Joseph. Joseph then wrapped the body in a linen cloth and placed it in a tomb hewn of a rock and rolled a stone against the door. Mary Magdalene and Mary the mother of Jesus saw where the body was laid (Mark 15:33–47). Matthew adds that Joseph was a disciple of Jesus, and that the tomb was new and belonged to him, with Mary Magdalene "and the other Mary" sitting opposite the tomb. In Matthew's account there is nothing of Pilate's amazement at Jesus' early death, only that Pilate ordered the body to be given to Joseph. The next day, the day after the Day of Preparation, writes Matthew, the chief priests and Pharisees went to Pilate, said that while "the imposter" was alive he said he would rise again after three days so the tomb should be secured till the third day, lest his disciples ask him why and tell the people he was risen from the dead. Evidently, the clerics and their sometime colleagues, the Pharisees, had tipped to the fact that when accused of stating that after its destruction he would rebuild the temple in three days, Jesus meant the temple of his body, not the Jerusalem sanctuary (Mark 14:54). In response to the chief priests' and Pharisees' request Pilate said they had a guard of soldiers sufficient to secure it, which they did by sealing the tomb (Matthew 27:62–66). In his account, Luke describes Joseph as "a good and

---

[1] Here (Mark 15:42–43) we encounter the reference that contradicts Mark's usual sequence since the Jewish day began at sundown or at approximately 6:00 P.M., the reference in Mark 15:42 is to the onset of Kridah, the 15th of Nisan, the crucifixion thus having occurred on Thursday.

righteous man" who, though a councilmember had not agreed to its plan. Luke describes Joseph as "waiting expectantly for the kingdom of God," adds that it was the Day of Preparation, the Sabbath's beginning, writing that the women who had come with Jesus from Galilee followed, saw the tomb and his body, returned to prepare spices and incense, and rested on the Sabbath (Luke 17:50–54). In the Fourth Gospel Joseph of Arimathea is described as a "secret" disciple, for fear of the Jews. Together with Nicodemus, Jesus' visitor by night, the two bring close to a hundred pounds of myrrh and aloes, wrap the body of Jesus in linen according to Jewish burial custom, and lay it in a brand new tomb. "And," the evangelist concludes, "because it was the Jewish day of Preparation, and the tomb was nearby, they laid Jesus there" (John 19:38–41). Despite his celebrated animus toward Jesus' adversaries, throughout the Gospel, in the aggregate called "the Jews," once more the evangelist nods toward recognition of their custom, noting that the work of burying Jesus was minimal, since the tomb lay near the site of crucifixion, thus only peripherally offending Jewish Sabbath law, and rendering Jesus or his body innocent of breaking it.

The Resurrection

An examination of the 16th chapter of Mark reveals that of the twenty verses normally included in this chapter, only eight have any real claim to genuineness. Verses 9–20 (the so-called "Aristion ending") have no actual support in the manuscript evidence or the testimony of the early Church. These verses are so clearly a collation of scenes from Luke's and Matthew's accounts that we may assign them to a period in which Mark had been long since dead (i.e., the middle of the second century?). The form and content of the addition to verse 8, which first appears in fifth century manuscripts of the New Testament, betrays its character as a later attempt at supplementation. A third insertion, not included in the NRSV, which records Jesus' reproach of the disciples' unbelief, is from the late fourth or fifth century—the "Freer Logion," named for the man who acquired it in England in 1906. Eight verses in all, then, are devoted to the theme of Jesus' resurrection, against fifty verses in Luke and twenty in Matthew. The irritatingly brief ending has given rise to speculation: Mark composed a longer ending, carelessly torn away by an ancient archivist, or the ending was removed because it did not harmonize with the narratives in the later rival Gospels which replaced it in favor and use, or, Mark intended a two-volume work, just as as Luke, only to be interrupted by martyrdom or death by natural causes.

These suggestions overlook what Mark may actually intended, an ending that comported with the theme underlying the entire Gospel, that is, the "Messianic Secret." Throughout the Gospel Jesus enjoins those he heals, along with their demonic tormentors, to keep silent. His audiences, to say nothing of his disciples, struggle to identify him in a welter of interrogatives, and when they finally do orders them to keep silent. In this book of the "Secret Epiphanies" Jesus is made known only in the Gospel's signature ("The beginning of the good news of Jesus Christ, the Son of God," Mark 1:1), and at its end in the centurion's confession, needing God himself to identify him at his baptism ("You are my Son, the Beloved," Mark 1:9) and at his transfiguration ("This is my Son, The Beloved," Mark 9:7).

Mark's brief section opens with the ending of Sabbath when the women (Mary Magdalene, Mary, the mother of James, and Salome) who bring spices to anoint the body of Jesus, and their arrival at the tomb on the first day of the week. The stone having been rolled away from the tomb they enter and encounter a young man robed in white, sitting on the right. The young man's habit is is reminiscent of Jesus' apparel at the Transfiguration (Mark 9:3; Luke 24:4; Matthew 23:3,4). The young man tells the women not to be alarmed, they seek Jesus of Nazareth who was crucified and has been raised, pointing to the spot where he had been laid. Then he tells the women to tell Peter Jesus is going ahead to Galilee, where they will see him. The reference to Peter suggests Paul's word concerning Jesus' first appearance to him in I Corinthians 15:5. Following this direction, the women flee from the tomb in terror and amazement "saying nothing to anyone," the Gospel concludes, "for they were afraid" (Mark 16:8). The "secret," obviously, is not even broken by the young man's word regarding Jesus' resurrection, since those to whom it is announced are too frightened to tell of it. Some seem to prefer to see the report of the women's silence as a contrast to the breach of Jesus' command to the healed to be silent, thus as a device for interpreting the Gospel. Use of the passive voice in the young man's word to the women "he has been raised" (*egerthe*, Mark 16:6), allows the inference that the event was not initiated by Jesus himself but by God. In Paul's first letter to the Corinthians he uses the passive voice of the aorist tense (*ophthe*, "he was shown to," not, as in the NRSV: "he appeared to Peter," I Corinthians 15:5), to allow for the same inference. Further, since the apostle indicates this narrative as transmitted to him (I Corinthians 15:3), it follows that such usage belonged to the narrative -confession of the community which preceded him.

The additions of Matthew, Luke, and John are too varied and numerous to allow any kind of chronological sequence.

The divergence of Matthew from his Markan exemplar is considerable. An anonymous visitor ("the other Mary") accompanies Mary Magdalene to the tomb. Absence of guards at the tomb in Mark is compensated for by the guards who behave as if dead at the earthquake. Mark's "young man" at the tomb (a *neaniskos*, of military age) has become an angel of the Lord who rolled away the stone. Unlike the women in Mark who are too fearful to tell anyone what they saw or heard, in Matthew they run to tell the disciples, only to encounter Jesus who says "Greetings! Take hold of his feet and worship him." Again, Jesus speaks to them, telling them not to fear but to tell "my brothers" to go to Galilee where they will see him. Matthew then contains a report of the chief priests' and elders' bribing the guards who were to say Jesus' disciples had stolen his body, that if Pilate got wind of the transaction they would put him at ease and keep the guards out of trouble. "And this story," writes Matthew, "is still told among the Jews to this day" (Matthew 28:11–16).[1] Matthew then writes that the eleven went to Galilee, to the mountain to which Jesus had directed them. In Mark there is no mention of a mountain, nor does Matthew give its name or location. The evangelist next writes that when the disciples saw Jesus, they worshiped him, "but some doubted" (Matthew 28:7). Is the meaning of that phrase that while the rest recognized Jesus at once, some couldn't believe their eyes? Or, does Matthew intend by it to state that the faith needed to acknowledge Jesus as Messiah and Son of God during his ministry was the same needed to see him raised; that while others beheld him with that eye of faith, "some" did not, could not? Matthew then concludes his report of the appearances with Jesus' commissioning the eleven to go and make disciples of all the nations, baptizing them in the name of the Father, Son, and Holy Spirit, teaching them to obey all that he commanded, remembering he would be with them to the end of the age (Matthew 28:16–20). The command to baptize by way of the Trinitarian formula suggests a nuancing of the actual event by Matthew, since it bears striking resemblance to Christian practice in Matthew's time. And, at the command to teach the nations obedience to Jesus' command may be a nuancing reflective of a certain (Jewish-Christian?) emphasis on faith as needing to issue in action, a significant feature of Matthew's Gospel. In all this the actuality of the event itself is not called into question but notice given the fact that nothing of Jesus' life and career has not been viewed from the Gospel writer's own perspective.

In Luke and John the detailed narratives yield a kind of genre of appearances, the sudden appearance and disappearance of the risen Lord, the fright of the witnesses; Jesus' rebuke of the disciples' lack of faith, and his role as interpreter of the event. In Luke's version the women enter the tomb and encounter two men in dazzling white. Bowing to the ground, the men—in concert—ask, "Why do you look for the living among the dead?" They remind the women Jesus told them the Son of Man would be handed over to be crucified, and on the third day would rise.[2] Remembering Jesus' words, the women return from the tomb to tell this to the eleven and "all

---

1. In the Strassburg manuscript of the *Toledoth Yeshu* ("Stories of Jesus"), an apocryphal work from the sixth and known to Christians in the thirteenth century, states that Jesus' body was removed, and his ascension proclaimed on the basis of the empty tomb, but that his body was found hidden in garden and dragged back to Jerusalem.

2. Cf. the divergence from the Son of Man's rising "after three days" in Mark's [passion predictions (8:31; 9:31; 10:34) and this rising "on the third day" in Matthew (16:21 ; 17:33; 20:19), and in Luke (8:32; 18:33).

the rest." In Luke's account, as in Mark's and Matthew's, Mary Magdalene is named as visitor to the tomb, but the names of those accompanying her are altered again, this time to Joanna, the mother of James, and "the other women with them." Luke then writes that the women's report seemed to "the apostles" to be an idle tale. Use of the term "apostles" here anticipates the later identification of the disciples as witnesses of the risen Lord, and their commissioning by him to go into the world.

Luke's additions to the resurrection narrative are extensive. He writes that following the women's report Peter runs to the tomb, sees the linen cloths laid aside and returns home amazed at what has happened. Thus, for Luke, Peter is the first disciple and the first male to arrive at a realization of Jesus' rising, a privilege later to catapult him to the head of the Jerusalem caliphate in the evangelist's second book. But Peter's recognition does not occur without palpable evidence in the grave clothes laid neatly by. And again, Jesus' appearance to Peter yields genre-like references to the resurrection: the visible appearance of Jesus unaccompanied by demonstrations of power as in, say, the theophanies of the Old Testament.

Luke then adds the lengthy narrative of the journey of the two disciples toward Emmaus, so far unidentifiable by modern methods, their encounter with Jesus whom they do not recognize, and who initiates the conversation with asking what they are discussing. One of them, named Cleopas (whose mother the Fourth Gospel reports was present at the crucifixion (cf. John 19:25), asks if the unrecognized companion is a stranger to "the things" having lately occurred in Jerusalem. The stranger asks "what things, and "they"—once more a response in concert—reply, "the things about Jesus of Nazareth, a prophet mighty in word and deed, handed over by "our" chief priests and elders to be put to death. "But we had hoped," added the two "that he was the one to redeem Israel," and it was already the third day since those things had taken place, as if to contest the promise of the rising "on the third day." The travelers add that some women of their group had been to the tomb, did not see Jesus' body, but reported seeing angels who said he was alive. The two added that some of their company went to the tomb, found it as the women had said, but did not see Jesus. At this point Luke commences to paint a portrait of Jesus left unfinished in his co-evangelists' records, that of Jesus as interpreter of scripture. After rebuking their slowness at believing what the prophets had said of the Messiah's suffering and entrance into glory,

> ...beginning with Moses and all the Prophets, he interpreted to them the things about himself in all the scriptures. (Luke 24:27)

Here Jesus is described as covering the lion's share of Old Testament utterance concerning the Messiah, i.e., "Moses and all the Prophets."

The portraiture is interrupted. At the travelers' urging Jesus agrees to stay with them, and at table, after taking and breaking the bread, they recognize him, and consent to the portrait as that of Jesus. "Were not our hearts burning within us while he was talking to us on the road, while he was penning the scriptures to us"? (Luke 24:32). The two then return to Jerusalem, find the eleven and the others, are told the Lord had risen and appeared to Simon, then recount what had happened to them "in the breaking of the bread." Recognition of Jesus in that "breaking of the bread" once more suggests a nuancing of the event from the perspective of early Christian practice, this time, of celebration of the Lord's Supper. Luke continues that Jesus appears, says "peace," rebukes the disciples for their terror, tells them to look at his hands and feet, that he is not a ghost but with flesh and bone just as they, after which he shows them his hands and feet. Then, in midst of their joy and wonder Jesus asks if they have anything to eat, and as if to satisfy their appetite for the concrete once more, eats a piece of broiled fish in front of them.

Finally, the portrait of Jesus as interpreter is resumed and fleshed out in the repetition of what had been said on the Emmaus road:

> These are the words that I spoke to you while I was still with you—that everything written about me in the law of Moses, the prophets, and the psalms must be fulfilled. (Luke 24:44)

This time the range of coverage includes the entire *Tanak*: *Torah*, *Nebim*, and *Kethubim*, the Law, Prophets, and the Psalms, the Writings. And it is precisely Luke's reference to this range, in contrast to Jesus' partial treatment of Old Testament utterance elsewhere, say in Matthew's Sermon on the Mount, or in Mark's and the other Synoptics' report of the debate over the Messiah as David's Lord, which completes the portrait. More, that Luke's portrait of Jesus as interpreter, concentrating on Messiah's death and entrance into glory, is evidence that for this evangelist this event is the "device" for scripture interpretation.

Then, Luke writes that Jesus opens the disciples' eyes to understand, and, as if with a final brushstroke adds that:

> It is written then, that the Messiah is to suffer and rise from the dead on the third day, and that repentance and forgiveness of sins is to be proclaimed in his name to all nations beginning from Jerusalem. (Luke 24:4 –47)

The scene ends with Jesus' promise to send upon them what the Father had promised, and thus to remain in the city till they are clothed "from on high," an event with which Luke begins his second volume, the descent of the Spirit at Pentecost.

At the end of his Gospel Luke reports the ascension. Jesus leads the disciples to Bethany, blessses them, and while blessing is carried up to heaven. The disciples worship him, return to Jerusalem, and are continually in the temple blessing God (Luke 24:50–53).

In the Fourth Gospel two chapters are devoted to the resurrection appearances. The first is to Mary Magdalene who comes alone to the tomb while it is still dark the first day of the week, sees the stone rolled away, runs to tell Peter and the other disciple whom Jesus loved, and reports the removal of Jesus' body. Peter and the other disciple set out for the tomb, the other disciple outruns Peter, looks into the tomb, sees the graveclothes lying there, but does not enter the tomb. Peter arrives, enters the tomb, sees the linen wrappings and the cloth that had been on Jesus' head rolled up in a place by itself. The other disciple also enters the tomb, sees and believes, then John adds "for yet they did not understand the scripture, that he must rise from the dead (John 20:1–10)." How, apart from the other women cited by the Synoptics, Mary Magdalene is the first and only witness to the empty tomb, though her sight is restricted since she does not enter. Behind the report of her informing Peter and the other disciple who in her word run to the tomb, may lie an apologetic, since a woman's testimony, though allowed in ancient Judism, was nevertheless open to suspicion. In addition, a legitimate testimony requires two witnesses, hence the appearance of Peter and the other disciple, who, initially, simply repeat Magdalene's' experience, and only enters the tomb after Peter has done so. But, the evangelist writes, "He believed. For as yet they did not understand the scripture, that he must rise from the dead" (John 30:7–8). The reference to the other disciple's believing while "they," i.e. the rest and Peter, did not yet understand the scripture, has an odd appearance. But it may be John's intent is to indicate that if the scripture had been understood there would have been no need to satisfy the appetite for physical evidence. It may also be that the status given scripture by this evangelist, that is, as efficient cause of the events of the passion, is to be seen here as well.

Significant status is given Mary Magdalene as the first and sole witness of the risen Lord. She is outside the tomb, weeping, looks in, sees angels in white sitting where the body of Jesus had lain, one at the head, the other at the feet. To their query why she weeps she repeats that she had told Peter and the other disciple "They have taken away my Lord, and I do not know where they have laid him" (John 20:13). She turns around, sees Jesus who asks why she is weeping, supposes him to be the gardener and asks him where he has taken the body so she may take it away. Jesus says, "Mary!" to which she responds in the Hebrew with "Rabboni!" for a which the evangelist furnishes the translation ("which means Teacher"), tells her not to hold him to her since he has not yet ascended to the Faather, but to tell his brothers that he is ascending to his and their Father, his and their God, after which Magdalene tells the disciples she has seen the Lord (John 20:11–18).

Fleeing for their lives at the crucifixion the disciples huddle together, bolt the door, and all of a sudden Jesus is there, no need of a key or a sledge to break tdown the door, as if the evangelist intends to make clear that there was nothing standing in his way; that he was master of every human convention—doors, roofs, walls, all the things humans erect for their security give way before him.

Then Jesus says, "peace," which is not a condition or situation left to humans to effect , but which is what God gives. And since Jesus gives peace and only God can give it, the conclusion to be drawn is that to Jesus belongs whatever it is that makes God God—an inference evangelist never tires of making throughout his entire Gospel. Then, John writes, when Jesus showed them his hands and his feet the disciples were glad at seeing the Lord.! They saw him in the flesh, though in a flesh they had never seen before, but with a body, with skin and sinew and bone, corporeal, recognizable.

Again, Jesus says "peace," then adds "as the Father has called me, so I send you." The redoubled "peace" applies first to the sight of him, then to his call. As if to say, "You're not just to sit there, basking in all this celebration; you have work to do." Significantly, in the gospel accounts of the extraordinary events of Jesus' life and career, there is no lingering at the site of the event. For that work Jesus breathed on them and said, "Receive the Holy Spirit." Incidentally, in opposition to the Church in the East the Church in the West confesses that the Spirit proceeds from the Father and the Son, as the Niceno-Constanopolitan reads: C*redo in Spiritum Sanctum, Dominum, et vivificantem, qui ex Patre Filioque procedit.* "At any rate, for that work ahead the disciples needed the Spirit, that love of the Father for the Son and love of the Son for the Father present, living, existing, manifest in a person. And the task "If you forgive thesins of any, they are forgiven them; if you retan the sins of any, they are retained" (John 18:23). Putting forgiving ahead of retaining Jesus gives priority to forgiveness, to addressing that preoccupation with self instead of with God and the neighbor (John 20:19–23).

Enter Thomas, called Didymus, the Twin. When told by the rest that they had seen the Lord, he said, "Unless I see the mark of the nails in his hands, put my finger in the mark of the nails and my hand in his side, I will not believe." It appears that Thomas was merely asking for what the disciples already got—a sight of Jesus' hands and side. Thomas was no more a positivist than the other eleven, who first came to faith when they saw Jesus turn the water into wine. The problem is that Thomas had come loose from the community. The conclusion to his story indicates that if he had been with the rest, he would have believed sooner and been spared the agony.

Thomas finally got what he wanted. Jesus appeared a second time, said "peace" a third time, as though it had not yet registered, at least not with Thomas, who finally got where he belonged. Jesus says, "Put your finger here and see my hands. Reach out your hand and put it in my side." Then he adds, "Do not doubt but believe," as though the sight of Jesus' hands and side were not enough to turn the tide, as though faith were something that was not tied to the evidence of the five senses. It is remarkable that Thomas gets what he wants, palpable, tangible, concrete evidence of Jesus' rising, and yet Jesus calls him to faith. Somehow, for Thomas, what he could see brought him to faith; somehow he needed the evidence of the eye to bring him to belief. "My Lord and my God!" he says. But the way by which he comes to his confession gets no stamp of approval from Jesus. "Have you believed because you have seen me? Blessed are those who have not seen me and yet have come to believe." "Blessed" said Jesus, not "happy." The blessing of God be on those who despite the temptation to be ruled by sight and sound alone, still hold to Jesus against tangible proof. Blessed are those who walk that arduous way (John 20:24–29).

To the narrative above the Fourth Evangelist appends a verse respecting the Gospel's purpose, that despite the number of signs performed in the disciples' presence not written "in this book," these were written to evoke faith in Jesus as the Messiah, the son of God, and by it may have life (John 20:30).

On the whole, the final chapter of the Fourth Gospel appears appendix-like. Following the solemn statement of purpose at the end of the last chapter it contains a congeries of events. In the first (John 21:1–14) Jesus shows himself to the disciples by the Sea of Tiberias, and as follows: Peter announces to Thomas, Nathaniel, the Zebedee and two others that he is returning to his former occupation: "I am going fishing." The rest get into the boat with him, but catch nothing during their nightly expedition. After daybreak and standing on the beach Jesus asks if the disciples have caught anything, to which they reply in the negative. He then tells them to cast their net over the right side, resulting in a catch none can handle. Peter, informed by the beloved disciple that their conversation partner is the Lord, puts on his clothes, and jumps into the sea, while the rest drag the net one hundred yards from the beach. Now ashore, they see a charcoal fire, and are ordered by Jesus to bring some of the catch. Peter then hauls the net ashore with its hundred and fifty-three fish, and with the net untorn. Jesus invites the group to breakfast, none of whom dares to ask who he is because they already know. Jesus then distributes bread and fish. The scene ends with the evangelist's note that this is the third time Jesus has appeared to the disciples following his resurrection.

The narrative contains at least three oddities calculated to befuddle the reader The first is that Peter, naked, covers himself before plunging into the sea (John 21:7), the second has to do with the precise number of fish dragged onto shore (John 21:11), and the third with the disciples' not daring to ask Jesus who he is "because they knew it was the Lord" (John 21:12). One would imagine uncovering and not the reverse before plunging into the water. Respecting the number of the catch, even by way of gematria, that is, of assuming the number one hundred fifty-three represents the value of particular terms or words, for some reason deliberately hidden from view, in what language would such occur, in Hebrew, Aramaic, or Greek? And if so, would those words somehow be a metaphor for a "great catch" in the Messianic age, or to some other event? Or, perhaps, to confound all the welter of subsequent scholarly interpretation, the disciples simply counted their catch? Lastly, why would anyone not dare to ask if they already knew the answer?

In the next scene (John 21:15-19) Jesus restricts his conversation to Peter, asking him if he loves him "more than these," to which Peter replies that the Lord knows he loves him. Jesus replies: "Feed my lambs." Jesus asks again, "Simon son of John do you love me?" Peter repeats his earlier answer, and Jesus says, "Feed my sheep." A third time Jesus puts the question to Peter who now troubled answers, "Lord you know everything; you know that I love you" (John 21:17) Jesus replies, "Feed my sheep," adds that when Peter was younger he girded himself and went wherever he wished, but when grown old would stretch out his hands, another would fasten his belt, and lead him where he did not want to go. At this point the evangelist intervenes, stating that Jesus was indicating what kind of death Peter would die , and for what purpose. The exchange ends with Jesus' word, "Follow me." Here, Jesus' thrice questioning Peter's love for him hides reminiscence of Peter's earlier threefold denial. Then, the prediction that when older Peter would stretch out his hands indicates how he would die and for what purpose, that is, as the death of Jesus a crucifixion to "glorify God" (cf. John:39b; 12:27-28, 41, and Luke 24:46). According to Origen of Alexandria (AD 184-253) cited in Eusebius, "Peter was crucified at Rome with his head downwards, as he himself desired to suffer."[3] Jerome (AD 327-420) writes: "At his, Nero's

---

3. Eusebius, *Ecclesiastical History*, Loeb Classical Library, III, 1. http://hup.harvard.

hands, Peter received the crown of martyrdom being nailed to the cross with his head towards the ground and his feet raised on high, asserting that he was unworthy to be crucified in the same manner as his Lord."[4]

The last scene (John 21:20-25) includes a final exchange between Jesus and Peter. Observing that the disciple "whom Jesus loved" was following him, and whom the evangelist further identifies as the one who reclined next to Jesus at the Supper and asked, "Lord, who is it that is going to betray you?" Peter asks Jesus, "Lord, what about him?" Jesus replies that it is none of Peter's affair if he wills that the observed should remain till he comes, and adds "Follow me!" Scotching the rumor spread through the community that the beloved disciple would not die, but that Jesus simply said, "If it is my will that he remain until I come," the evangelist concludes his Gospel with the statement that "this is the disciple" who testifies to and has written "these things," and whose testimony "we" know is true. Then he adds that Jesus did many other things which if written down the world itself could not hold the books containing them (John 21:24). This last verse is curious, has all the earmarks of a testimony to the Gospel's veracity by someone belonging to the evangelist's community" ("we know"). Further, the remainder of the sentence, beginning with "there are many other signs that Jesus did," and ending with the first person singular ("I suppose") suggests a representative of the evangelist's community has put the period to his Gospel.

The infinitely larger question remains regarding the identity of the "disciple who is testifying to these things and has written them." Dispute over the identity of the Gospel's author has existed for years. For example, according to the oldest list of New Testament Gospels and epistles, the Muratorian Canon, originally written in Greek in about the year AD 170, refers to John the disciple of Jesus as the Gospel's author.[5] On the other hand, the ecclesiastical historian Eusebius (AD 260/265-339/340) cites a statement of Papias of Hierapolis (ca. AD 60-163) from which it could be inferred that a disciple of John named Aristion, wrote down what the apostle had said.[6]

The Gospel narratives of the resurrection differ so markedly that the attempt to arrange them in some sort of chronological order is bound to fail. First of all, Matthew and Luke, normally dependent on Mark for their outlines, leave little evidence of any collaboration or dependence here. In fact, the first evangelist's report dare not be measured against the more advanced

---

edu/features/loeb/digital.html

4 Jerome, *De Viriis Illustribus*, Loeb Classical Library, Chapter 1. http://hup.harvard.edu/features/loeb/digital.html

5. Cf. Aland, Kurt, editor, *Synopsis Quatuor Evangeliorum* (Stuttgart: Deutsche Bibelgesellschaft, 1985), 38.

6. Ibid., 531.

pieces of Matthew and Luke. Mark records that the Risen Lord has appeared, as is clear from 16:7: "Go, tell his disciples and Peter that he is going ahead of you into Galilee; there you will see him, just as he told you." Need Mark have engaged in more detail? Does not his indirectness suit a Gospel of the "secret epiphanies"? Must an evangelist who deals briefly with Jesus' words and omits the story of his birth and childhood report appearances go beyond his earthly life to satisfy the desire for completeness? Next, the very least the historian must concede is that something must have happened to allow for such a "reaction" as has occurred the last two thousand years. There can be no doubt that Mark, Matthew, Luke, and John believed Jesus of Nazareth had been raised from the dead, and the fact that their reports do not agree is as much an argument in their favor as against it. Ultimately, the resurrection of Jesus Christ is a matter to be believed or rejected, a posture, a stance a perspective for which historical research may clear the way, but even that case, even if historical research could bring one to take note and affirm what is written here, that still would not constitute more than mere opinion. Trust in the one who rose, sharing his life, and evidencing this in thought, word and deed is the consequence to which the evangelists themselves intend to bring us.

PART FIVE

Summary

Summary

From these observations of the life and career of Jesus of Nazareth, what kind of portrait emerges? Who was Jesus, and what did he intend? And are there parallels to his story that detract from his uniqueness, relegate him to a pantheon filled with other gods and super-humans, and to the extent that devotion to him would simply be equal in value to the devotion to any other religious figure? The Fourth *Eclogue* of the Roman poet Virgil (700–19 BC), tells of the birth of a boy (possibly: the text is obscure) by way of parthogenesis, a savior, who in his maturity will become divine and rule the world, understood by some to predict the reign of Augustus Caesar. The Greek sophist Pilostratus (ca. AD 170–247) compiled eight books of the life and career of Apollonius of Tyana (ca. AD 15–100), replete with miracle stories and tales of second sight. But however similar to Jesus of Nazareth such figures may be proved to be, they still do not argue for a common origin, since "similarity is not identity." And, as for the miraculous, it is crystal clear that, for example, the healing miracles performed by Jesus differ by far from those of other healers by their lack of any hint of self-aggrandizement, and total concentration on aid to the afflicted. Modern scholarship can deny historicity to the healing and nature miracles in favor of the exorcisms which allow for psychological interpretation. However, in every instance but one, the healing of the blind man of Bethsaida (Mark 9:22–26), the healing does not occur in stages but at once. Hence the exorcisms are no less vulnerable to elimination by way of modern research than the other miracles of Jesus. Toward the end of the Old Testament period, the miraculous in terms of a penetration or invasion of the continuum of cause and effect has disappeared, then re-emerges with the telling of the story of Jesus. For Jesus' mighty deeds herald the advent of the radically new; a fissure in that "tomorrow, and tomorrow, and tomorrow, creeps in its petty pace from day to day." They announce deliverance from captivity to the old and the ordinary. And this is precisely what he intended, by calling to the radical transformation involved in repentance and faith and offering deliverance from evil. If Jesus' performance is restricted to isolated portions of Galilee and Judea, it promises a newness one day to envelop the world.

It is certainly true that Jesus challenged the religious persuasions belonging to his part of the world. In fact, his attacks on the ecclesiastical leaders of his country led to his crucifixion. Some of his bitterest attacks concern members of the ruling class in Judaism, the chief priests, in charge of relegating daily life and the worship of God. "Truly I tell you, the tax collectors and the prostitutes are going into the kingdom of God ahead of you" (Matthew 21:31). Not even the reform movement in Judaism, born out of struggle against pagan rule and desecration of Judaism's most sacred place, its temple, escaped his ire. He railed against the burden of duties they required of the Jew who would be devout, in number reaching to three hundred and sixteen: "They tie up heavy burdens, hard to bear, and lay them on the shoulders of others; but they themselves are unwilling to lift a finger to move them" (Matthew 23:4). The attacks were caustic and radical enough to link together the warring religious parties in Judaism, Pharisees and priests, to plot to kill him.

Jesus' association with those called "sinners," that is, with tax-gatherers and the like, render his behavior unique and open to attack. According to the three Synoptics he calls Matthew, a hated publican, a minion of Rome, to follow him (Mark 2:13-17; Matthew 9:9-13; Luke 5:27-28). The positioning of Matthew's call early in Mark's Gospel is hardly accidental. It heralds the type of person with whom Jesus will deal throughout. Later, at table with Mathew and others, the Pharisees and scribes, hot for reform in Judaism, ask his disciples, "Why does your teacher eat with tax collectors and sinners?" to which he replies, "Those who are well have no need of a physician, but those who are sick," then adds, "I have come to call not the righteous but sinners" (Matthew 9:10-13). There is irony in Jesus' use of those terms "well" and "righteous." They hide their opposites. The Pharisees need a physician, belong with those they call "sinners." The difference lies in their self-appraisal. Jesus invites himself to the home of another tax-collector named Zachaeus (Luke 19:1-10). The fact that this man is wealthy ("If I have defrauded anyone of anything, I will pay back four times as much," vs. 8), is of absolutely no matter to Jesus. His critics note that "he has gone to be the guest of one who is a sinner," vs. 7).

Jesus deals with women in public. In the Fourth Gospel he converses at length with the woman at the well near Sychar, a woman married five times, and now living with a man without benefit of clergy (John 4:7-26). He parries with the Canaanite (Mark 7:24-30; Matthew 15:21-28), an act a rabbi careful to preserve respect would scarcely do, added to which he would allow to trap him in his speech (she said, "Lord, help me." He answered, "It is not fair to take the children's food and throw it to the dogs." She said, "Yes, Lord, yet even the dogs eat the crumbs that fall from their masters' table"). To the consternation of his table partners he allows a woman to invade the party and anoint him. When his partners complain of the "waste," he replies that she has done him a good service; a kind of prolepsis, an anticipation of his burial (Mark 14: 3–9; Matthew 26:6–13; John 12:1–8).[1] In a narrative that has little support and has gone the rounds,[2] a woman caught in adultery, presumably by the scribes and Pharisees is made to stand before Jesus while he is teaching in the temple. Her accusers state that the law of Mosses demands that such women be stoned and ask what he has to say. He stoops down, writes with his finger on the ground, then in reply to further questioning straightens up and says, "Let one among you who is without sin be the first to throw a stone at her." The scene may be apocryphal, but there is nothing in it uncharacteristic of Jesus.

Viewed from the purely human aspect, Jesus displays a choler that current portraiture of him would studiously avoid. After the attack on two of the tree Galilean towns which witnessed his deeds of power ("Woe to you, Chorazin! Woe to you, Bethsaida!"). Jesus leaves the best for last, sets his own home town degrees beneath Sodom, Gentile sinhole of corruption ("And you, Capernaum, will you be exalted to heaven? No, you will be brought down to Hades," Matthew 11:21–23). But this tempestuousness is contrasted with the aspect of "gentle Jesus, meek and mild," taking children in his arms, gentle toward female outcasts and in the open (!),wept above Jerusalem, weeping at the death of Lazarus, and caring for his mother from his cross. There is a double-sidedness, a kind of *communicatio idiomatum* (communication of properties) adhering to his behavior, reflective, perhaps, of his nature but evoked by circumstance, by adversary or follower. Jesus reflects the same attitude toward habits of the mind. For example, there is simplicity in his admonition to lay aside every care: "Consider the lilies of the field, how they grow; they neither toil nor spin, yet I tell you, even Solomon in all his glory was not clothed like one of these" (Matthew 6: 28b–29). But he applauds the shrewd steward who commits fraud, reducing amounts debtors owed his master in hope of a *quid pro quo* on dismissal

---

1. In John's account the place and cast of characters are changed. The event takes place in the home of Mary and Martha, not in the home of Simon the leper. Mary, not an unnamed woman, performs the anointing, and Judas Iscariot raises the complaint, not "some...who said to themselves, etc."

2. The earliest manuscripts and other witnesses do not contain John 7:53–8:11. The verses appear, wholly or in part, after John 7:36, John 21:25, Luke 21:38 or Luke 24:53.

(Luke 16:1–9); he enjoins the lepers to adhere to ecclesiastical-legal custom and tradition and show themselves cured to the priest (Luke 17:14), and advocates doing whatever those who sit in "Moses' seat" teach them (Matthew 23:2). These "properties" are "communicated" in the charge to be "wise as serpents *and* innocent as doves" (Matthew 10:16). And this to say nothing of his taste for structuring his speech, his use of triads, dear to the heart of the Psalmist, prophet and evangelist, especially Mark; for the heuristic[3], urging his hearers to find something out for themselves; saying "No" and meaning "Yes"[4]—provided all this is not the invention of the evangelis to discuss which belongs elsewhere. Just these few examples ae sufficient to indicate Jesus was not an anti-intellectual, but could astonish his audience with his learning: "How does this man have such learning, when he has never been taught?" (John 17:15).

Surprisingly, in Matthew's and Luke's account the women at the tomb are first to hear of Jesus' resurrection (Matthew 28:5–6; Luke 24:5–7), and in the Gospel of John (20:11–18), he first appears to Mary Magdalene. In the first instance the women's testimony would be of no value in a Jewish court. Incidentally, Luke writes that when the women reported to the disciples what they had heard, it "seemed to them an idle tale, and they did not believe them" (Luke 24:11). In the second instance, the third (cf. Luke 8:2) and fourth evangelist have allowed the inference that the woman to whom Jesus first appeared was the one from whom he had cast out seven demons. By the time the longer ending of Mark appeared, the inference had congealed to a certainty that the one from whom he cast out the demons was the one to whom he first appeared (Mark 16:9), thus opening the Gospel accounts to the charge of drawing their evidence from the hallucinations of a deranged female. Thus, Jesus' treatment of women extends to the point of rendering vulnerable the account of his death and rising, at least initially.

---

3. The current pope missed this aspect of Jesus' language in altering the petition, "and lead us not into temptation." It was the disciple's affair to ferret out what it meant, viz., that "God indeed tempts no one to sin, but we pray in this petition that God would so guard and presesrve us that the devil, the world, and our own flesh many not deceive us, nor lead us into error and unbelief, despair and other great and shameful sins; but that,when so tempted we may finally prevail and gain the victory." The quotation is from the old *Lutheran Hymnary*, "Including the symbols of the Evangelical Lutheran Church" (Minneapolis: Augsburg Publishing House, 1935), lii.

4. Cf. The striking example of *litotes* raised to the enth power in the narrative of the Syrophoenician, or Canaanite woman. Once in Mark, twice in Matthew Jesus refuses to heal her daughter, but when she resolutely persists in petitioning him, he says, "you may go—the demon has left your daughter" (Mark 7:28). In Matthew, he replies, "Woman, great is your faith! Let it be done for you as you wish" (Matthew 15:28).

Jesus also treats with the ritually unclean, as with the woman suffering from flow of blood (Mark 5:25-34; Matthew 9:20-22; Luke 8:43-48).[5] And, he exhibits no abhorrence of lepers, but engages with them for their healing (Mark 11:40-45; Matthew 9:1-4; Luke 5:12-16)[6], even to the point of touching the leper and risking defilement (Matthew 9:2-4).[7]

But these events only marginally characterize Jesus. They are like the lines and fissures of the face. They may enhance or disfigure, but the face could be without them and it would be readily recognizable. What with all the summoning to discipleship, the exorcisms, the miracles of healing and nature miracles, with all the disputing, what characterizes Jesus of Nazareth, to which his words and deeds are warped or bent is that he is marked for, intent on, faced toward death. Of the Gospels, the clues to this strange identity are most evident in Mark's Gospel. In chapter one Jesus' proclamation of the kingdom follows the arrest of the Baptist, indicated by the same verb-form as is used of Jesus' passion (Mark 1:14); an omen of what is to come. In chapter two, Jesus speaks of himself in oblique fashion as the bridegroom who in days to come will be taken from the "wedding guests" (Mark 2:20). Chapter three contains the first reference to Judas "who betrayed him" (Mark 3:19). In the parable of the sower in Chapter four Jesus speaks of the seed fallen among thorns and choked (Mark 4:7). In chapter five the scene is composed of tombs, drowning, sickness, and death. Chapter six again contains the destinies of Jesus and the Baptist, reporting the latter's death and Herod's word on hearing of Jesus' activity that he Baptist had been raised from the dead and hearing of Jesus (Mark 6:4-16). In chapter seven Pharisees and scribes come down from Jerusalem to spy out the disciples' neglect of ritual cleansing (Mark 7:1-2). Chapters eight, nine and ten contain the three passion predictions (Mark 8:31; 9:31; 10:33-34). In chapter eleven the authorities look for a way to kill Jesus (Mark 11:19). Chapter twelve contains the parable of the vineyard, on hearing which his enemies want to arrest him (Mark 12:12). The "little apocalypse" of chapter thirteen includes

---

5. *Leviticus* 15:25-27 describes such a woman throughout *the time of her* discharge as unclean. The Michnah tractate *Niddah* ("The Menstruant") opens with the following: "Shammai says: For all women it is enough that they be deemed unclean only from their time of suffering a flow," Danby *The Mishnah*, 745. Obviously, as long a the woman suffers a flow, she is unclean

6. Leviticus 13 and 14 describe person s afflicted with leprosy, in chapter thirteen with diagnosis by a priest, chapter fourteen with purification. Leviticus 13:45 reds: "The person who has the leprous disease...shall cover his upper lip and cry out, 'Unclean, Unclean.'"

7. Cf. Leviticus 7:21: "When any one of you touch ay unclean thing—human uncleanness or an unclean animal or any unclean creature—and then eats its flesh from the Lord's sacrifice of well-being, you shall be cut out off from your kin."

prediction of persecution "because of my name" (Mark 13:13). Then follows the passion chapters fourteen and fifteen, in which Mark gives himself over to scrupulous detail. When read backwards, the Gospel can easily be seen to concentrate on the death motif, beginning by way of inference then climaxing in the cry of dereliction from the cross (Mark 15:34).

> The life of Jesus was as swift and straight as a thunderbolt. . . .The primary thing that he was going to do was to die. He was going to do other things equally definite and objective, we might almost say equally external and material. But from first to last the most definite fact is that he is going to die. . . .From the moment when his star goes up like a birthday rocket to the moment when the sun is extinguished like a funeral torch, the whole story moves on wings with the aped and direction of a drama, ending in an act beyond words. . ..[8]

If the Gospel writers' use of Old Testament passages in connection with the passion is not meant to establish the integrity of the biblical word, but to assign the initiative to the biblical word, that it is the agent by which the events of the passion occur, then the conclusion that may be drawn is that Jesus has no alternative but to suffer; he is fated, destined for it. At the Last Supper Jesus says to the disciples, "The Son of Man goes as it is written of him" (Mark 14:21), a word suggestive of a line from a world and a millenium away:

> The moving finger writes; and having writ, Moves on: nor all thy Piety nor Wit Shall have it back to cancel half a Line.Nor all thy Tears wash out a Word of it.[9]

The agony in the garden ending in his submission to the Father's will is intended to emphasize that feature. But there is an older tradition, reaching back to the epistles of Paul which antedate the Gospels. More, that tradition antedates the epistles of Paul, and to which he refers and nuances. The tradition is reflected in the Christ-hymn of Philippians, chapter two, in which Christ Jesus, who though "in the form of God, did not regard equality with God as something to be exploited, but humbled himself, taking the form of a slave. . .. And being found in human form, he humbled himself and became obedient to the point of death—even death on a cross" (Philippians 26:8). For this reason, for his obedience, the hymn continues, "God highly

---

8. Chesterton, G.K. *The Everlasting Man* (San Francisco: Ignatius Press, 2008), 207-208.

9. *The Rubayat of Omar Khayyam*. Translated by Edward Fitzgerald (Edinburgh and London: T.N. Foulis, MDCCCCV), LI.

exalted him and gave him the name that is above every name" (Philippians 2:9). According to this tradition, Jesus had an alternative. The agony in the garden reflects a struggle between two wills, that of Jesus and that of his Father. The fact that he submits his will to the Father's does not denote fate or destiny, the absence of an alternative, but rather an obedient submission of his will to the will of the Father. Closely aligned with this concept is the declaration in Hebrews that "in the days of his flesh" Jesus' "prayers and supplications, with loud cries and tears" were heard because of his "obedient submission." The epistle writer continues: "although he was a Son," that is, his essence hidden the deity, in his historical life "he learned obedience through what he suffered." For this reason, "he became the source of eternal salvation for all who obey him" (Hebrews 5:7–10), just as in the Christ-hymn he was given "the name that is above every name."

Perhaps these two traditions, if they are such, are not irreconcilable. When Matthew, for example, indicates what event takes place in order to fulfill the prophetic word, that word occurs "through the prophet." But Matthew will also write that what is fulfilled had been spoken "by the Lord" through the prophet (Matthew 1:22; 2:1). The word of the prophet, then, is the agent , not the initiator of the event's fulfillment. God is initiator, who speaks the word fulfilled by the event. And to this God Jesus is obedient. This means that the events of Jesus' passion are not caused by the prophetic word, in the aggregate conceived as fate or destiny, but rather by the God who speaks through it and to whom Jesus submits. And since the events are so intimately connected with the word they fulfill, so that they would not occur were it not for the word they fulfill, they take on the feature of submission to the one through whose word they occur. This is the meaning behind Jesus' word: "The Son of Man goes as it is written of him." (Mark 14:21; Matthew 26:24).

A Final Reflection on the Resurrection of Jesus

Initially, a few observations need making. First, the fact that there are "constants" within the narraatives of the resurrection leaning toward genre does not undermine historicity, but reflects the habit of earliest Chirstianithy. Constants and genres were necded to transmit the gospel in its oral, pre-written form. The suggestion that in this stage the gospel underwent radical changes in form and content reflects a certain exceptionalism, criticism from a "high horse," the notion that current transmission of historical events has evolved to a higher level than in any earlier period, that a developed oral transmission of tradition took place less in the observance than in the breach. Next, as the Tübingen scholar Ernst Käsemann (1906–1980 indicated, access to the past is mediated; the Gospels which narrate the Christian message are embedded in the life of the earthly Jesus. This, for those who revere the risen Jesus, revelation is indissobly connected with his "earthly corporeality."[1] Third, as Nils Dahl of Oslo University and Yale (1911–2001) stated, what the Gospel writers tell and how they tell it is determined by their faith in the crucified and risen Christ.[2] These comments ring the changes on the thesis of Martin Kähler of Bonn and Halle-Wittenberg (1835–1912) over a half-century earlier, that the risen Lord is not the historical Jesus *behind* the Gospels, but the Christ of apostolic preaching.[3] Lastly, due to the access to history through narration, due to the Gospels' having been written from the perspective of faith, thus that the earthly—historical Jesus is the existential-historical, preached Christ, attempts to separate the "historical Jesus" from the "Christ of faith" will always be attended by frustration, however legitimate.

1. Cited in *Jesus Handbuch*, 79.
2. Cited in the *Jesus Handbuch*, 474.
3. Cited in the *Jesus Handbuch*, 67.

In his Gospel, Matthew records that the disciples went to Galilee, to the mountain where Jesus had directed them, writing that "when they saw him, they worshipped him; but some doubted" (Matthew 29:17). In classical and New Testament *Koine* Greek the term for "doubt" is a compound of the terms "two," or "double" *(dis-)* plus "standing" *(stasis)*, hence to waiver, to be of two minds, but may also denote absence. The one group of disciples worships while the other leans toward, or outright denies Jesus' appearance. This dual, immediate reaction to Jesus' appearance is lacking in the other Gospels which separate in time belief from non-belief in his appearance. In Mark's Gospel such dual, immediate reaction is absent, because the women are too afraid to report their experience. In Luke the resurrection as announced by the women is sloughed off by the disciples as an "idle tale" (Luke 24:11). In the Fourth Gospel, Thomas demands empirical evidence of Jesus' rising, but reference to the contrary on the part of the others is lacking. This immediate, dual reaction in Matthew allows for a perspective according to which, in the encounter with reality, perception precedes conception. For some of the disciples the concept of Jesus' rising emerges from their perception, for the others perception did not lead to conceiving that Christ had been raised, only to the "absence" *(distasis)* of faith. This does not require construing the resurrection of Jesus as a creation of the disciples' imagination, nor lack of it in the doubters or deniers. The tree that falls in the forest without anyone seeing or hearing it, does not mean the event did not occur. The resurrection of Jesus could occur apart from belief or unbelief in it. Insistence on perception prior to conception does not dissolve the perceived objects. The appearance of Jesus does not "need" the disciples' conception of it any more than that tree in the forest needs an observer or auditor. Faith (or unbelief) in the resurrection shares, in kind, if not in degree, the nature and character of the human habit of thought. This view does not prove the resurrection of Jesus, nor does it disprove it. The best it can achieve is to indicate the plausibility that Jesus' rising originated in the overwhelming experience of his appearances to a few of his followers after his death, which then were interpreted by aid of traditional modes, and connected with aspects of Jesus' earthly activity.[4] On the other hand, what this view can actually achieve is to allow for positing what it is that drives perception toward conception of the object, Jesus' rising.[5] That state or condition that drives thought toward perception of its object is, for lack

---

4. A paraphrase of the conclusion drawn to the section on Resurrection, Appearances, and Instructions of the Risen One in the *Jesus Handbuch*, 492.

5. James, William. *Percept and Concept and Their Practical Uses.* "Whether our concepts live by returning to the perceptual world or not, they live by having come from it. It is the nourishing ground from which their sap is drawn." p. 7.

of a better term, *need*—garden variety need. It is the need, or the desire—the urge to believe—that urges perception toward the concept of it, or to its denial. It is need that moves the organs of perception to vary, thus the objects of perception that seem to vary.[6] With respect to the resurrection of Jesus, the need for it is greater with the one than the other group. It is thus the need, the desire, the will, in essence the humanity that gives birth to the move toward grasping the object. Human thought is a mendicant, a beggar.[7] Its object does not need me to be, to be there; it is a given," a gift, an act of grace, as the old theologians would put it, *extra nos*, or as Luther's catechism has it, "without our prayer."

> For this tangled absurdity of a Need, Even a Need-love, which never fully acknowledges its own neediness, Grace substitutes a full, childlike and delighted acceptance of our Need, a joy in total dependence. We become "jolly beggars."[8]

To the objection that need is the engine hauling the totality of human thought and discovery, the answer is that there is nothing human without need, that need is as much an initiator of scientific discovery as the need for the existence of a God. The present crop of biologists is as needy in the aggregate as the impoverished derelict. The biologist's insistence that faith is an infection against which I "need" (he will never refer that condition to himself) to be inoculated, just as loudly, boisterously, raucously, reflects a need, a longing, a desire, a passion to eliminate religious faith from the scene. There is no movement from the percept to the concept of it, apart from the need for it. The need is prior, driving toward perception and conception. Because I am the object of the love of God, and the universe is entangled in my destiny (Romans 8:20–21) I can see it, hear it, taste it, touch it, feel it. The question how it is that the need for it is stronger in the one than in the other, requires a theological explanation. With the one, the weight of the need is on the side of a percept leading to a conceept of Jesus' rising, while with the other the weight falls on the side of a perception of its absence. The observation has not determined the outcome, but the need and weight given it. This need has to do with the activity of a transcendent God in love with the world, and to such effect that it tore him in two to answer my need. Needy mortal that I am, needing a world, an entire universe

---

6. Blake, William, "Jerusalem" in David V. Erdman, *The Poetry and Prose of William Blake* (Garden City, New York: Doubleday, 1970), 175.

7 This is, perhaps, what Luther had in mind when almost with his last breath, he said, "Wir sind bettler, *hoc est verum*." The last words Luther ever wrote. Contained in his Göttingen sermon on I Corinthians 1:26–31.

8. Lewis, C.S., *The Four Loves* (NY: Harcourt, 1988), 131.

to impinge upon me "from without," I witness to a God who has deigned to place in me such weight as drives my need to a perception and thus a conception of the resurrection of Jesus of Nazareth risen from the dead. And, if I yield to the weight of belief in it, why should I "refuse to budge an inch until I have (all the) objective evidence?"[9] I concede that if Mathew only intended to write that at Jesus' appearing the disciples could not believe their eyes, in other words could not manage the welter of perceptions, using Matthew's narrative as the occasion for this reflection topples, but only the occasion, not the argument.

To engage in any further argument would be to indicate that research is not limited to an object as such, say, to the event of the resurrection as such, but requires attention to its effects. As noted above,[10] scholars, following the lead of Hans-Georg Gadamer, call this the consciousness of the history of the texts' effects prior to and independent of the researcher. Taking the narrative of Jesus' rising as the 'text,' two thousand years have witnessed to its effect in the confession of it, as well as the resistance to it, the obliquy heaped upon it, a riot of commotion engined by that "text," that event.

> If for this life only we have hoped in Christ, we are of all people most to be pitied. But in fact Christ has been raised from the dead, the first fruits of those who have died. (I Corinthiuans 15:9–10)

---

9. James, William, *The Will to Believe and Other Essays in Popular Philosophy, and Human Immortality* (Digireads.com Publishing, 2010), IX.

10. Cf. p.3.

Appendix

Glossary

1. Adoptionist—The view according to which Jesus was adopted as the Son of God at his baptism.
2. Apocalypse—A text containing the revelation of what is to occur at the end of time.
3. Apocrypha—Biblical or related writings not forming part of the accepted canon of Scripture.
4. Apologist—A person who offers an argument in defense of something controversial.
5. Apostle—A witness to the resurrected Jesus sent to proclaim the Gospel.
6. Atonement—(In religious contexts) reparation or expiation for sin.
7. Beatitude—The blessings listed by Jesus in the Sermon on the Mount (Matt. 5:3–11).
8. Blasphemy—The act or offense of speaking sacrilegiously about God or sacred things; profane talk.
9. Centurion—The commander of a century (100 soldiers) in the ancient Roman army.
10. Demythologize—Reinterpret what are considered to be mythological elements of (the Bible).
11. Dogma—A principle or set of principles laid down by an authority as incontrovertibly true.
12. Doxology—A liturgical formula of praise to God.

13. Epiphany—The manifestation of Christ to the Gentiles as represented by the Magi (Matthew 2:1-12).

14. Epistle—A letter.

15. Epistemology—The theory of knowledge, especially with regard to its methods, validity, and scope. Epistemology is the investigation of what distinguishes justified belief from opinion.

16. Eschatology—The part of theology concerned with death, judgment, and the final destiny of the soul and of humankind. "Christian hope is concerned with eschatology, or the science of last things"

17. Etiology—The investigation or attribution of the cause or reason for something, often expressed in terms of historical or mythical explanation.

18. Evangelist—A person who seeks to convert others to the Christian faith, especially by public preaching. Matthew, Mark, Luke, John.

19. Exodus—A mass departure of people, especially emigrants. The departure of the Israelites from Egypt.

20. Exorcism—The expulsion or an evil spirit from a person or place.

21. Gnostic—Adhering to a religion that denies physical matter or corporeality.

22. Gospel—"God-spell" or the "Good News" of Jesus Christ.

23. Hellenist—A specialist in the study of Greek language, literature, culture, or history, or an admirer of the Greek culture and civilization. A person who adopted the Greek customs, language and culture during the Hellenistic period, especially a Hellenized Jew.

24. Heretic—A person holding an opinion at odds with accepted doctrine of a particular religious faith.

25. Hierophany—(From Greek hiero-, "sacred," and phainein, "to show") is a term designating the manifestation of the sacred.

26. Historicity—Historical authenticity.

27. Hypocrite—A person who puts on a false appearance of virtue or religion.

28. Liturgy—A form or formulary according to which public religious worship, especially Christian worship, is conducted.

29. Logos—The Word of God, or principle of divine reason and creative order, identified in the Gospel of John with the second person of the Trinity incarnate in Jesus Christ.

30. Messianic—A position, expectation or text having to do with the Messiah.

31. Mishnah—The most important section of Jewish codified law in the Talmud.

32. Obdurate—Stubbornly refusing to change one's opinion or course of action.

33. Parable—A story, often with a single point, drawn to illustrate an aspect of existence.

34. Pharisee—A member of a reformed movement in Judaism concentrating on strict observance of Mosaic law.

35. Piety—The quality of being religious or reverent.

36. Pilgrimage—A pilgrim's journey.

37. Qumran—A sect headquartered at the west bank of the Dead Sea, in opposition to Jewish officialdom.

38. Rhetoric—The art of effective or persuasive speaking or writing, especially the use of figures of speech and other compositional techniques.

39. Sadducee—A member of a Jewish sect for whose political advantage it cooperated with Roman rule, and in doctrine denied the afterlife.

40. Samaritan—a member of a people inhabiting Samaria in biblical times, or of the modern community in the region of Nablus claiming descent from them, adhering to a form of Judaism accepting only its own ancient version of the Pentateuch as Scripture.

41. Sanhedrin—«sitting together,» hence «assembly» or «council» were assemblies of either twenty-three or seventy-one elders

42. Septuagint—a Greek version of the Hebrew Bible (or Old Testament), including the Apocrypha, made for Greek-speaking Jews in Egypt in the 3rd and 2nd centuries BC and adopted by the early Christian Churches.

43. Soteriology—the doctrine of salvation.

44. Synoptic—Relating to the first three Gospels (Matthew, Mark, Luke), their relationship of similarity and difference.

45. Syntax—The arrangement of words and phrases to create well-formed sentences in a language.

46. Talmud—The body of Jewish civil and ceremonial law and legend comprising the Mishnah and the Gemara. There are two versions of the Talmud: the Babylonian Talmud (which dates from the 5th century AD but includes earlier material) and the earlier Palestinian or Jerusalem Talmud.

47. Testament—Something that serves as a sign or evidence of a specified fact, event, or quality.

48. Torah—(in Judaism) the law of God as revealed to Moses and recorded in the first five books of the Hebrew scriptures (the Pentateuch) a scroll containing the Torah.

49. Transfiguration—a complete change of form or appearance into a more beautiful or spiritual state.

50. Vulgate—the principal Latin version of the Bible, prepared mainly by St. Jerome in the late 4th century, and (as revised in 1592) adopted as the official text for the Roman Catholic Church.

(Source: Google dictionary, edited by Roy A. Harrisville)

Questions for Reflection

Part I

1. How was the Virgin Birth explained by the ancient church?
2. What was the influence of Assyria on the Northern Kingdom of Galilee and its implications?
3. What was Hamann's response to the visit by the Magi? Was it an illusion?
4. How is Herod portrayed? What are some of his characteristics? How do we know?
5. Provide an outline of the "Infancy Gospel of Thomas."
6. Where was the Dead Sea community located? Was John a member? How do we know?
7. Provide examples of OT references to John the Baptist.
8. When John asks Jesus, "Who are you?" what does Jesus say?
9. Who were the gnostics? The Mandeans?
10. What do we mean by a Christological context?
11. What is the "adoptionist tradition?" Which Gospel is least affected by it and why?
12. What is the Messiah tradition? Provide examples from the OT.

Part II

13. What does "repentance" mean in Hebrew?

14. What is meant by the "Rule of God?" What does it have to do with salvation?
15. Compare and contrast examples of the language of John with that of the other evangelists.
16. What characterizes the questions of Nicodemus to Jesus? Was he an early scientist? Legalist? Does he reflect an ontological world view?
17. Give examples of references to "dark" and "light" in the Gospels. What is meant by "doing the light" as opposed to "seeing the light?"
18. How are Samaritans different from the Jews of the NT?
19. Describe how the passage from the Brothers Karamozov sheds light on the temptations of Jesus.
20. Why does Jesus command the disciples to silence? What is meant by the "Messianic Secret" in Mark?
21. How would you define a zealot in today's world? Compare and contrast zealots in the NT with examples from today.
22. What is meant by the "paradigm of the Kingdom?" Why is it "patient?" What is it waiting for?
23. Give examples of linguistic references, analogies, symbols or terms used in the miracle stories. How do these references inform the story?
24. What is Alfred Einstein's view of religion and science? How does he defend his views and why?
25. Choose one of the parables and explain why it's either confusing or ironic.
26. What is eschatology? Give examples of eschatological threads in the parables of Jesus.
27. Choose one of the "hard sayings" of Jesus and explain why it's difficult to hear or understand.
28. Explain the gap between what the OT law demands and room for "conscience." What part does conscience play in repentance? How is it related to the "freedom of the Christian" (op. cit. Luther)?
29. Describe the difference between Pharisees and Sadducees.
30. At what point in all four Gospels do the authorities plan to kill Jesus? What did he do that got him noticed?
31. How did Jesus teaching with authority in the synagogue at Capernaum differ from usual rabbinic teaching?

32. How is the Messiah tradition related to the stories of Moses?
33. What led to the Maccabean revolt?
34. Explain the problem of "memory" for the disciples (Luke 12:49; John 2:22). How is memory tied to the future event of the resurrection?
35. What is the Davidic ancestry of the Messiah? Why is this significant?
36. Why did Jesus denounce the Scribes in Mark 12:38–40 and Luke 20:45–47?

Part III

37. Choose one of the Beatitudes and explain the contrasting metaphors contained in them (light/dark/children/poor) (Matt 5:13–14).
38. How is forgiveness part of the community (Luke 17)? To what extent is it individual?
39. Explain the relationship between the Advocate and Christ.
40. How is OT Scripture determined to be NT destiny?
41. What is the meaning of the symbol of the veil of the temple being torn in two at the crucifixion?
42. Explain the case of "doubting Thomas." How does it contribute to the transmission of the community's message of the resurrection? Why was Thomas singled out?

Summary

43. What is the significance of the "Christ Hymn" in Philippians 26:8?

Final Reflections

44. Explain how perception can influence conception. How does this duality relate to subjectivity in perception? What are some examples from philosophy that would underscore this duality (Kant, Plato, etc.)?
45. What does it mean to "abide in the word (John 15:10)?" How might this inform faith?

Bibliography

Bacon, Benjamin W. *Is Mark a Roman Gospel*. MA: Harvard University Press, 1919.
———. "The 'Son of Man' in the Usage of Jesus," *Journal of Biblical Literature*, XLI (1922).
Blake, William. "Jerusalem" in David V. Erdman, *The Poetry and Prose of William Blake*. Garden City, New York: Doubleday, 1970.
Bloch, Ernst. *Religion im Erbe, Eine Auswahl aus seinen religionsphilosophischen Schriften*, edited by Jürgen Moltmann. Suhrkamp: Frankfurt am Main, 1959, 1961, 1964, 1966.
Bultmann, Rudolf. *Geschichte der synoptischen Tradition*. Gottingen: Vandenhoeck & Ruprecht, 1961.
Case, Shirley Jackson. *Jesus, a New Biography*. Chicago: University of Chicago Press, 1927.
Charles, R.H. *The Apocrypha and Pseudepigrepha of the Old Testament*. Oxford: Clarendon Press, 1913.
———. *The Book of Enoch*. Santa Cruz, Internet Sacred Text Archive, 1917, XLVI, https://www.sacred-texts.com/
Chesterton, G.K. *The Everlasting Man*. San Francisco: Ignatius Press, 2008.
Danby, Herbert. *The Mishnah*. MA: Peabody, 2012.
Dante Alighieri, *The Inferno*. Translated by Allen Mindelbaum, New York: Bantam Books, 1980.
Dio Cassius, *Roman History*. Translated by Earnest Cary. *Loeb Classical Library*, Cambridge: Harvard University Press, 1916.
Dostoyevsky, Fyodor. *The Brothers Karamazov*. Translated by Constance Garnett. NY: Dover, 2001.
Edmunson, Mark. *The Death of Sigmund Freud*. NY: Bloombury, 2010.
Ehrman, Bart D. *Did Jesus Exist?:The Historical Argument for Jesus of Nazareth*. New York: Harper Collins, 2012.
Eusebius, *Ecclesiastical History*, Loeb Classical Library. http://hup.harvard.edu/features/loeb/digital.html
Gospel of Thomas. Translated by B. M. Metzger, in *Synopsis Quattuor Evangeliorum*, edited by Kurt Aland. Stuttgart: Deutsche Bibelgesellschaft, 1985.
Hamann, Johann Georg. „Kreuzzüge des Philologen." *Sämtliche Werke*, 2: Schriften über Philosophie/Philologie/Kritik. 1758–1763. Vienna, 1950.

Homeric Hymns. Translated by Hugh G. Evelyn-White. Cambridge: Harvard University Press, 1914.

Hume, David. *An Enquiry Concerning Human Understanding, The Harvard Classics,* edited by Charles W. Eliot. New York: P.F. Collier & Son, 1909–1914.

James, William. *The Will to Believe and Other Essays in Popular Philosophy, and Human Immortality.* Digireads.com Publishing, 2010.

———. *Percept and Concept and Their Practical Uses.* https://foundations301.files.wordpress.com/2009/09/percept-and-concept2.pdf

Jerome. *De Viriis Illustribus.* Loeb Classical Library, http://hup.harvard.edu/features/loeb/digital.html

Jesus Handbuch, edited by Jens Schröter und Christine Jacobi. Tübingen: Mohr Siebeck, 2017.

"John 8 and the Birth of Jesus" by Asif Iqbal and published by *Bismika Allahuma* on October 15, 2005.

Käsemann, Ernst. *Kirchliche Konflikte,* Gottingen: Vandenhoeck & Ruprecht: 1981.

———. "Die Gegenwart des Gekreuzigten," *Kirchliche Konflikte,* Göttingen: Vandenhoeck & Ruprecht, 1982.

Kümmel, Werner Georg. *Verheißung und Erfüllung. Untersuchungen zur eschatologischen Verkündigung Jesu;* AThAT 6; Basel 1945, Zürich: Zwingli Verlag, 19532, 19563.

Lewis, C.S. *God In The Dock, Essays on Theology and Ethics,* edited by Walter Hooper, Grand Rapids: William B. Eerdmans Publishing Company, 1970.

———. *Mere Christianity,* New York: Harper Collins, 1952.

———. *The Four Loves,* New York: Harcourt, 1988.

Lightfoot, J.B. *The Apostolic Fathers,* Part II, London: Macmillan and Co., 1889.

Luther, Martin. Collected Works. *Weimar Ausgabe.* http://luther.chadwyck.co.uk/ Accessed May 16, 2020.

———. "Temporal Authority: To What Extent It Should Be Obeyed," Vol. 45: *Christian in Society II.* Translated by Schindel, J.J. Revised by Brandt, Walther I., Philadelphia: Fortress Press, 1962.

Lutheran Hymnary. Minneapolis: Augsburg Publishing House, 1935.

Macaulay, Thomas Babington. "The Battle of the Lake Regillus," *Lays of Ancient Rome,* XL, London: Longmans, Green, Reader, & Dyer, 1867.

Metzger, Bruce M. *The Text of the New Testament: Its Transmission, Corruption, and Restoration.* Oxford University Press: 2005.

The Mishnah. Translated From The Hebrew With Introduction And Brief Explanatory Notes by Herbert Danby, Oxford University Press, 1933.

Nestigen, James Arne. "The End of the End: The Role of Apocalyptic in the Lutheran Reform," *Word & World* 15, no. 2 (Spring 1995): 204.

Parsons, John J. *Hebrew for Christians.* https://www.hebrew4christians.com/About_HFC/about_hfc.html

Piper, Otto A. "The Virgin Birth: The Meaning of the Gospel Accounts," *Interpretation,* no. 2 (1964): 142.

———. "The Origin of the Gospel Pattern," *Journal of Biblical Literature* 78, no. 2 (1959): 123.

Resch, Alfred. *Agrapha,* Ausserkanonische Schriftfragmente. Leipzig: J.C. Hinrichs'sche Buchhandlung, 1906.

Ritschl, Albrecht. *Der biblische Stoff der Lehre,* Bonn: A. Marcus u. C. Weber's Verlag, 1900.

Robbins, Vernon K. "The Chreia," *Greco-Romn Literature And The New Testament*, edited by David E. Aune, Atlanta: Scholars Press, 1988.
Rubayat of Omar Khayyam. Translated by Edward Fitzgerald, New York: Doubleday, 1938.
Sanhedrin. Translated by Jacob Schachter and H. Freedman. London: Soncino Press, 1935.
Santala, Risto. *The Midrash Of The Messiah*. Finland: Tummavuoren Kirjapaino Oy, 2002.
Schechter, Solomon. *Fragments Of A Zadokite Work*. Cambridge: At the University Press, 1910.
Schweitzer, Albert. *The Quest of the Historical Jesus*. Translated by W. Montgomery, London: A & C Black, 1910.
Shaw, Martin and Peracy Dearmer, *The English Carol Book, First Series*. London: A. R. Mowbray & Co., Ltd., 1913.
Soncino Babylonian Talmud. Translated by Rabbi Dr. I. Epstein., London: The Soncino Press, n.d.
Stuhlmacher, Peter. *Historical Criticism and Theological Interpretation of Scripture*. Translated by Roy A. Harrisville, Minneapolis, Augsburg, 1977.
Synopsis Quatuor Evangeliorum, edited by Kurt Aland, Stuttgart: Deutsche Bibelgesellschaft, 1985.
Tertullian, *De Oratione*, (Tertullian's tract on The Prayer), edited and translated by Ernest Evans, 1953, S.P.C. K. 1953.
Tractate Sanhedrin, Mishnah and Tosefta. Translated by Herbert Danby, London: Society For Promoting Christian Knowledge, 1919.
Vermes, Geza. *The complete Dead Sea scrolls in English*. London: Penguin Books, 2004.
Vielhauer, Philipp and George Strecker. *New Testament Apocrypha: Gospels and Related Writings*, edited by Schneemelcher, Wilhelm and Wilson, Robert McLachlan, Louisville: Westminster John Knox Press, 1991.
Virgil. *Eclogues. Georgics. Aeneid: Books 1–6*. Translated by H. Rushton Fairclough. Revised by G. P. Gold. Loeb Classical Library 63, Cambridge, MA: Harvard University Press, 1916.
Wellhausen, Julius. *Pharisäer und die Sadducaer*. Bamberg: Greifswald, 1871.
"What Life Means to Einstein: An Interview by George Sylvester Viereck," *The Saturday Evening Post*, October 26, 1929.

Index

NEW TESTAMENT

Matthew

Reference	Page
1:21	14
1:22	4, 199
1:21	14
1:22	4, 199
2:1	199
3:10	14, 16
3:11	13, 70
3:12	19
3:14	12, 59
3:15	14
3:17	14
4:10	26
4:13	109
4:2	25
4:7	26
5:1	66, 119
5:3	126
5:13–14	114
5:14–15	63
5:20	114
5:21–43	114
6:1–6	116
6:16–18	116
6:19–34	115
6:28b-29	195
7:6	116
7:7–8	76
7:24–27	65
8:3	20
8:5	35
8:5–13	109
8:6	54
8:11	152
8:18–20	117
8:22	117
8:23–27	45
9:20–22	72, 197
9:1	109
9:1–4	197
9:2–4	197
9:9	194
9:14–17	68
9:15	69
9:18	109
9:27	35
9:35	118
9:37–38	118
10:37	78, 123, 132
10:17–25	122, 124
10:40–42	123, 132
10:1–6	122
10:5–6	23
10:5–15	129
10:11	12
10:16	196
10:16–23	130
10:24–25	131
10:24–26	54

Matthew (continued)

10:26–28	131
10:26–33	123
10:26	123
10:29–33	131
10:37–39	123
10:38–39	132
10:45	108
11:20–24	109, 146
11:2	16
11:2–19	132
11:4–5	16
11:6	51
11:11	16
11:13	133
11:14	86
11:21–23	195
11:22–34	45
11:25	146
12:12–13	143
12:22	33
12:24	131
12:29	69
12:31–32	99
12:35	89
12:38–42	101
12:39	102
12:43–4	33
13:3–9	53, 55
13:9	70
13:13	54, 98
13:24–30	53, 54
13:31–32	53, 55
13:32–33	55
13:44	54, 55
13:45–46	54, 55
13:47–50	54
13:54–55	83
13:57	83
13:58	83
14	119
14:2	104
14:26	119
14:31	119
15:4–6	79, 100, 101
15:1–20	99
15:7–9	100
15:21	35
15:21–28	194
15:29	47
15:32–39	144
15:32–50	45
15:38–52	144
16:1–2	101
16:5–12	103
16:7–10	48
16:12	103
16:24–25	118
17:24–27	45, 50
17:14–21	33
17:17	74
17:20–21	74
18:6–7	120, 124
18:23–35	54, 59
18:1–5	120
18:8–9	124
18:15–16	124
18:19–20	124
19:13–15	120, 144
19:16–22	145
19:17	145
19:23–30	124
20:1–16	54
20:24–28	121
21:18–22	45, 75
21:2	127
21:12–13	104
21:20	76
21:23	85
21:25	85
21:28–32	59
21:31	194
21:33–41	70
21:45	71
22:18	86, 89
22	86
22:1–14	65
22:2	66
22:3	88
22:4, 6	66
22:14	86
22:19	87
22:22	88
22:33	89
22:36	89

22:46	107
23:1–36	107
23:1–7	146
23:2	196
23:3, 4	180
23:4	80
23:13	80
23:13–28	146
23:25	80
23:27	80
23:29	80
24:9–14	124, 141
24	140
24:1–2	140
24:3–8	140
24:15–25	141
24:28	141
24:29–31	141
24:32–36	141
24:34	64
24:36	65
24:42–51	65
25:1–13	54
25:14–30	56
25:27	57
25:39	142
26:39	99, 155
26:1–3	88
26:3	90
26:6–13	195
26:17–20	151
26:24	199
26:29	152
26:49–50	157
26:53	160
26:52–53	158
26:63	162
27:24–26	169, 170
27:6–26	166
27:15–23	166
27:19	167
27:29	170
27:32	170
27:38	172
27:42–43	27
27:51–53	175
27:54	175
27:62–66	177
28:5–6	196
28:7	181
28:11–16	181
28:16–20	181
28:15	118
28:18	146
29:17	201
36:29	152

Mark

1:22	27, 34, 85
1:27	34, 37, 85
1:7	12, 13, 70
1:1	15, 179
1:21	31, 109
1:32	31, 34
1:34	31, 32
1:4	36
1:9	180
1:11	14
1:13	36
1:14	197
1:14	86
1:18	29
1:20	29
1:21–28	32
1:23–24	31
1:25	31
1:27–28	32
1:30	36
1:31	36
1:32–34	109
1:40	36
1:41	36
1:45	37
2:1	109
2:1–12	109
2:6–7	37
2:13–17	194
2:18–22	68
2:20	197
2:27	82
3:1	36, 109
3:3, 5b	36
3:3–9	70
3:5	36, 143
3:6	32

Mark (continued)

Reference	Page
3:11	31, 70
3:13	30, 119
3:19	197
3:27	69
3:28–30	99
3:30	99
4:32	55, 131
4:3–9	55
4:7	197
4:8	55
4:12	98
4:21–25	63
4:24–30	55
4:26–29	53
4:27	70
4:30–32	55
4:34	53
4:35–41	45
5:25–34	72, 197
5:2–7	31
5:8	31
5:13	31
5:20	32
5:21–43	36
5:30	127
5:42	37
6:4	83, 143
6:30–44	45, 144
6:35	47, 48
6	143
6:1	109
6:2	34
6:3	83
6:4–16	197
6:6	143
6:30–31	36
6:31	47
6:33–37	36
6:34	47
6:38	48
6:39	48
6:41	48
6:42–43	36
6:43	48
6:45–52	49
6:45–53	45
7:10–13	79, 101
7:1–2	197
7:1–12	99
7:6–8	100
7:24–30	194
7:31	36
7:32	36
7:35	36
7:37	37
8:31	157, 197
8:1–10	45
8:2	144
8:2–3	47
8:4	47
8:5	48
8:6	48
8:7	180
8:8	48
8:11–12	101
8:12	102
8:14–21	103
8:16	103
8:17–21	48
8:19–20	48
8:21	48
8:22–25	109
8:30	142
8:31	157, 197
8:31–9:1	122
9:2	119, 154
9:31	157, 197
9:42	120, 124
9:3	180
9:17–18	31
9:22–23	74
9:22–26	193
9:22–27	75
9:23	75
9:24	75
9:25	31
9:26	32
9:28–29	32
9:30	142
9:31	157
9:33–39	120
9:39	120
9:41	124
9:42	120, 124

9:43–48	124	13:32	65, 131
10:2–9	115	13	130
10:19	78, 125	13:1–2	140
10:13–16	120, 144	13:6	140
10:17–22	146	13:7	140
10:17–31	128	13:8	141
10:18	145	13:9	141
10:21	145	13:9–13	141
10:23	75	13:11	156
10:28	126	13:13	198
10:33	157	13:21–23	156
10:33–34	197	13:28–37	141
10:35–43	128	13:33–37	141
10:41–45	121	13:58	156
10:46	43	13:28–31	53
10:7–22	144	13:30	64
11:12–14	45, 75	13:30–31	141
11:20–25	128, 134	13–15	156
11:23	76, 134	14:36	5, 99, 142
11:2	127	14:1–2	88, 152
11:13	129	14:3–8	140, 156
11:15	104	14:3–9	153, 195
11:15–19	104	14:34	154, 156
11:19	197	14:37	154, 156
11:20–25	134	14:21	198, 199
11:21	76	14:61	78, 162
11:22–24	76	14:62	78, 162
11:28	85	14:1	90
11:30	85	14:3	154
11:40–45	197	14:10	157
12	86, 95	14:11	157
12:17	87, 88	14:12–16	151
12:34	90, 129	14:13–16	127
12:12	71, 197	14:18	157
12:1–9	70	14:18, 42	153
12:13	86	14:21	157
12:14	86	14:22–24	152
12:19	88	14:25	152
12:24	88	14:29–33	153
12:27	107	14:37, 38	154
12:28–34	129	14:40	156
12:35	106	14:41–42	156
12:35–37	78	14:42	157
12:37	125	14:44	157
12:38–40	107	14:45–46	157
12:40	108	14:47	158
12:41–44	126	14:51–52,	158
13:3	119, 156	14:53	160

Mark (continued)

14:53–65	162
14:54	177
14:59	162
15:39	14, 175
15:1–5	165
15:6	166
15:6–15	166
15:15	169
15:16–20	170
15:21	170
15:23	27
15:29	173
15:32	175
15:33–47	177
15:34	198
15:34–35	174
15:37	174
15:38	14
16:8	84, 180
16:6	180
16:8	84
16:9	196
23	170
39–40	48

Luke

1:51n-52	62
2:25	20
3:16	12, 13, 70
3:9	16
3:17	16
3:22	14
4:36–38	85, 109
4:24	83, 144
4:2	25
4:2–29	83
4:3	109
4:4	26
4:6	83
4:8	26
4:21	83
4:30	83
5:12–16	197
5:27–28	194
5:33–39	68
6:46–49	53, 65
6:10	143
6:17	66
6:18	33
6:20	126
6:20b-23	113
6:27–29	115
7:1–10	109
7:14–43	59
7:27	12
8:43–48	72, 197
8:5–8	55, 70
8:2	196
8:9	54
8:22–25	45
8:32	63
8:45–46	127
9:10–17	109, 144
9:10	45
9:23–27	118
9:24	75
9:46–48	120
9:57–58	117
9:60	117
9:62	117
10:12–15	109, 146
10:4–12	118
10:16	123
10:25	89
10:25–37	71
10:28	90
10:29	129
10:29–37	23
11:1–4	58
11:5–8	57
11:9–13	76
11:14	33
11:15	20–42
11:16	101
11:21–22	69
11:29	102
11:29–32	101
11:37–41	99
11:39–44	146
11:39–40	101
11:46–52	101
11:42–44	101
11:50–51	101
12:1	80, 103

12:11–12	122, 124	18:9–14	59
12:2–9	123	18:16–18	63
12:10	99	18:18–25	145
12:12–19	124	18:24–30	125
12:16–21	68	18:28	126
12:21	68	19:1–10	194
12:35–48	65	19:12–27	56
12:39	65	19:26	57
12:49	65	19:27	57
12:51–53	141	19:30	127
13:1–5	133	19:45–46	104
13:5	57	20:45–47	107, 108
13:6–9	57	20:40	89, 90
13:14–23	141	20	86
13:15	141	20:2	85
13:20	53	20:4	85
13:20–21	55	20:9–16	70
13:29	152	20:19	71
14:7–11	68	20:20	86
14:7–14	53, 55	20:34–35	88
14:15–24	65	21	140
14:25–33	123	21:1–14	126
14:28–32	123	21:5–6	140
15	57, 72	21:7–11	140
16:1–9	68, 196	21:12–19	141
16:9–14	59	21:20–24	141
16:10	125	21:25–28	141
16:11–12	126	21:29–33	63
16:13a, 13b	126	21:29–36	141
16:25	118	21:32	64
17:5–6	74, 75	21:41–44	78
17	134	22:15	142, 147
17:1–2	124	22:43–44	147, 155
17:1–3a	120	22	157
17:3–4	124	22:1–2	88
17:5–6	74	22:2	90
17:5–10	134	22:7–13	151
17:7–10	59	22:29–31	170
17:11–19	23	22:61–62	161
17:14	196	22:10–12	127
17:20–23	134	22:16	152
17:50–54	178	22:17	169
18:1–8	57, 58	22:22–24	169
18:15–17	120, 144	22:24–30	121
18	61	22:25, 26	171
18:1	59	22:26	88
18:7–8a	58	22:36–37	176
18:9	62	22:37	158

Luke (continued)

22:39-4	145
22:44	145
22:48	157
22:50	158
22:51	158
22:54	160
22:60	161
23:4-5	168
23:26	170
23:34	171
23:38	172
23:39-43	173
24:11	196, 201
24:4	180
24:4-47	183
24:5-7	196
24:32	183
24:37	119
24:44	183
24:46	187
24:50-53	184
29:34-35	88

John

1:14	7, 8
1:1	7
1:3	7
1:4	7
1:6, 8	7
1:10, 11	7
1:13	8
1:18	8
1:27	13
1:29	13
1:34	21
1:36	13
1:38	21
1:43-45	109
1:45	3
1:48	21
1:49	21
2:22	85, 105, 106, 162
2:1-11	37, 48, 51
2:1-12	45
2:2	51
2:4	51
2:11	52
2:13-17	104
2:16-17	84
2:18	105
2:18-22	85
2:19	84
2:20	85
2:21	85
3:2a, 2b	21
3:6	21
3:8	21, 53
3:10	21
3:12	22
3:13	22
3:16	23, 99
3:26	13
3:28-29	13
4:2	13
4:2-3	8
4:7-26	194
4:9	24
4:21	105
4:36b-54	38
4:46-54	48
5:1	90
5:1-18	90
5:2-47	38
5:14	91
6:1-15	38, 45
6:5	48, 152
6:14-15	49, 90
6:16-21	49, 109
6:1	90
6:6	48
6:9	90
6:15	45
6:15-30	102
6:16	39
6:35	103
6:39	157
6:53	147
6:65	147
6:67	147
7:3-4	92
7:5	92
7:8a, 8b	92
7:11	92
7:25-31	93

7:26	93	14:26	21
7:27	93	15:1–6	136
7:40–44	97	15:1–8	137
7:42–44	94	15:7	76
7:45–52	95	15:21	139
8:20	52, 126	16:12–15	138
8:39–59	39	16:2	54
8:48	71	16:24	139
8:52	152	16:25	53
9:1–3	91	17:1	22, 52, 92, 155
9:1–14	39	17:15	196
9:13–34	96	18:1–11	145
9–21	54	18:10	155
9:35–41	54	18:11	158
10:1–5	54	18:13–14	160
10:18–2	97	18:23	185
10:22–39	97	18:25–27	161
11:1–57	39	18:28–30	171
11:4	138	18:28–40	167
11:6	148	18:49	166
11:15	148	19:1	169
11:33	147	19:7	97
11:36	147	19:17	170
11:38	148	19:18	193
11:38–53	84	19:22	172
11:41b-42	47	19:25b–27	172
11:42	48	19:31–37	176
11:47, 49	90	19:38–41	178
11:47–53	88	19:39–40	23
11:53	104	20:1–10	184
12:27–28	148, 187	20:11–18	185, 196
12	157	20:13	184
12:1–8	195	20:19–23	185
12:21	109	20:24–29	186
12:23	52	20:28	52
12:24	54	20:30	186
12:26–28	155	21:1–14	186
12:3	98	21:7	187
12:40	98	21:11	187
13:1	52	21:12	187
13:1–11	151	21:15–19	187
13:3	135	21:17	187
13:16	54	21:20–25	188
13:17	135	21:24	188
13:18	135	23:105	166
13:34	135	27	52
14:12	22, 92	30:7–8	184
14:15–31	136	30:39b	187

John (continued)

41	187

Acts

1:13	28
1:18	164
2:23	98
2:30	107
5:37	87
5:37	142
19:1–6	13

Romans

8:22–23	138
8:16	154
8:20–21	202

I Corinthians

15:3,	180
15:5,	180
1:26–31	202

Philippians

2	198
2:9	199
26:8	198

Hebrews

5:7	145
5:7–10	199

James

1:5	77
1:6	77
4:3	77

I Peter

1:18–19	99

I John

4:2–3	8

Revelation

13:8	99, 158
4:7	174
11:15	87

OLD TESTAMENT

Genesis

1	118
1:1	7
1:1	30
4:8	101

Exodus

3:14	25, 89
2:13–14	137
3:6	88
12:46	176
17:1–7	95
18:21	58
21:37	58
22:22–23	108
22:3	58
23:20	11
23:25	26
30:13ff.	126
34:22	92

Numbers

27:6–11	70
19:11–22	71
20:13	95
15:30	163
9:12	176

Deuteronomy

6:4–5	71, 89, 129
18:15	12, 18, 94
4:7	47
6:7	89
6:13	26
6:16	26
8:13	26
10:18–19	71

10:20	79
18:18–19	12
19:15	22
25:5–6	88
29:23	110

Psalms

2:7	173
19:25	173
22	174
22:6	173
22:16	176
31:22	174
34:20	176
41:9	135
69:9	173
69:21	171

Proverbs

17:2	20

Isaiah

53:5	99, 170
53:12	158, 173
6:9	54, 98
1:9–10	110
7	4
7:14	4
11:1–9	106
40	12
40:3	11
42	83
50	170
53:23	154
56:7b-8	105

Ezekial

16:48–50	110

Daniel

2:28	140
2:13	141
9	142
11	141
12	141

Joel

2:12	16

Micah

5:2	95
7:6	131

Zechariah

12:10	176

Malachi

3:1	11, 132

APOCRYPHA

Enoch

55:4	32

Testament of Levi

18	32

Testament of Zebulun

9	33

Assumption of Moses

10:1	33

www.ingramcontent.com/pod-product-compliance
Lightning Source LLC
Chambersburg PA
CBHW060600230426
43670CB00011B/1906